# EUROCALL Conference

Évora, Portugal
11-14 September 2013

**Proceedings**

*20 years of EUROCALL:*
*Learning from the Past, Looking to the Future*

Linda Bradley and Sylvie Thouësny (Eds.)

Published by Research-publishing.net
Dublin, Ireland; Voillans, France
info@research-publishing.net

© 2013 by Research-publishing.net
Research-publishing.net is a not-for-profit association

20 Years of EUROCALL: Learning from the Past, Looking to the Future.
2013 EUROCALL Conference, Évora, Portugal, Proceedings
Edited by Linda Bradley and Sylvie Thouësny

The moral right of the authors has been asserted

All articles in this book are licensed under a Creative Commons Attribution-Noncommercial-No Derivative Works 3.0 Unported License. You are free to share, copy, distribute and transmit the work under the following conditions:
- Attribution: You must attribute the work in the manner specified by the publisher.
- Noncommercial: You may not use this work for commercial purposes.
- No Derivative Works: You may not alter, transform, or build upon this work.

Research-publishing.net has no responsibility for the persistence or accuracy of URLs for external or third-party Internet websites referred to in this publication, and does not guarantee that any content on such websites is, or will remain, accurate or appropriate. Moreover, Research-publishing.net does not take any responsibility for the content of the pages written by the authors of this book. The authors have recognised that the work described was not published before (except in the form of an abstract or as part of a published lecture, or thesis), or that it is not under consideration for publication elsewhere. While the advice and information in this book are believed to be true and accurate on the date of its going to press, neither the authors, the editors, nor the publisher can accept any legal responsibility for any errors or omissions that may be made. The publisher makes no warranty, expressed or implied, with respect to the material contained herein.

**Trademark notice**: product or corporate names may be trademarks or registered trademarks, and are used only for identification and explanation without intent to infringe.
**Copyrighted material**: every effort has been made by the editors to trace copyright holders and to obtain their permission for the use of copyrighted material in this book. In the event of errors or omissions, please notify the publisher of any corrections that will need to be incorporated in future editions of this book.

Typeset by Research-publishing.net
Cover design: © Raphaël Savina (raphael@savina.net)
Photos: © Fany Savina (fany.savina@gmail.com)
Fonts used are licensed under a SIL Open Font License

ISBN13: 978-1-908416-12-4 (Paperback, Print on Demand, Lulu.com)
ISBN13: 978-1-908416-13-1 (Ebook, PDF file, Open Access, Research-publishing.net)
ISBN13: 978-1-908416-14-8 (Ebook, Kindle Edition, Amazon Media EU S.à r.l.)
ISBN13: 978-1-908416-15-5 (Ebook, ePUB file, Open Access, Research-publishing.net)

Legal deposit, Ireland: The National Library of Ireland, The Library of Trinity College, The Library of the University of Limerick, The Library of Dublin City University, The Library of NUI Cork, The Library of NUI Maynooth, The Library of University College Dublin, The Library of NUI Galway.

Legal deposit, United Kingdom: The British Library.
British Library Cataloguing-in-Publication Data.
A cataloguing record for this book is available from the British Library.

Legal deposit, France: Bibliothèque Nationale de France - Dépôt légal: novembre 2013.

# Table of Contents

| | |
|---|---|
| vii | Foreword |
| x | Conference Committees |
| 1 | Establishing an Online Vocabulary Levels Test by Using Flash Incorporating COPS Theory<br>*Kazumi Aizawa and Tatsuo Iso* |
| 7 | Conceptions of Personal Learning Environments Among EFL Teachers at Upper Secondary Level in Sweden<br>*Christopher Allen* |
| 14 | Speech Acts in a Virtual World: Design and Implementation<br>*Panagiotis Arvanitis* |
| 18 | An Investigation into Multi-level Components of Online Reading Fluency<br>*Andrew Atkins* |
| 25 | Critically Evaluating Prensky in a Language Learning Context: The "Digital Natives/Immigrants Debate" and its Implications for CALL<br>*Silvia Benini and Liam Murray* |
| 31 | Non-native Speakers Learning Swedish Together in Virtual Interaction<br>*Hilkka Bergman and Kristiina Tedremaa-Levorato* |
| 38 | Videogame-like Applications to Enhance Autonomous Learning<br>*Anke Berns and Concepción Valero-Franco* |
| 45 | A Constructionist Approach to Student Modelling: Tracing a Student's Constructions Through an Agent-based Tutoring Architecture<br>*Katrien Beuls* |
| 51 | Separating Fact and Fiction: The Real Story of Corpus Use in Language Teaching<br>*Alex Boulton* |
| 57 | German-French Case Study: Using Multi-Online Tools to Collaborate Across Borders<br>*Regina Brautlacht and Csilla Ducrocq* |

Table of Contents

64     Online Role-plays: Combining Situational and Interactional Authenticity in Foreign Language Learning
*Maria de Lurdes Correia Martins, Gillian Moreira, and António Moreira*

71     Discourse Markers in Italian as L2 in Face to Face vs. Computer Mediated Settings
*Anna De Marco and Paola Leone*

78     Developing Phonological Awareness in Blended-learning Language Courses
*Carmela Dell'Aria and Laura Incalcaterra McLoughlin*

86     Written Corrective Feedback and Peer Review in the BYOD Classroom
*Daniel Ferreira*

93     E-xperience Erasmus: Online Journaling as a Tool to Enhance Students' Learning Experience of their Study Visit Abroad
*Odette Gabaudan*

98     A Facebook Project for Japanese University Students (2): Does It Really Enhance Student Interaction, Learner Autonomy, and English Abilities?
*Mayumi Hamada*

106     A Chinese-French Case Study of English Language Learning via Wikispaces, Animoto and Skype
*Laura M. Hartwell and Bin Zou*

112     Listeners' Responses in Interaction Through Videoconferencing for Presentation Practices
*Atsushi Iino, Yukiko Yabuta, and Yoichi Nakamura*

117     The Use of New Technologies for the Teaching of the Igbo Language in Schools: Challenges and Prospects
*Modesta I. Iloene, George O. Iloene, Evelyn E. Mbah, and Boniface M. Mbah*

123     The European Project TILA
*Kristi Jauregi, Sabela Melchor-Couto, and Elina Vilar Beltrán*

129     Using Smart Phones in Language Learning – A Pilot Study to Turn CALL into MALL
*András Kétyi*

| | |
|---|---|
| 135 | Data-Driven Learning of Speech Acts Based on Corpora of DVD Subtitles<br>*S. Kathleen Kitao and Kenji Kitao* |
| 141 | Expert Views on How Language Education May Develop in the Next 20 Years and What CALL Could Contribute<br>*Ton Koenraad* |
| 149 | iTILT and SmartVET: 2 EU Projects to Promote Effective Interactive Whiteboard Use in Language and Vocational Education<br>*Ton Koenraad, Shona Whyte, and Euline Cutrim Schmid* |
| 158 | Learning French Through Ethnolinguistic Activities and Individual Support<br>*Celia Lafond and Nadia Spang Bovey* |
| 164 | Interactive Whiteboards in Japanese Education<br>*Gordon Liversidge* |
| 169 | Exploring Culture-related Content in the COCA with Task-based Activities in the EFL Classroom<br>*António Lopes* |
| 175 | Creating and Nurturing a Community of Practice for Language Teachers in Higher Education<br>*Teresa MacKinnon* |
| 183 | Podcasts for Learning English Pronunciation in Igboland: Students' Experiences and Expectations<br>*Evelyn E. Mbah, Boniface M. Mbah, Modesta I. Iloene, and George O. Iloene* |
| 188 | Understanding Presence, Affordance and the Time/Space Dimensions for Language Learning in Virtual Worlds<br>*Susanna Nocchi and Françoise Blin* |
| 194 | The Impact of Employing Mobile Technologies and PCs for Learning Coursera Online Lectures and TOEIC Practice Kit<br>*Hiroyuki Obari* |
| 200 | Developing a Virtual Learning Community for LSP Applications<br>*Panagiotis Panagiotidis* |

## Table of Contents

**206** Toward Mobile Assisted Language Learning Apps for Professionals that Integrate Learning into the Daily Routine
*Antonio Pareja-Lora, Jorge Arús-Hita, Timothy Read, Pilar Rodríguez-Arancón, Cristina Calle-Martínez, Lourdes Pomposo, Elena Martín-Monje, and Elena Bárcena*

**211** Developing Swedish Spelling Exercises on the ICALL Platform Lärka
*Dijana Pijetlovic and Elena Volodina*

**218** Automatic Selection of Suitable Sentences for Language Learning Exercises
*Ildikó Pilán, Elena Volodina, and Richard Johansson*

**226** Further Investigation Into the Reuse of OERs for Language Teaching
*Hélène Pulker*

**231** Categorization of Digital Games in English Language Learning Studies: Introducing the SSI Model
*Pia Sundqvist*

**238** Use of Discussion Board and PaperShow in Translation Class
*Mika Takewa*

**244** Designing Pro-telecollaboration Teacher Training: Some Insights Based on the OCEAN Personality Measures
*Anna Turula*

**250** Do Students Share the Same Experience in an Online Language Exchange Programme? – The Chinese-French eTandem Case
*Jue Wang Szilas, Ling Zhang, and Claudia Berger*

**258** $C^4$ (C quad): Development of the Application for Language Learning Based on Social and Cognitive Presences
*Masanori Yamada, Yoshiko Goda, Hideya Matsukawa, Kojiro Hata, and Seisuke Yasunami*

**265** Author Index
**267** Name Index

# Foreword

Portugal was very glad to receive, for the first time, the annual conference of the European Association for Computer Assisted Language Learning (EUROCALL). The University of Évora welcomed EUROCALL. The venue was the beautiful historic city of Évora, a UNESCO World Humanity heritage site. The conference took place in the Main Building of the University, Colégio do Espírito Santo (Holy Spirit College), with its charming rooms covered by old "azulejos" (white and blue tiles). In addition to Évora's reputation for academic excellence, the city offers an outstanding beauty, embraced by its fortress walls, filled historic memories in each street, each home, each inhabitant. Its squares and monuments tell us national history, religion and culture episodes and its townsfolk are proud of both past and present times.

This year's host comprised the University of Évora, the school of Social Sciences and the Department of Linguistics and Literatures (DLL). The School of Social Sciences is one of the largest units within the University of Évora. It is composed of eight departments of various sizes, five of which are situated in the Holy Spirit College building and three others in the Pedro da Fonseca College building. The DLL is a dynamic and proactive department, which takes account of the changing needs and trends of society and the increasingly competitive labour market while maintaining its vocation in the humanities. Offering courses at undergraduate level (1st cycle), Masters degrees (2nd cycle) and Doctorates (3rd cycle), predominantly in the areas of languages, linguistics, literatures and cultures for which it possesses highly qualified teachers, it seeks to satisfy the demands of a labour market where language and cultural skills have become increasingly indispensable.

EUROCALL 2013's theme was *20 Years of EUROCALL: Learning from the Past, Looking to the Future*. The conference seeked to establish an overview of EUROCALL's twentieth anniversary. As a professional organization, EUROCALL has been aiming, along its 20 years of existence, to promote innovative research, development and practice in the area of Computer Assisted Language Learning (CALL) and Technology Enhanced Language Learning (TELL) in education and training. During 20 years the organization has brought together educators, researchers, PhD students, administrators, designers of software and language learning systems, government representatives, equipment and software suppliers and other professionals involved in CALL and TELL. Some of the areas covered during the conference were:

- Recent developments in mobile learning;
- Language learning in virtual environments;
- Synchronous communication in language learning;

- European Language Portfolio, self assessment and ICT;
- Challenges of e-learning: the role of the institution;
- E-learning: student expectations and experience;
- Successes of e-learning through the eyes of the student;
- The use of new technologies for language teaching in schools;
- Promoting the use of new technologies amongst language teaching professionals;
- Developments in the pedagogy of online learning;
- Corpora and language learning;
- Courseware design;
- Cross-sector collaboration through e-learning;
- Supporting less widely taught languages through CALL;
- Improving intercultural competence through language learning;
- Managing multimedia environments;
- Distance and collaborative learning;
- Self access and learner autonomy.

Concerning the academic programme, many of the 150 delegates took the opportunity of attending one of the seven workshops offered. The workshops had the following titles: *Tools for CLIL Teachers*; *In search of L1-L2 equivalence with the help of comparable corpora*; *SIG workshop: Research and Publishing in CMC and Virtual Worlds*; *Integrating Telecollaborative Exchanges into Foreign Language Higher Education – INTENT*; *KungFu Writing – Commenting in the clouds*; *Virtual Worlds SIG Workshop*; *Using Pedagogic Corpora in ELT*.

From Wednesday afternoon until Saturday, there were nearly 80 individual presentations (45 minute presentations or 30 minute presentations), divided into Research, Research and development, and Reflective practice. There were also the SIG meetings, which had the following titles: *Mobile assisted language learning for professionals: integrating learning into the daily routine*; *CMC SIG Symposium: Forget the old, let's hear from the new!*; *Virtual world; Teacher Education*; *NLP*; *Corpus CALL*. This year there was a SIG meeting dedicated to the country which hosted the conference: *CALL in Portuguese speaking countries/Aprendizagem de línguas com o auxílio de computadores na Lusofonia*. This meeting joined investigators and teachers who work and study in Portuguese, allowing them to share experiences and knowledge.

EUROCALL 2013 followed EUROCALL 2012's newly founded tradition of awarding a poster. Posters presented at the conference were eligible for the EUROCALL "Award for the best poster" in two categories: post-graduate and non-postgraduate. Winners are named on the EUROCALL website and their poster is also published on the site. In addition, the authors received a certificate from EUROCALL, a free online membership for one year and a voucher.

The conference hosted three excellent keynote speakers who gave insightful presentations. Thierry Chanier gave a viewpoint on the place of CALL within the digital humanities, Christopher Jones spoke about Fulfilling the promise of the Web-delivered Language Instructions, and finally, Ana Gimeno gave a perspective of EUROCALL's twenty years, and future expectations in CALL. All the speeches have been archived in EUROCALL's member area: https://educast.fccn.pt/vod/channels/1c2al6i8gm.

The social programme allowed delegates to relax and enjoy the centre of Évora, with its beautiful and traditional housings and monuments. Delegates were also asked to join in in traditional singing and dancing with local students (*tunas*), and to listen to *cante alentejano*, men and women in traditional dress singing *a capela*.

EUROCALL 2013 continued the tradition of extending the conference experience to the virtual community. The keynote speeches were recorded and are now available to the virtual community. The VS also had a blog with delegates commenting on the parallel sessions they were attending, as well as plenty of tweets via EUROCALL's own Twitter account.

Authors of all accepted presentations (papers and posters) and present at the conference were able to send a 1500 word text (not including abstract and bibliography) for publication in the proceedings. All in all, 41 papers are included in these proceedings.

The local organising committee wishes to show our appreciation to the EUROCALL Executive Committee for all their help in making this year's celebration in Évora a reality. Thank you to those presenters who submitted their paper, and last but not least, to all the presenters and delegates for making EUROCALL 2013 the success it was.

Maria João Marçalo and Ana Alexandra Silva<br>
Universidade de Évora, Portugal

# Conference Committees

The 2013 EUROCALL Conference on *20 Years of EUROCALL: Learning from the Past, Looking to the Future* was organised by the University of Évora in Portugal.

## Programme Committee

**Programme chairs**
- Françoise Blin, *Dublin City University, Ireland*
- Peppi Taalas, *University of Jyvaskylä, Finland*

**Committee members**
- Christine Appel, *Universitat Oberta de Catalunya, Spain*
- David Barr, *University of Ulster, UK*
- Françoise Blin, *Dublin City University, Ireland*
- Alex Boulton, *Université 2, Nancy, France*
- Claire Bradin Siskin, *Excelsior College, US*
- Angela Chambers, *University of Limerick, Ireland*
- Jozef Colpaert, *University of Antwerp, Belgium*
- John Gillespie, *University of Ulster, UK*
- Muriel Grosbois, *Université de Paris 4, France*
- Nicolas Guichon, *Université de Lyon 2, France*
- Sarah Guth, *Università degli studi di Padova, Italy*
- Regine Hampel, *The Open University, UK*
- Mirjam Hauck, *The Open University, UK*
- Trude Heift, *Simon Fraser University, Canada*
- Francesca Helm, *Università degli studi di Padova, Italy*
- Phil Hubbard, *Stanford University, USA*
- Liam Murray, *University of Limerick, Ireland*
- Sue K. Otto, *University of Iowa, USA*
- Hans Paulussen, *University of Leuven, Belgium*
- Mathias Schulze, *University of Waterloo, Canada*
- Lesley Shield, *Freelance CALL Consultant, UK*
- Oranna Speicher, *University of Nottingham, UK*
- Glenn Stockwell, *Waseda University, Japan*
- Peppi Taalas, *University of Jyvaskyla, Finland*
- Maija Tammelin, *Aalto University School of Economics, Finland*
- June Thompson, *Editor, ReCALL*
- Cornelia Tschichold, *Swansea University, UK*

## Local Organising Committee

- Fernando Gomes, *University of Évora, Portugal*
- Maria João Marçalo, *University of Évora, Portugal*
- Ana Alexandra Silva, *University of Évora, Portugal*

## EUROCALL Executive Committee 2012/2013

### President and vice-president
- Françoise Blin, Presisent, *Dublin City University, Ireland*
- Peppi Taalas, Vice-President, *University of Jyväskylä, Finland*

### Members, elected and co-opted officers
- Kent Andersen, *Byggeri & Bygningsservice, øvrige, Odense*
- Alex Boulton, *University of Lorraine, France*
- Mirjam Hauck (elected), *Open University, UK*
- Francesca Helm (elected), *University of Padova, Italy*
- Maria João Marçalo, *University of Évora, Portugal*
- Oranna Speicher (elected), *University of Nottingham, UK*
- Sylvi Vigmo (co-opted), *The University of Gothenburg, Sweden*

### Appointed officers
- John Gillespie, Treasurer, *University of Ulster, Coleraine, Northern Ireland*
- Toni Patton, Secretary, *University of Ulster, Coleraine, Northern Ireland*

# Establishing an Online Vocabulary Levels Test by Using Flash Incorporating COPS Theory

## Kazumi Aizawa[1] and Tatsuo Iso[2]

**Abstract**. The present study aims to demonstrate how the estimation of vocabulary size might be affected by two neglected factors in vocabulary size tests. The first factor is randomization of question sequence, as opposed to the traditional high-to-low frequency sequencing. The second factor is learners' confidence in choosing the correct meaning for a given target word. A new online vocabulary size test was developed for the purpose of the study with the two factors in mind. The results of the test revealed that (1) randomizing question sequences did not have significant effects on the score of the vocabulary size test and (2) even though the learners who had a mastery level of 8000 words showed higher confidence in high frequency words than the learners with a smaller vocabulary, such confidence faded as early as 4000 frequency level of JACET 8000. The findings are discussed in detail in terms of the scale or the length of vocabulary size tests as well as the need for incorporating confidence in the estimation of vocabulary size.

**Keywords**: vocabulary size, multiple-choice test, confidence level.

## 1. Introduction

It is widely accepted that the knowledge of vocabulary is one of the most important and fundamental assets one would hope to attain in order to carry out a task involving verbal communication more successfully. Accordingly, many attempts have been made to measure the outcome of vocabulary learning.

---

1. Tokyo Denki University, Tokyo, Japan; aizawa@cck.dendai.ac.jp
2. Reitaku University, Chiba, Japan

**How to cite this article**: Aizawa, K., & Iso, T. (2013). Establishing an Online Vocabulary Levels Test by Using Flash Incorporating COPS Theory. In L. Bradley & S. Thouësny (Eds.), *20 Years of EUROCALL: Learning from the Past, Looking to the Future. Proceedings of the 2013 EUROCALL Conference, Évora, Portugal* (pp. 1-1). Dublin/Voillans: © Research-publishing.net.

Such attempts yielded vocabulary tests of many kinds that are appreciated and enjoyed among teachers and researchers who recognize the importance of vocabulary and wish to have deeper insights into the nature of vocabulary and its growth. Among such tests, vocabulary size tests have received most attention so far. A few examples would be Vocabulary Levels Test (VLT) (Nation, 1990) and Yes/No Test (Meara, 1992).

Despite their popularity, however, there are few studies conducted on the limitations of the vocabulary size tests (Aizawa, 2006a, 2006b; Aizawa & Iso, 2007). Although it has been shown that the test scores from which the learner's vocabulary size is estimated vary depending on the types of vocabulary tests, we have yet to see how several factors of a vocabulary size test could affect the results. One such factor is the sequence of questions. We believe this is an important issue when the time required to complete a vocabulary size test becomes longer, since learners can become more susceptible to fatigue in the latter part of the test.

Confidence is also a factor that has not been paid attention to. Researchers and practitioners intuitively know that learners do not necessarily answer questions with the same degree of confidence when taking a vocabulary test, especially when it is a multiple-choice test. Some questions will be answered highly confidently while others with lower confidence or with no confidence at all when guesswork is employed. What we do not know yet is how the concept of confidence can be incorporated in the design of vocabulary size tests by means of Clustered Objective Probability Scoring (COPS) (Shizuka, 2004), for example. The present study, therefore, discusses how such vocabulary test factors might affect the estimation of learners' vocabulary size.

## 2.  Study

### 2.1.  Purpose

The current study primarily aims to investigate how the ordering of questions affects the estimate of learners' vocabulary size. It also attempts to include the measurement of learner confidence in a vocabulary test and investigates the relationship between the estimated vocabulary size and learners' confidence in answering each question of a vocabulary test. Research questions are as follows.

- What are the effects of randomizing the order of questions in a vocabulary size test?

- How does confidence interact with learners' vocabulary levels as well as the frequency levels of vocabulary?

## 2.2. Participants

A total of 159 Japanese learners of English from two universities participated in this study. Among them, 65 subjects came from one university where they majored in English. It was expected that their overall English proficiency was slightly higher than the rest of the subjects, 94 to be exact, who were technology majors from another university.

## 2.3. Instrument

The Flash VLT is a multiple-choice type of test that measures learners' receptive vocabulary size (cf. for example, Schmitt, Schmitt, & Clapham, 2001). A set of three question items is displayed at the upper side of the screen. To answer, a test taker simply drags the solid circle attached to an English word and drops it to fill one of the small holes directly below the corresponding Japanese word. A hole marked with a double circle should be filled if a test taker is 90-100% confident that s/he chose the correct answer. Likewise, a hole with a single circle indicates medium confidence and one with a triangle shows that s/he does not have confidence at all.

The test adopted the target words from JACET 8000 (JACET, 2003). The list is divided into eight levels based mostly on frequencies, with each level containing a thousand words. From each level, 30 words were randomly chosen as question items. During the selection of the items, an effort was made to keep the ratio of the part of speech to as close as that of the original subsists so that the question items are the better representatives. The total number of question items is 240 (30 words x 8 levels).

Two slightly different versions of the same test were prepared for the purpose of the study: FIXED and RANDOM. In the FIXED version, the 80 sets of three target words are in descending order of word frequency. The RANDOM version only differed from the FIXED version in the sequence of the question items. Each time the test started, the same 80 sets of target words were automatically randomly sequenced except the first three sets. The order of the first three sets were fixed in order to identify the subjects who did not understand the directions of the test and failed to choose correct answers to the target words that they most likely have already learned before.

## 2.4. Procedure

All the subjects took both versions of the test with exactly one week in between. Half of the subjects took the FIXED version first, and then took the RANDOM version. The order of the two versions was reversed for the other half of the subjects. All of the subjects finished each version of the test within 40 minutes.

## 3. Results and discussion

The scores of the two versions of the Flash VLT was compared to find out if randomizing the question sequence of a vocabulary size test would yield different outcomes when compared to the traditional "higher-to-lower frequency" order. The results showed that the estimated vocabulary sizes obtained from the two versions of the same test did not statistically differ (see Table 1 and Figure 1). Moreover, when the test results were examined by each frequency band, it was apparent that the subjects performed in the same manner in the two versions. Considering that the subjects were to repeat the form-meaning matching task more than 200 times, it was expected that fatigue would negatively affect the subjects' performance in the FIXED version, especially since the words with lower frequency were arranged toward the end of the test.

Table 1. Descriptive statistics of the vocabulary size ($N = 159$)

|  | Mean* | SD |
|---|---|---|
| FIXED | 5924.2 | 949.5 |
| RANDOM | 5907.0 | 949.1 |

* The maximum possible vocabulary size was 8000.

Figure 1. Comparison between FIXED and RANDOM ($N = 159$)

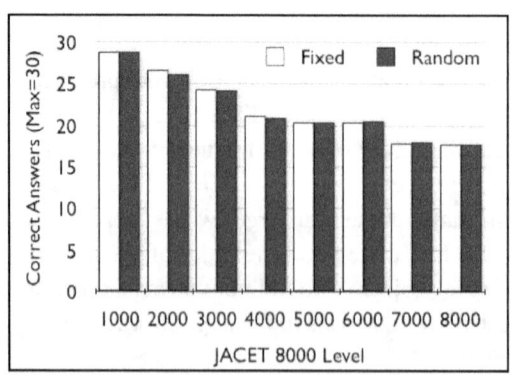

As for the relationship between confidence and learners' vocabulary levels as well as word frequency, the overall results were generally in accordance with our expectation. The larger the vocabulary the subjects acquired, the more confident they were. Also, the less frequent the target words became, the less subjects showed confidence. The results indicate that flash VLT successfully elicited learners' judgments on their own confidence.

On closer examination (Table 2), there were clear patterns in the decline of confidence across the vocabulary level groups. The subjects in groups below 4000 vocabulary level lost their confidence as early as 2000 level target words, whereas those in G4000, G5000, and G6000 maintained their confidence that they had when dealing with 1000 level words at least until the end of 2000 level target words. Further, the groups with the highest vocabulary levels, G7000 and G8000 continued to be as confident until 3000 level words as they were dealing with 1000 level words. What can be inferred from here is that obtaining a passing grade of 80% at a certain level frequency level in vocabulary size test does not necessarily ensure that learners are dealing with questions with high confidence. The question is what it means to have a 6000 vocabulary level when such learners are not very confident in dealing with 4000 level words. Apparently, the concept of vocabulary level (and vocabulary size as well) needs to be reconsidered with confidence in mind if learners' size of vocabulary is to be quantified.

Table 2. Distribution of the answers with "high" confidence (%)

| | N | JACET 8000 Levels | | | | | | | |
| --- | --- | --- | --- | --- | --- | --- | --- | --- | --- |
| | | 1000 | 2000 | 3000 | 4000 | 5000 | 6000 | 7000 | 8000 |
| G1000 | 25 | 85 | 59 | 53 | 42 | 44 | 42 | 34 | 30 |
| G2000 | 27 | 92 | 77 | 62 | 53 | 47 | 49 | 39 | 38 |
| G3000 | 48 | 97 | 86 | 78 | 59 | 56 | 58 | 40 | 43 |
| G4000 | 23 | 97 | 90 | 82 | 72 | 61 | 65 | 52 | 52 |
| G5000 | 11 | 98 | 94 | 87 | 72 | 69 | 67 | 53 | 59 |
| G6000 | 13 | 99 | 96 | 89 | 75 | 70 | 69 | 48 | 54 |
| G7000 | 5 | 100 | 98 | 94 | 80 | 73 | 77 | 63 | 63 |
| G8000 | 4 | 100 | 98 | 94 | 90 | 90 | 90 | 84 | 85 |

## 4. Conclusions

The findings of this study confirmed the traditional testing methodology of receptive vocabulary size in terms of how the question items should be sequenced. They also demonstrated how confidence should be taken into account when estimating the size of vocabulary. For further research, it will be of high importance to investigate how to incorporate learners' confidence in the calculation of vocabulary size estimations through vocabulary size tests.

## References

Aizawa, K. (2006a). Rethinking Frequency Markers for English-Japanese Dictionaries. In M. Murata, K. Minamiide, Y. Tono, & S. Ishikawa (Eds.), *English Lexicography in Japan*. Tokyo: Taishukan.

Aizawa, K. (2006b). Is Frequency of Words Related to Difficulty of Words? *Paper presented at the BAAL/IRAAL*.

Aizawa, K., & Iso, T. (2007). Estimating Word Difficulty: The Divergence From Frequency Levels. *Annual Review of English Language Education in Japan (ARELE), 18*, 111-120. Retrieved from http://ci.nii.ac.jp/lognavi?name=nels&lang=en&type=pdf&id=ART0009707101

JACET. (2003). *JACET List of 8000 Basic Words*. Tokyo: The Japan Association of College English Teachers.

Meara, P. (1992). *EFL vocabulary tests*. University of Wales, Swansea: Center for Applied Language Studies.

Nation, I. S. P. (1990). *Teaching and learning vocabulary*. New York: Newbury House.

Schmitt, N., Schmitt, D., & Clapham, C. (2001). Developing and exploring the behaviour of the two new versions of the Vocabulary Levels Test. *Language Testing, 18*(1), 55-88. doi: 10.1177/026553220101800103

Shizuka, T. (2004). *New horizons in computerized testing of reading*. Osaka: Kansai University Press.

# Conceptions of Personal Learning Environments Among EFL Teachers at Upper Secondary Level in Sweden

## Christopher Allen[1]

**Abstract**. In recent years, virtual learning environments (VLEs) or course management systems (CMSs) have become commonplace in European higher education as well as making inroads into primary and secondary schools. VLEs such as *Moodle*, *Blackboard* and *It's Learning* offer educational institutions standardised packages in the form of a range of administrative, pedagogical and communicative tools. Teachers of English as a foreign language (EFL) at secondary and tertiary levels are certainly no exception to this trend, employing VLEs as learning platforms to support a variety of ICT-based learning activities and tasks. VLEs have however attracted criticism from some quarters in that they may sometimes be seen merely as virtual embodiments of the classroom with all the restrictions which the 'physical' classroom has traditionally entailed. Furthermore it has been argued that VLEs have failed to embrace the full advantages of Web 2.0 technologies or acknowledge trends towards informal learning afforded by social media. The response to this criticism has been the envisioning of personal learning environments (PLEs) which utilise the plethora of free, often collaborative online resources and tools now available to teachers and learners. This paper explores the conceptualisation of PLEs among upper secondary school teachers of English in Sweden on the basis of Dabbagh and Reo's (2009) model of social collaboration and interactivity in the educational workplace.

**Keywords**: personal learning environment, sociocultural, collaborative learning.

---

1. Department of Languages Linnaeus University Kalmar, Sweden; christopher.allen@lnu.se

**How to cite this article**: Allen, C. (2013). Conceptions of Personal Learning Environments Among EFL Teachers at Upper Secondary Level in Sweden. In L. Bradley & S. Thouësny (Eds.), *20 Years of EUROCALL: Learning from the Past, Looking to the Future. Proceedings of the 2013 EUROCALL Conference, Évora, Portugal* (pp. 7-13). Dublin/Voillans: © Research-publishing.net.

# 1. Introduction

## 1.1. General

Over the previous decade, the use of virtual learning environments or learning management systems (LMSs) has become commonplace in universities and schools. Often originating in requirements to deliver course materials on a distance basis, such learning platforms have begun to assume a more central position in the Web 2.0 educational workplace, frequently in the form of blended systems which combine online access with campus/classroom activities.

This dominance has however recently been called into question. Advocates of PLEs have argued that VLEs are merely virtual extensions of the traditional classroom with the pedagogical limitations which this entails. PLEs on the other hand can provide learners with an authentic and more genuinely sociocultural learning experience in the truest Vygotskian sense than that offered by institutionalised learning platforms, mirroring informal learning fostered by digital interaction beyond the classroom (Livingstone, 2001). This paper examines the extent to which a focus group of EFL teachers in Swedish upper secondary schools have been successful in harnessing these freely available resources in providing a collaborative learning experience.

## 1.2. VLEs

VLEs have been widely adopted by universities and schools and have come to embody the trend towards social interaction, connectivist learning and user-generated content loosely subsumed under the heading of Web 2.0. While these benefits are readily acknowledged, the rise of and over-reliance on VLEs can be seen as a further manifestation of the ongoing confrontation between educational tradition and technology. Weller (2007), cited in Conole (2008), sees VLEs merely as virtual extensions of the traditional 'bricks and mortar' classroom with all the constraints which this analogy entails, contriving to perpetuate the behaviouristic model of one-way knowledge transfer.

## 1.3. VLEs and PLEs in English language teaching

The theoretical underpinnings of the Web 2.0 technologies embodied in VLEs and PLEs lie in the work of Vygotsky (1978) who envisaged learning as a sociocultural activity mediated by psychological or physical tools in a social context. The importance of sociocultural theory in English Language Teaching has been increasingly recognised and is inherent in collaborative, activity-based approaches such as task-based learning (Ellis, 2003; Nunan, 2004; van Lier, 2007; Willis, 1996). Within the decentralised Swedish school system, VLEs such as *Moodle*, *Blackboard* and *It's Learning* are being increasingly adopted as a result of decisions at municipal level.

Figure 1. A sample personal learning environment

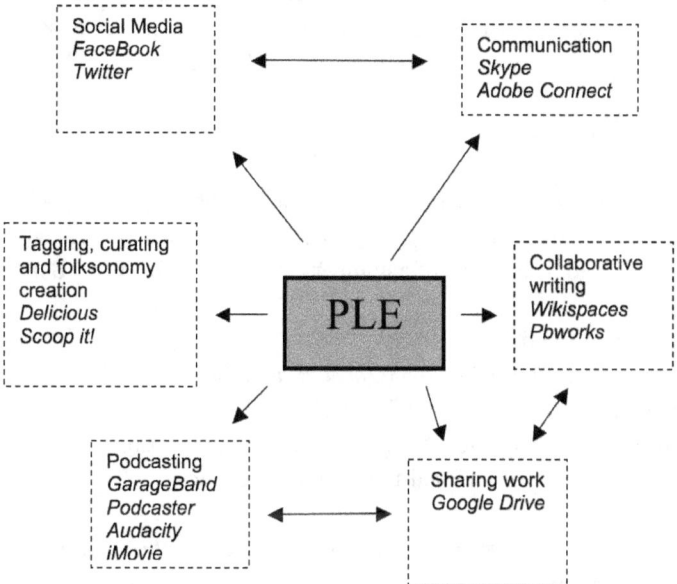

Following Dabbagh and Reo (2009), it is possible to characterise digital learning activities in terms of different degrees of social collaboration and interactivity. In their model, level 1 refers to the use of tools for the individual's own private use only with no thought towards sharing or collaboration. Level 2 is characterised as 'basic interaction and sharing' while level 3 encompasses fully-fledged social networking (Figure 1).

## 2. Method

### 2.1. Background

In 2012, the Swedish municipality in question introduced a scheme by which all first and second year upper secondary school pupils were provided with a *MacBook Air* for their personal use for the duration of their studies. Typical proficiency levels in English among pupils in Swedish upper secondary schools range between B1 and C1 in the CEFR system[2].

## 2.2. The participants

A focus group of 10 upper secondary school EFL teachers from a single municipality in southern Sweden was interviewed for the study. These teachers all had L1 Swedish with varying degrees of experience, typically combining English with another subject such as Swedish, modern languages, history or social science. Of the teachers interviewed, 8 were aged under 40 years.

## 2.3. Interviews and data-collection

Interviews were semi-structured with questions focusing on the teacher's use of PLE tools and resources in their language teaching. Teachers were asked to describe their use of PLE tools in terms of a number of loosely-defined ICT domains:

   A: Social media (*FaceBook*, *Twitter*, etc)
   B: Podcasting and digital media (*GarageBand*, *Audacity*, *iMovie*, etc)
   C: Collaborative writing (e.g. wikis, etc)
   D: Information management: tagging, filtering and curation
   E: Video conferencing and real-time communication

Interview respondents were then asked to assess the extent of their involvement in accordance with the following levels based on Dabbagh and Reo (2009), ranging from Level 0 (no use) to level 3 denoting extensive use in teaching (Table 1).

Table 1. Levels of collaboration

| Level | Description |
| --- | --- |
| 0 | **No utilisation** (I did not make any use of this area of ICT either personally or in my teaching) |
| 1 | **Private information / management / resource creation** / use (I use the tool / resource for my private use and management of information which I do not intend to share with others) |
| 2 | **Basic interaction / sharing** (I enable public views, set up a personal profile, and configure tools for resource sharing) |
| 3 | **Social networking** ( I configure resources to pool pupils' knowledge or content via comments, RSS feeds, etc, actively building online networks and communities, enabling information 'push' by subscription, etc). |

---

2. http://www.skolverket.se/om-skolverket/publikationer

## 3. Results

The results of the interviews and questionnaire responses are summarised in Table 2 below, which presents a set of average scores for the level of collaborative learning (on the 0-3 scale described above).

Table 2. Average level scores for the ten respondents for each collaborative ICT domain

| Area | Average level | Examples of activities |
|---|---|---|
| A: Social Media | 1.6 | Class and homework instructions, links, sharing of documents, texts and pictorial sources |
| B. Podcasting and digital media | 0.2 | 2 examples of literature projects using video |
| C. Collaborative writing and blogs | 0.0 | Not used in the classroom |
| D. Information management | 0.0 | Not used in the classroom |
| E. Video conferencing and real-time communication | 0.0 | Not used in the classroom |

It was clear from the results of the survey that the teachers in question were increasingly looking towards Area A, Social Media as their conceptualisation of a PLE. The main areas of *FaceBook* usage included the dissemination of links with an English language content, the sharing of documents, general administration and the publication of instructions in preparation for classroom activities.

Only one respondent however described their use of *FaceBook* at level 3. Three participants in the study mentioned their use of *Google Drive* and one participant mentioned *Wikispaces* with a very similar purpose in mind, that of creating a customised 'mini' VLE. *Twitter* was an underused resource for teaching although a number of teachers reported using this privately.

Areas B-E were however underexploited in terms of opportunities they presented for collaborative learning. In particular it was noted that teachers had not really come to terms with collaborative writing in the form of wiki tools or blogs. Teachers were unfamiliar with the blogging of leading international EFL practitioners and theorists. Podcasting and video production were mentioned as activities by two of the teachers; all participants in the study expressed their interest in receiving training in the technicalities of podcast and video production using tools such as *GarageBand, iMovie* or *Windows Moviemaker*.

As would be expected of teachers with daily classroom contact with their pupils, the use of video conferencing and real-time communication was insignificant although two teachers mentioned the occasional use of *Skype* to come into contact with pupils unable to attend regular classroom lessons.

## 4. Discussion and conclusion

Within a wider international computer-assisted language learning context, the results of the study are interesting in that they represent a preliminary evaluation, albeit on a very small scale, of a major municipal investment in a relatively resource-rich context, what Dudeney, Hockly, and Pegrum (2013) characterise as a *High-tech (H)* classroom environment. At the time of writing, teachers were approximately one academic year into this investment and perhaps it is a little too early to draw any significant conclusions.

Although developed for a wider e-learning context, Dabbagh and Reo's (2009) four level model has nevertheless shown some potential in the analysis of degrees of social collaboration in EFL learning environments at upper secondary level. While there are some difficulties involved in the demarcation of the learning levels, especially level 2 (basic interaction/sharing) and level 3 (social networking), it is argued that the model can serve as the basis for increasingly sophisticated comparisons of trends as teachers progressively come to terms with the use of Web 2.0 tools in the promotion of collaborative learning in modern languages.

In a wider perspective, the teachers' use of social media and tools such as *Google Drive* marks a clear move away from what Dudeney et al. (2013) see as a coursebook-driven approach (where activities promoting digital literacies are seen as extensions of the traditional EFL textbook). Instead the point of departure would appear to be the planning of activities around a division of digital literacy into four focus areas (Dudeney et al., 2013; Hockly, 2012). The results of the survey suggest that any ICT in-service training programme needs to go beyond presentations of subject-specific lists of websites and resources, encompassing not only what might be crudely put as 'button pushing' but also a wider social constructivist/collaborative framework.

**Acknowledgements**. The author would like to thank the Department of Languages, Linnaeus University for the opportunity to attend the 2013 EUROCALL conference in Portugal.

# References

Conole, G. (2008). New Schemas for Mapping Pedagogies and Technologies. *Ariadne, 56*. Retrieved from http://www.ariadne.ac.uk/issue56/conole/

Dabbagh, N., & Reo, R. (2009). Back to the Future: Tracing the roots and learning affordances of social informatics for tertiary Teaching. In L. Ward & C. McLoughlin (Eds.), *Web 2.0-based e-learning: Applying Social Informatics for Tertiary Teaching* (pp. 1-20). Hershey: Igi Global.

Dudeney, G., Hockly, N., & Pegrum, M. (2013). *Digital Literacies*. Pearson.

Ellis, R. (2003). *Task-based Learning and Teaching*. Oxford: Oxford University Press.

Hockly, N. (2012). Digital Literacies. *ELT Journal, 66*(1), 108-112. doi: 10.1093/elt/ccr077

Livingstone, D. W. (2001). Adults' informal learning: Definitions, finds, gaps, and future research. *NALL Working Paper # 21-2001*. Toronto: Ontario Institute for Studies in Education. Retrieved from http://www.lindenwood.edu/education/andragogy/andragogy/2011/Livingstone_2001.pdf

Nunan, D. (2004). *Task-Based Language Teaching: a comprehensively revised edition of designing tasks for the communicative classroom*. Cambridge: Cambridge University Press.

van Lier, L. (2007). *The Ecology and Semiotics of Language Learning: a Sociocultural Perspective*. Norwell, MA: Kluwer Academic Publishers.

Vygotsky, L. S. (1978). *Mind In Society*. Cambridge, MA: Harvard University Press.

Weller, M. (2007, December 6). My personal work/leisure/learning environment. *The Ed Techie*. Retrieved from http://nogoodreason.typepad.co.uk/no_good_reason/2007/12/my-personal-wor.html

Willis, J. (1996). *A Framework for Task-based Learning*. Longman.

# Speech Acts in a Virtual World: Design and Implementation

## Panagiotis Arvanitis[1]

**Abstract**. In the first half of the twentieth century, notions such as linguistic structures and student's linguistic capacity were the traditional elements of any language teaching. These notions are yielding their place to the functional use of language and how language is being shaped by the different communicative situations. This communicative approach of teaching a foreign language has led the redefinition of learning objectives and general principles of the teaching act. The emphasis is on student's communicative ability, therefore communication plays a key role in teaching Language - Civilisation. In the Common European Framework of Reference for Languages: Learning, Teaching, Assessment (CEFR), we find the key notion of speech acts. The interest in this project is the relationship between traditional speech acts and simulated situations in Virtual Worlds. Furthermore, there is an interest in finding out if it is possible to develop learner's language skills by teaching and using speech acts in these environments. In the above context, in this paper we first illustrate current needs in teaching and learning second languages, then we discuss the design of a Virtual world and finally its implementation for teaching speech acts of French language in higher education.

**Keywords**: language teaching and learning, speech acts, virtual worlds, higher education.

## 1. Introduction

The effort of teaching a foreign language through language, culture and civilisation of others still occupies all those involved in the linguistic educational process. In recent decades, the main principles of second language teaching focus on

---

1. Aristotle University of Thessaloniki, Thessaloniki, Greece; arva@frl.auth.gr

**How to cite this article**: Arvanitis, P. (2013). Speech Acts in a Virtual World: Design and Implementation. In L. Bradley & S. Thouësny (Eds.), *20 Years of EUROCALL: Learning from the Past, Looking to the Future. Proceedings of the 2013 EUROCALL Conference, Évora, Portugal* (pp. 14-17). Dublin/Voillans: © Research-publishing.net.

teaching language and culture as a whole, with a great concern about the means of communication in specific socially-based situations.

In the first half of the twentieth century, notions such as linguistic structures and student's linguistic capacity were the traditional elements of any language teaching. With the significant contribution of Halliday (1978) and Hymes (1984), these notions are yielding their place to the functional use of language and how language is being shaped by the different communicative situations. This new communicative approach of teaching a foreign language has led to the redefinition of learning objectives and general principles of the teaching act. The emphasis is on student's communicative ability. Therefore, communication plays a key role in teaching Language - Civilisation. Simultaneously, with discourse analysis, it becomes clear that communication is accomplished through written and oral texts. From these texts, linguistic elements derive their significance and meaning; consequently, linguistic elements can not be considered as isolated teaching objectives, but as functional communication structures and conventions inextricably linked with text types.

Furthermore, the use of information and communication technologies (ICT) has widely spread in second language learning and teaching environments. Learners are now interacting with a variety of semiotic modes through image, video, sound, and new forms of written and spoken texts in a complex multilingual communicative universe.

## 2. Speech acts

Speech acts are the core of teaching. Around them, curricula and author textbooks are articulated and they are in perfect relation and connection with both communicative situations and textual genres. It should be noted that genres offer the most appropriate medium for the cultivation of linguistic and metalinguistic skills, including awareness of the relationship between the structural and social aspects of language (Halliday & Hasan, 1991).

Speech acts were primarily detected in the "communicative approach" to teaching foreign language in 1970, an approach which has brought radical changes in the methodology of teaching a foreign language. In the Common European Framework of Reference for Languages: Learning, Teaching, Assessment, which is widely adopted and accepted as the European standard for teaching and learning foreign languages, we find again the key notion of speech acts. Speech acts are at the heart of teaching and the core development of communicative language skills in the sense that they describe what learners can do with language in specific contexts or in a particular communicative situation (Council of Europe, 2001).

According to CEFR, learner's communicative language competence is activated in the performance of the various language activities involving reception, production, interaction or mediation (interpretation or translation). Each of these types of activity is possible in relation to texts in oral or written form, or both.

## 3. Virtual worlds

In an era of "digital globalization", the increasing use of open technological platforms, such as CMC, VLS, LCMS, Blogs, Wikis, social networking sites, and online gaming platforms and simulation environments, affect the entire adulthood of young learners. A whole new generation – often described by researchers with terms such as "Net generation" (Oblinger & Oblinger, 2005), "new millennium learners" (OECD, 2008), or "digital natives" (McLester, 2007; Prensky, 2001) – lives, entertains and gets educated by digital technologies and media. In this web generation (2.0), users are no longer simple consumers of the information provided by the websites' administrators, but are now in a position to participate, communicate and cooperate with other users, as well as to create and publish any type of multimedia information and create new content or even their own personal websites.

Virtual Worlds are 3-Dimensional MUVEs (Multi-User Virtual Environments) in which users can move and interact with each other. Virtual Worlds can be simple or very complex environments that simulate specific sites and locations from rooms or buildings, to entire cities or islands. Today's concept of "virtual world" refers to a type of online community that is implemented using a computer simulated 3D environment in which users can interact with each other with audio and text and use or create objects in it (Miah & Jones, 2011). Nowadays, a growing number of virtual environments and worlds are available to users (Bainbridge, Lutters, Rhoten, & Lowood, 2010).

In the case of foreign language learning, a key challenge for the foreign language teacher has always been the design of a learning environment that brings learners close to the natural environment and the native speakers of the target language. For the purposes of our study, learning scenarios are especially developed and designed with French as the main reference language. The scenarios aim at the development of communicative language skills and are based in speech acts, which are associated with the levels of language proficiency, as defined by the CEFR.

## 4. Conclusions

In order to design, develop and schedule training scenarios for communicative language education and training of learners in virtual worlds, a teacher must take into account the kind of experiences that are expected to occur to the users/learners, such as partial immersion in a social interaction, participation, and collaboration with someone for a purpose. Furthermore, we propose to take into account specific speech acts for the development of communicative language skills.

## References

Bainbridge, W. S., Lutters, W., Rhoten, D., & Lowood, H. (2010). The Future of Virtual Worlds. In W. S. Bainbridge (Ed.), *Online Worlds Convergence of the Real and the Virtual* (pp. 289-302). London: Springer-Verlag. doi: 10.1007/978-1-84882-825-4_23

Council of Europe. (2001). *Common European Framework of Reference for Languages: Learning, teaching, assessment* (CEFR). Retrieved from http://www.coe.int/t/dg4/linguistic/Cadre1_en.asp

Halliday, M. A. K. (1978). *Language as social semiotic*. London, England: Edward Arnold.

Halliday, M. A. K., & Hasan, R. (1991). *Language, context, and text: aspects of language in a social-semiotic perspective*. London, England: Oxford University Press.

Hymes, D. H. (1984). *Vers la compétence de communication*. Collection «Langues et apprentissage des langues». Paris, France : Hatier-Crédif.

McLester, S. (2007). Technology Literacy and the MySpace Generation: They're Not Asking Permission. *Technology & Learning, 27*, 16-22.

Miah, A., & Jones, J. (2011). Virtual Worlds. In G. A. Barnett (Ed.), *Encyclopedia of Social Networks*. London: SAGE.

Oblinger, D. G., & Oblinger, J. L. (2005). (Eds.). *Educating the Net Generation*. Educause e-books. Retrieved from http://www.educause.edu/ir/library/pdf/pub7101.pdf

OECD. (2008). New Millennium Learners. Initial findings on the effect of digital technologies on school-age learners. *OECD/CERI International Conference*. Retrieved from http://www.oecd.org/dataoecd/39/51/40554230.pdf

Prensky, M. (2001). Digital natives, digital immigrants, part 1. *On the Horizon, 9*(5), 1-6. doi: 10.1108/10748120110424816

# An Investigation into Multi-level Components of Online Reading Fluency

## Andrew Atkins[1]

**Abstract**. This paper provides a discussion of the results of a cross-sectional examination of linguistic and non-linguistic variables that are predicted to influence L2 reading fluency. The study is part of a larger, longitudinal mixed-methods study into reading fluency development using online Timed Reading (TR) with participants from a mid-to-high level private university in western Japan. The larger study will also be briefly explained to provide some background. For the study presented in this paper, participants read two, short, equivalent, graded, online texts against a clock and then answered comprehension questions without recourse to the texts. A custom-made web application was used to administer the readings. The texts used were all 300-words long and graded using tools available on *The Compleat Lexical Tutor* website (Cobb, 2003) to be within the first 1,000 words of English. Data from a battery of tests that included a paper-based vocabulary size test (Nation & Beglar, 2007), and a computer-based word-recognition reaction time test were recorded. These data were triangulated with graded text reading performance data to assess the relative importance of the components assessed. The relationship between the measured variables is explained using correlation and regression analysis, providing insight for reading researchers and teachers.

**Keywords**: reading fluency, word recognition, reaction time, online reading, vocabulary size.

## 1. Introduction

The ability of students to read in a fluent and efficient manner is of concern to many educators in English as a Foreign Language (EFL) contexts as the ubiquitous nature of the Internet, at least for the foreseeable future, makes reading a skill

---

1. Kinki University, Higashi-Osaka, Japan; andrew@kindai.ac.jp

**How to cite this article**: Atkins, A. (2013). An Investigation into Multi-level Components of Online Reading Fluency. In L. Bradley & S. Thouësny (Eds.), *20 Years of EUROCALL: Learning from the Past, Looking to the Future. Proceedings of the 2013 EUROCALL Conference, Évora, Portugal* (pp. 18-24). Dublin/Voillans: © Research-publishing.net.

necessary for their lives. This paper is an attempt to investigate reading fluency for a group of first-year students studying at a Japanese university and tries to discover which components from a set of predicted variables have the greatest influence on reading fluency.

The recent interest in Asian classrooms in reading fluency is a backlash against the traditional focus on intensive reading (Gorsuch & Taguchi, 2010). Some of the most promising techniques investigated to date to address this issue have been extensive reading (Day & Bamford, 1998; Waring, 1997), repeated reading (Gorsuch & Taguchi, 2008; Samuels, 1979/1997), and timed reading (Chang, 2010; Underwood, Myskow, & Hattori, 2012). This paper will utilise only timed reading to investigate reading fluency.

Bernhardt (1991, 2005) identifies that the various aspects of vocabulary knowledge may account for 50 per cent of the variability in language ability, and it is interesting to explore to what extent reading fluency is influenced by lexical knowledge, as suggested by Meara's (1996) *dimensions* of lexical knowledge.

The need for research into reading fluency cannot be stressed enough, as expounded by Segalowitz (2010), who explains the notion of fluency gaps. He suggests that L2 learners are often unsatisfied by their deficiency in the L2, as compared to their L1, especially where fluency is concerned. Segalowitz (2010) also discusses another type of fluency gap, a between-individual fluency gap, which is more the focus of this paper. This paper hopes to contribute to the field by providing information about the factors that make for more fluent readers, and why some students are more successful in achieving fluency than others.

## 2. Method

### 2.1. Participants

A total of 134 participants from 3 intact classes were recruited to take part in this study. The students were from a small national university in western Japan and were taking required English classes as part of their Economics related majors. The participants came from the Economics faculty in the university and had an average age of 19 years. There was a gender bias with 33 female subjects (24.6%) and 101 male subjects (75.4%). Students at the university were not divided in ability-based streams, but rather assigned in a relatively random manner to groups. There were however some scheduling constraints that made assignment not entirely random.

## 2.2. Materials

*2.2.1. Timed reading*

The instruments at the backbone of this research were 26 randomly assigned tests of timed reading delivered using a web application. The treatment consisted of two equivalent reading passages, each with 6 comprehension questions. The passages were controlled for vocabulary load (Webb & Nation, 2008) and the questions were designed to test understanding and not memory.

The application was a simple web application, built using PHP, Javascript and a MySQL database. Students' reading time and scores were then recorded in the database (Atkins & Cole, 2011).

*2.2.2. Vocabulary size test*

Nation and Beglar's (2007) Vocabulary Size Test (VST) was used to provide data for receptive vocabulary knowledge. Only the first five levels of the fourteen-level test were used as these were felt to be the most relevant for the purpose of this investigation. The test consists of ten test items for each one thousand-word level. Timed reading is designed to promote fluency and as a result the lexical load is intentionally low.

*2.2.3. Word recognition reaction time test*

This test was designed to check students' word recognition skills. Using the Compleat Lexical Tutor website (Cobb, 2003), 40 randomly generated Anglo-Saxon words from the second 1,000 words of English, and randomly generated plausible 20 non-words from Meara's (1996) list of 100 plausible-non-words were made into a reaction time test using the Compleat Reaction Timer v.4 (Cobb, 2003). Reaction times were recorded by the program and sent by email to the researcher.

## 2.3. Procedures

The first five levels of the VST (Nation & Beglar, 2007) were administered in week four of the school year, taking 40 minutes to administer. In week 20, two randomly assigned timed reading passages were administered, the *word recognition reaction time practice test* was administered, and this was followed by the *word recognition reaction time test*.

## 2.3.1. Analytical approach

To account for variation in performance and uncontrollable differences in the difficulty of the reading passages the mean adjusted word per minute (WPM) for the 2 passages administered in week 20 was used as the dependent variable. The higher the number the more proficient a reader is assumed to be.

The VST gave raw scores from 10 for each of the five levels tested and a raw total score for all five levels combined. A higher number suggests greater vocabulary knowledge.

The *word recognition reaction time test* provides us with an average reaction time for distinguishing whether a word is known or not. It also provides us with an error score. The reaction time shows how fast a participant can distinguish a word from a non-word.

Multiple correlation was used to examine the relationship between the dependent TR variable and independent variables. Hierarchical linear regression was also used. All analyses were carried out using SPSS 17.0 for Windows.

## 3. Discussion

Many of the variables in this study correlate with varying degree with reading fluency. Some of the variables measured also correlate with each other, as in some cases they are measuring the same thing.

The TR passages and tests themselves are another issue that must be considered. The data obtained was from a much larger study of timed reading performance. In this study the metric used is the mean of performance on two randomly assigned passages. Even with the greatest care taken to make the passages equivalent, there are so many factors that it is not possible to control for.

The regression results suggested that receptive vocabulary (VST) accounts for the greatest amount of variance in the criterion variable for reading fluency. This accounted for 21% of the variance, less than in Bernhardt (1991), although both studies found that vocabulary was the most influential predictor. Word recognition reaction time accounted for 6.9% of the variance in the model, but this figure must be interpreted with caution as in some cases fast reaction times came at the expense of a high number of errors, and vocabulary size had a large effect on errors made.

## 4. Conclusions

Although the results of this study have suggested that vocabulary size and word recognition account for a significant proportion of reading fluency, the quality of the instruments used dictates the quality of the results. The dependent variable is perhaps not completely valid as it is really comparing apples with oranges as the participants actually read completely different passages on different subjects. This problem will be reduced in the parent study by using mean times for a series of readings. Reading fluency is a very personal thing and influenced by not only the text itself, but also what the reader brings to the text on a particular day. It would be better to assess it over a longer period of time and with a variety of passage themes, and perhaps try to control vocabulary more. It is also conceivable that the controlled nature of the texts reduces the influence of vocabulary size on performance, and this is worthy of further investigation.

Although simplicity is often the best strategy in research design, the complex nature of reading fluency makes simplicity untenable. In this study more than 70% of the variance in the regression model is unaccounted for, which is comparable to Bernhardt (1991). Although, as discussed, the dependent criterion variable in this study may not be truly valid, it is also certain that other variables need to be measured. These should include some measure of grammatical knowledge, some tests of a greater variety of individual differences, and some measure of cultural knowledge and schema for the passages used. Shiotsu (2009) used a more comprehensive battery of tests in his study and this study would benefit from some of those tests, especially the sentence-level reading ability test and a further word recognition exercise. Shiotsu (2009) also makes the recommendation that "future research should employ standardised test scores or proficiency ratings" (p. 36). Athough the VST is not standardised, it has been used with thousands of students in Japan and around the world, which at least in part satisfies Shiotsu's (2009) recommendation.

This research provides little in the way of pedagogical implications; however, it has provided some valuable insight and knowledge that will be included in the parent study where some of the data used in this paper was taken from. The parent study is a reading and writing fluency parallel growth study. It is hoped it will provide some much needed information for L2, and especially EFL educators to help them prepare students to use language more fluently and effectively. Further examination of reading fluency and its component parts can only lead to greater understanding of what is needed in the classroom to create students who can use English to make their futures brighter.

**Acknowledgements.** I would like to thank Tom Cobb for his inspiration and invaluable advice on this paper.

## References

Atkins, A., & Cole, S. (2011). The development of an online timed reading program. In E. Forsythe, T. Gorham, M. Grogan, D. Jarrell, R. Chartrand, & P. Lewis (Eds.), *CALL: What's your motivation? Collected papers on the cutting edge of language learning practice.* Nagoya, Japan: JALT CALL SIG.

Bernhardt, E. B. (1991). *Reading development in a second language.* Norwood, NJ: Ablex Publishing Corporation.

Bernhardt, E. B. (2005). Progress and procrastination in second language reading. *Annual Review of Applied Linguistics, 25*, 133-150. doi: 10.1017/S0267190505000073

Chang, A. C.-S. (2010). The effect of a timed reading activity on EFL learners: Speed, comprehension, and perception. *Reading in a Foreign Language, 22*(2), 284-303. Retrieved from http://nflrc.hawaii.edu/rfl/October2010/articles/chang.pdf

Cobb, T. (2003). *The Compleat Lexical Tutor* [Website]. Retrieved from http://www.lextutor.ca

Day, R. R., & Bamford, J. (1998). *Extensive reading in the second language classroom.* Cambridge: Cambridge University Press.

Gorsuch, G., & Taguchi, E. (2008). Repeated reading for developing reading fluency and reading comprehension: The case of EFL learners in Vietnam. *System, 36*(2), 253-278.

Gorsuch, G., & Taguchi, E. (2010). Developing reading fluency and comprehension using repeated reading: Evidence from longitudinal student reports. *Language Teaching Research, 14*(1), 27-59. doi: 10.1177/1362168809346494

Meara, P. (1996). The dimensions of lexical competence. In G. Brown, K. Malmkjaer, & J. Williams (Eds.), *Competence and Performance in Language Learning* (pp. 35-53). Cambridge: Cambridge University Press.

Nation, P., & Beglar, D. (2007). A vocabulary size test. *The Language Teacher, 31*(7), 9-13. Retrieved from http://jalt-publications.org/files/pdf/the_language_teacher/07_2007tlt.pdf

Samuels, S. J. (1979/1997). The method of repeated readings. *The Reading Teacher, 50*(5), 376-381.

Segalowitz, N. (2010). *Cognitive bases of second language fluency.* New York: Routledge.

Shiotsu, T. (2009). Reading Ability and Components of Word Recognition Speed: The Case of L1-Japanese EFL Learners. In Z. Han & N. J. Anderson (Eds.), *Second Language Reading Research and Instruction: Crossing the Boundaries* (pp. 15-39). Ann Arbor: University of Michigan Press.

Underwood, P., Myskow, G., & Hattori, T. (2012). The effect of speed reading instruction on Japanese high school students' English reading comprehension. *Journal of International Education Research, 8*(1), 27-39. Retrieved from http://journals.cluteonline.com/index.php/JIER/article/view/6693/6768

Waring, R. (1997). Graded and extensive reading - questions and answers. *The Language Teacher*, *21*(5), 9-12. Retrieved from http://jalt-publications.org/files/pdf/the_language_teacher/tlt_21.05.pdf

Webb, S., & Nation, I. S. P. (2008). Evaluating the vocabulary load of written text. *TESOLANZ Journal, 16*, 1-10. Retrieved from http://www.tesolanz.org.nz/includes/download.aspx?ID=106692

# Critically Evaluating Prensky in a Language Learning Context: The "Digital Natives/Immigrants Debate" and its Implications for CALL

## Silvia Benini[1] and Liam Murray[2]

**Abstract.** More than 10 years have passed since the first introduction of the term "digital natives" in Prensky's (2001a, 2001b) two seminal articles. Prensky argues that students today, having grown up in the Digital Age, learn differently from their predecessors, or "digital immigrants". As such, the pedagogical tools and methods used to educate the Natives are outdated. Consequently, many educational professionals became convinced that the ways in which today's students think and learn have been qualitatively changed by their use of information and communication technology (ICT). Indeed, the analogy introduced by Prensky is very appealing, however, no significant empirical evidence exists to support this conjecture and neither facts nor evidence tested in everyday practice have been provided. This paper aims to critically examine the underlying "digital native" theory by reviewing some recent studies questioning the existence of digital natives and presenting some of the current findings from a major case study. The study involves Irish secondary school students and their approach and use of new technologies for language learning. By monitoring and interviewing the students and their teachers, it is intended to provide evidence and information to reflect on some key topics such as the use of ICT for language learning during and outside the class, the analysis of students' skills (as putative digital natives) within language learning, and the attitude of teachers and tutors toward technologies. Overall, it is intended to examine if the current evidence resulting from this study validates Prensky's digital native theory.

**Keywords**: digital natives, digital immigrants, ICT, education, language learning.

---

1. School of Languages, Literature, Culture and Communication, University of Limerick, Ireland; silvia.benini@ul.ie
2. School of Languages, Literature, Culture and Communication, University of Limerick, Ireland

**How to cite this article**: Benini, S., & Murray, L. (2013). Critically Evaluating Prensky in a Language Learning Context: The "Digital Natives/Immigrants Debate" and its Implications for CALL. In L. Bradley & S. Thouësny (Eds.), *20 Years of EUROCALL: Learning from the Past, Looking to the Future. Proceedings of the 2013 EUROCALL Conference, Évora, Portugal* (pp. 25-30). Dublin/Voillans: © Research-publishing.net.

## 1. Introduction

In 2001, the terms digital natives and digital immigrants were brought to our attention by Marc Prensky (2001a, 2001b). Digital natives refer to people born in the Digital Era; also called the "iGeneration", described as having been born with "digital DNA" (Zur & Zur, 2011). In contrast, digital immigrants relate to those who grew up in a pre-computer world. According to Prensky (2001a, 2001b), in the most general terms, digital natives speak and breathe the language of computers and the culture of the web in which they were born. On the contrary, digital immigrants learn to adapt to a new digital environment, dealing with technology not as naturally as those who grew up with it.

While Prensky (2009) has started to move away from the digital natives/immigrants distinction, the terms have become highly popular, appearing regularly in articles, blog posts, columns and books mostly in general (Bennett, Maton, & Kervin, 2008) and higher education (Jones & Shao, 2011) contexts.

Many of the arguments about the technological skills, educational preferences and approaches of the Net Generation students have been based on conjectures and assumptions (Bennett, Maton, & Kervin, 2008), showing a lack of empirical research. The same can be said about the so-called digital immigrants. These terms became part of our "common sense" without having been much explored in their true nature and everyday practice. Furthermore, there have been very few comparisons on students' and teachers' perceptions and use of technology (Waycott, Bennett, Kennedy, Dalgarno, & Gray, 2010), especially in secondary level institutions.

Research shows that there are many variables that go into creating the stereotypical digital native. The location, for example, seems to be a very important factor. In the US there is a different level of web technology and computer usage among the same demographic of digital natives in Australia (Kennedy, Judd, Dalgarno, & Waycott, 2010; Margaryan, Littlejohn, & Vojt, 2011) and those in the UK (Stoerger, 2009). In South Africa, as well, only 26% of the population might be described as digital natives (Brown & Czerniewicz, 2010). Broos and Roe (2006) indicate that socioeconomic factors as well as race, gender and educational background play an important role in how and how much people use technology. Finally, the access to technology and the utilisation of it in both quality and quantity should be something to take into great consideration.

The qualitative research introduced in this paper aims to investigate the student and teacher perspective on the use of ICT both as an everyday tool and as a language learning and teaching tool in a secondary level education environment. By examining the perspective of students and teachers in parallel it is possible to evaluate the evidence of a digital native/immigrant divide. Moreover, this study aims to gain a better understanding of the role technology plays in supporting learning in general and language learning in particular, providing an insight into what students and teachers perceive to be the benefits and/or limitations of using technology in their educational experience.

## 2. Method

The study reported in this paper is part of an on-going PhD project. The research employed a mixed-method approach (Creswell & Clark, 2007), conducting in-depth qualitative interviews alongside surveys and classroom observations. This large case study was conducted in two secondary schools both located in the Munster region, Republic of Ireland. The first is a mixed community school (School A), which is particularly orientated towards ICT and an overall commitment to innovation. The majority of students here are equipped with notebooks or tablet computers as are all of the teachers. The second school is a Catholic female school (School B). Here the environment and the teaching reflect a more traditional book-based approach, with small class sizes, a close teacher-student relationship and a limited access to one computer lab for all classes. The participants of the study were 2nd, 3rd and 5th year students and their Italian and Irish language teachers. The data elicitation phase lasted 18 weeks and started by asking the participants to complete pre-interview questionnaires to discover their perceptions and uses of technologies. During the 12th-15th week of the data collection phase, semi-structured and focus-group interviews were held to investigate the students' and teachers' use and access to technology particularly in relation to Irish and Italian language learning and teaching. In this paper we will introduce some of the data collected in the two schools, presenting selected quotations and appropriate analysis in order to address several of our noted research concerns.

## 3. Results and discussion

The first main question introduced to the students by both the questionnaires and the interviews was respectively *"Do you own any piece of technology?"* and *"Do you have access to any of the following piece of technology: laptop, computer, mobile phone? If yes, how often do you use it/them?"*. The response was unanimous. All students in both schools owned a mobile phone and a laptop (shared in some cases) and they were using these tools on a regular daily basis.

The second question addressed by the questionnaire to both teachers and students referred to the importance of ICT for language learning and teaching and here the responses varied:

> "Not vital. I think you need to be taught how to speak a language. You can't learn from being on a computer" (2nd year student, School B).

> "It isn't because there is one computer room for the whole school and we rarely use it" (2nd year student, School B).

> "Not to me specifically but some teachers rely on it for teaching methods" (Female 5th year student, School A).

Students in both schools are reporting that technology is not essential to learning but recognise that some tutors depend on it. Echoing this sentiment, some tutors agreed, whereas older teachers disagreed:

> "Very important. It is the conduit through which I can reach the students" (Male Irish Language Teacher, School A).

> "I do not make great use of ICT in my classes. I am teaching for over 25 years and tend to fall back to traditional teaching methods. Occasionally I use ICT. Lack of resources is a definite obstacle" (Female Irish Teacher, School B).

The teachers were interviewed on the digital natives/immigrants divide and, in this respect, they were asked if today's teachers and students recognise this concept. Some of their answers reveal deep similarities to those of their students:

> "I'm not one for tags, it's unfair. You are what you are. Digital native and immigrants makes no sense, you're not labeled because of your date of birth. There are many people who are engaging technology and they have become literally dependent on it. Many people are just not interested in technology. They [students] have not been trained. My own daughter she was born with the computer but that doesn't necessarily mean that you assume all this automatically just because you're born next to a computer. That doesn't necessarily mean that you understand it" (Female Italian Language Teacher, School B).

On digital immigrants:

"Certainly it is changing because newly qualified teachers are not immigrating towards it [technology], they're there really. But certainly we still have the older teachers in teaching struggling, either avoiding it or catching up or learning like myself" (Male Irish Language Teacher, School B).

On digital natives:

"In my opinion it's just a trendy name and I hear this a lot; if you want to put a title on it, well they are digital natives because they are born with it, it is in their environment, they are using the technology but the technology is using them as well; it is not the case for them to be productively using the technology or choosing and controlling the technology that, to me, would be a digital native, whereas a lot of people are just passive" (Male Irish Language Teacher, School B).

## 4. Conclusions

The initial findings of this on-going research highlight that the notion of students and teachers facing a digital divide is not as simple as Prensky (2001a, 2001b) has argued. In everyday life all participants use many of the same technologies (mobile phone, tablets, Web 2.0, etc.), but the types of activities they are undertaking and the concerns they have are very different. This became clearer when approaching the educational environment issue. For some students the idea of using technologies for language acquisition was stimulating yet not essential.

All teachers had a positive attitude towards ICT as a pedagogic method, yet there was a reported reliance on ICT from student and teacher groups. In one school, there remains a very strong traditional book-based and teacher centred approach which does not imply a negative attitude towards ICT inclusion. Access to ICT appears to be a greater concern in both schools.

We argue that the digital native learner sees these new generic tools as part of their realities. Yet, when it comes to their educational use, many questions remain unanswered: are educational standards rising, where is the "added value" in this normality and do we have better language learners?

**Acknowledgements**. Strong support for this project has been provided by the School of Languages, Literature, Culture and Communications, University of Limerick. The authors would like to acknowledge the support, availability and collaboration of the staff members of the two targeted schools and all their students.

# References

Bennett, S., Maton, K., & Kervin, L. (2008). The 'digital natives' debate: A critical review of the evidence. *British journal of educational technology, 39*(5), 775-786. doi: 10.1111/j.1467-8535.2007.00793.x

Broos, A., & Roe, K. (2006). The digital divide in the playstation generation: Self-efficacy, locus of control and ICT adoption among adolescents. *Poetics, 34*(4-5), 306-317. doi: 10.1016/j.poetic.2006.05.002

Brown, C., & Czerniewicz, L. (2010). Debunking the 'digital native': beyond digital apartheid, towards digital democracy. *Journal of Computer Assisted Learning, 26*(5), 357-369. doi: 10.1111/j.1365-2729.2010.00369.x

Creswell, J. W., & Clark, V. L. P. (2007). *Designing and conducting mixed methods research.* Wiley Online Library.

Jones, C., & Shao, B. (2011). *The net generation and digital natives: implications for higher education.* York, UK: Higher Education Academy. Retrieved from http://oro.open.ac.uk/30014/

Kennedy, G., Judd, T., Dalgarno, B., & Waycott, J. (2010). Beyond natives and immigrants: exploring types of net generation students. *Journal of Computer Assisted Learning, 26*(5), 332-343. doi: 10.1111/j.1365-2729.2010.00371.x

Margaryan, A., Littlejohn, A., & Vojt, G. (2011). Are digital natives a myth or reality? University students' use of digital technologies. *Computers & Education, 56*(2), 429-440. doi: 10.1016/j.compedu.2010.09.004

Prensky, M. (2001a). Digital natives, digital immigrants, part 1. *On the Horizon, 9*(5), 1-6. Retrieved from http://www.marcprensky.com/writing/Prensky%20-%20Digital%20Natives,%20Digital%20Immigrants%20-%20Part1.pdf

Prensky, M. (2001b). Digital natives, digital immigrants, part 2: Do they really think differently? *On the Horizon, 9*(6), 1-6. Retrieved from http://www.marcprensky.com/writing/Prensky%20-%20Digital%20Natives,%20Digital%20Immigrants%20-%20Part2.pdf

Prensky, M. (2009). H. sapiens digital: From digital immigrants and digital natives to digital wisdom. *Journal of Online Education, 5*(3), 1-9.

Stoerger, S. (2009). The digital melting pot: Bridging the digital native-immigrant divide. *First Monday, 14*(7). doi: 10.5210%2Ffm.v14i7.2474

Waycott, J., Bennett, S., Kennedy, G., Dalgarno, B., & Gray, K. (2010). Digital divides? Student and staff perceptions of information and communication technologies. *Computers & Education, 54*(4), 1202-1211. doi: 10.1016/j.compedu.2009.11.006

Zur, O., & Zur, A. (2011). *On digital immigrants and digital natives: How the digital divide affects families, educational institutions, and the workplace.* Zur Institute - Online Publication. Retrieved from http://www.zurinstitute.com/digital_divide.html

# Non-native Speakers Learning Swedish Together in Virtual Interaction

### Hilkka Bergman[1] and Kristiina Tedremaa-Levorato[2]

**Abstract**. This paper aims to give an overview of a cooperation project launched three years ago, under which students who study Swedish at two universities across the Baltic Sea have a chance to complete a part of relevant courses in their study programmes together in an online course. The primary goals of joint studying are: to encourage students from different nationalities to actively communicate with one another, using Swedish as the lingua franca (communicative and social competence), to motivate students to use a range of sources in Swedish to get information, and to give the participants a chance to gain new knowledge about their neighbouring country and the student life there (internationalisation competence). The common difficulties in carrying out joint studies at two different universities (Guth, Helm, & O'Dowd, 2012), e.g. timetabling and technical problems, are overcome by focusing on asynchronous dialogue and by choosing a technically workable platform with good technical support from one of the partner universities. The authors consider the cooperation a very positive experience, easy and inexpensive to implement, and highly recommend it to their colleagues. Our experience confirms what previous studies (Guth et al., 2012) have already outlined: despite the belief that foreign languages should be learned face-to-face and preferably with native speakers, students seem to appreciate using information and communication technology for connecting up with other people using the target language as their lingua franca. We also feel that these exchanges are particularly suitable for the teaching of less commonly taught languages and offer all parties both change and satisfaction.

**Keywords**: collaborative learning, virtual interaction, less-taught languages, non-native speakers, target language as lingua franca.

---

1. Turku University of Applied Sciences, Turku, Finland; hilkka.bergman@turkuamk.fi
2. Tallinn University, Tallinn, Estonia

**How to cite this article**: Bergman, H., & Tedremaa-Levorato, K. (2013). Non-native Speakers Learning Swedish Together in Virtual Interaction. In L. Bradley & S. Thouësny (Eds.), *20 Years of EUROCALL: Learning from the Past, Looking to the Future. Proceedings of the 2013 EUROCALL Conference, Évora, Portugal* (pp. 31-37). Dublin/Voillans: © Research-publishing.net.

## 1. Introduction

Comparing language learning today with language learning 20 years ago, it is evident that changes are significant. The difference is particularly noteworthy in the use of online technologies and not only in language teaching methodology. Paper textbooks and exercise books have been replaced by electronic ones, and fast Internet connections give the language learner an opportunity to use (unlimited) audiovisual material accessible on the Internet. Online projects also bring language learners all over the world into contact with one another and create opportunities for authentic communication.

The authors, who work as Swedish language lecturers at Turku University of Applied Sciences and Tallinn University, wished to give their students a possibility to complete a part of their Swedish language course in virtual collaboration with the partner university. Hereby, we present an overview of the cooperation that has been ongoing for three years by now.

## 2. Method

### 2.1. Students and language levels

The prerequisite for successful cooperation in language learning is a more or less equal level in language proficiency; differences in language proficiency can be a challenge to successful collaboration (Guth et al., 2012). The Finnish students who participated in the project had studied Swedish both in the comprehensive school and upper secondary school, and were on B1+/B2 language level. The students studying Swedish at Tallinn University start from zero and by the time of the joint study they are also on the same level.

Similar prerequisite skills make the formulation of tasks and communication between the students considerably easier. The number of students participating was 12 (Turku) and 9 (Tallinn) in 2011, 20 (Turku) and 7 (Tallinn) in 2012, and 18 (Turku) and 10 (Tallinn) in 2013.

### 2.2. Web platform

As Finnish and Estonian higher education institutions use different study environments, a decision on which platform to use had to be made first. As Turku University of Applied Sciences has been offering different online courses for students for a long time, and as the used platform Optima has also a Swedish language version, it was the most appropriate choice for the implementation of the joint study. The students of Tallinn University received a temporary user name and password in Optima.

## 2.3. Tasks

The primary goal of the joint online course was to encourage students to use Swedish as lingua franca when communicating with the students of the partner university. Therefore, group work formed a large part of the joint study. The first task consisted of presentations of the students' personal and academic backgrounds followed by a peer discussion on the virtual forum. Students were divided into Estonian-Finnish pairs and could comment each other's presentations on the forum and ask questions.

The next task was listening comprehension by following television and radio programmes in Swedish and commenting on them in a diary. The students wrote down a brief summary of the programme and complemented it with a small glossary of new vocabulary that was used in the programme. In addition, students evaluated their listening skills with reference to the Common European Framework of Reference for Languages[3].

The third task was to discuss current social topics that they had given in their individual essays in groups. Argumentation was carried out on the virtual discussion forum the following week. Some exemplary themes were given for the students, for instance:

- Should Turkey become/not become a member of the EU?
- Smoking in public places must be/should not be forbidden.
- Higher education should be/should not be free of charge.
- Nature needs our help.
- Present-day society – a consumption society?

Some examples of the topics proposed by students:

- Marriage or living together?
- The dangers of wind energy.
- Children have a right to home care.

---

3. http://www.coe.int/t/dg4/linguistic/Source/Framework_en.pdf

Thereafter, the students were divided into groups of 4-5 members and the communication continued on the virtual forum. All students had to read through their group members' essays and give argumentations for or against the opinions presented there.

## 3. Discussion

As our wish was to offer an online course with active feedback, the students received comments from both their peers and their teacher. In the case of the first task we also exchanged roles between ourselves, so that students would receive feedback not only from their own teacher but also from the so-called guest teacher. When working out the tasks, both lecturers took part again, since the joint course consisted of varied types of tasks.

In a joint study where group work comprises a large part of the study, it is of special importance that all the participants follow the given deadlines. When the deadline of a particular task was coming closer, we therefore sent a reminder by email. In the authors' opinion, the students were very committed to completing the tasks, and there were only a few cases when a student forgot about the deadline. We believe that students tend to consider their studies of value if they are credit-bearing and part of the study programme (O'Dowd, 2013).

In joint teaching, it is also important that the partner teachers have common visions, approaches and practices in their teaching (O'Dowd, 2013). We believe that a reliable teacher-partnership is vital to long-term collaboration and successful co-teaching. An online course can definitely be prepared online as well, but we presupposed that a physical meeting makes planning considerably easier, something that was also confirmed by our own experience.

### 3.1. Feedback from students

After the period of joint study, all students were asked to fill in a feedback questionnaire, in which they answered the following questions:

- How would you evaluate your language development during the course? Which sub-skills (reading, writing, online communication, listening, cultural competence) developed the most/least during the course?

- What did you like the most about the joint study? What kind of tasks suit best for an online course?

- Did you encounter any difficulties in using Optima? Was the timetable suitable for the course? Did you understand the feedback provided by the teacher?

- How would you evaluate the cooperation with the partner university on a scale from 10 (very good) to 1 (very bad)? Please explain your answer.

- Would you be interested in a similar joint study also with other higher education institutions and not only in the framework of language training? Why?

- Do you have any remarks or suggestions for modification?

All of the respondents noted that their language skills developed during the course. As the answer to the most developed sub-skill, listening, writing, and online communication were mentioned. Interesting was the fact that students evaluated the development of cultural competence very differently. In the opinion of approximately half of the students, this developed most of the sub-skills, and in the opinion of approximately the other half, the least.

When answering question number 2, it was mentioned that the tasks were varied and interesting and the reading and commenting of fellow students' texts exciting.

None of the students experienced problems with understanding the use of Optima or the instructions. The timetable was considered suitable and the majority also stated that they looked at the feedback provided by the teacher.

The feedback clearly indicated that students liked to study internationally. The evaluation of the participants in 2013 was on average 7.2 in Estonia and 8.2 in Finland on a scale from 10 to 1. Among other issues, students mentioned the following about the joint study:

- "a new way to study language";
- "a good way to learn to know Finnish/Estonian students";
- "thanks to online communication, language use seemed natural";
- "I learned a lot, also from other participants in the course";
- "exciting, good variation in study routine".

None of the students had anything negative to say about the joint study. It is evident that in students' opinion the internationality gave the course extra value and the form of study was motivating. Let us use the formulation of one of the students' feedback: "More similar sort of studies!".

## 3.2. Recommendations

Online studies suit well for several different types of tasks: reading comprehension, writing (analysis, report, summary), listening comprehension, translating, vocabulary and grammar exercises, and different assignments for group and pair work on communication forums. In our opinion, the best solution is to integrate a joint online course into an already existing course. In the present case, Estonian students "visited" the course *Svenska på nätet* (Swedish on the Net) during five weeks, after which both groups continued their respective Swedish language courses in Finland and Estonia.

In comparison to "ordinary studies", online studies require a more detailed planning and precise instructions (Koli, 2008), but in the authors' opinion, this one-time amount of time spent is rewarding. Relying on our experience, we can say that the course is easily manageable if the task for each coming week opens only after having completed the previous one. The teachers, on their side, have to strive for a good learning atmosphere and make the game rules clear for the students.

## 4. Conclusions

The project has turned out to be viable, key factors being students at approximately the same language level, partner teachers with similar aims and practices, good adaptation to existing study programmes and a workable platform. In all three years, students have evaluated the joint study project as successful and they have noted that it has been exciting and motivating.

It has been successful also in the opinion of the authors. As we had counted with the fact that we do not meet our students face-to-face, we were ready to interrupt at any moment if anybody would have problems with Optima or the instructions. The students, however, managed everything. Virtual communication is so natural and usual to present-day youth, that it should be used by teachers in creating virtual classrooms.

Successful online learning presupposes very thorough planning and preliminary work. In the authors' opinion online cooperation is also variation for the teacher; besides the physical classroom, they must create a virtual one, which is different from the former. Considering more and more complex economic situations at higher education institutions, we believe that such a joint study also has good future prospects.

## References

Guth, S., Helm, F., & O'Dowd, R. (2012). *University Language Classes Collaborating Online.* A Report on Integration of Telecollaborative Networks in European Universities. Retrieved from http://intent-project.eu/sites/default/files/Telecollaboration_report_Final_Oct2012.pdf

Koli, H. (2008). *Verkko-ohjauksen käsikirja*. Helsinki: FinnLectura.

O'Dowd, R. (2013). Telecollaborative Networks in university Higher Education: Overcoming Barriers to Integration. *The Internet and Higher Education, 18*(July), 47-53. doi: 10.1016/j.iheduc.2013.02.001

# Videogame-like Applications to Enhance Autonomous Learning

### Anke Berns[1] and Concepción Valero-Franco[2]

**Abstract**. This paper presents the results of an ongoing study which has been carried out with a group of German Foreign Language students at the University of Cadiz since 2012. The purpose of the study was to analyze the impact of videogame-like applications on foreign language learning and their motivational potential to increase learning beyond the classroom. The paper presents the results of a comparative study of several learning tools: a videogame-like application, a J-CLIC application and several Paper-based learning materials and their impact on students' foreign language learning. All three applications were designed by us for the specific purpose of the present study and in line with our target students' language proficiency and needs. In order to measure the impact of each application on students' learning, we designed a four part pre- and post-test, which was filled in by each student once before using the application and twice after using it. Additionally, we gathered personal feedback from the users by giving them an anonymous questionnaire.

**Keywords**: videogame-like applications, foreign language learning, virtual learning environments, motivation.

## 1. Introduction

The current pilot study aims to explore the possibilities and benefits of integrating 3-D videogame-like applications in the area of tertiary foreign language learning. The starting point of our study was the increasing need to provide our students with the learning tools that are able to motivate them towards autonomous learning in order to widen and foster what has previously been introduced in the classroom.

---

1. University of Cadiz, Spain; anke.berns@uca.es

2. University of Cadiz, Spain

**How to cite this article**: Berns, A, & Valero-Franco, C. (2013). Videogame-like Applications to Enhance Autonomous Learning. In L. Bradley & S. Thouësny (Eds.), *20 Years of EUROCALL: Learning from the Past, Looking to the Future. Proceedings of the 2013 EUROCALL Conference, Évora, Portugal* (pp. 38-44). Dublin/Voillans: © Research-publishing.net.

Since our target students are beginners, our interest focuses on the A1.1 level of the Common European Framework of Reference for Languages (CEFR) and the exploration of the learning tools that meet the specific needs of our learners. Amongst those is especially the necessity to acquire basic vocabulary and grammar skills which is often done through different kinds of drill-based activities that include reading, writing and listening. Moreover, with the increasing use of blended learning, teachers are expected to provide their students with additional tools for the autonomous learning beyond the classroom. This is often done by using Virtual Learning Environments (VLEs) as these enable teachers to provide a wide range of different learning contents and tools which students can access anytime and anywhere. On the one hand, this implies an enormous gain since it allows students to access materials whenever they need to and, on the other, teachers to follow students' learning process and, if necessary, to revise and add learning materials (Berns, González-Pardo, & Camacho, 2013).

## 2. Method

### 2.1. Materials

In order to analyze the impact of videogame-like applications on A1.1 level students' foreign language learning and their motivation towards autonomous learning, we have designed a 3-D videogame-like application, called the Supermarket game, as well as two alternative learning tools: a J-CLIC application and a Paper-based learning material. By doing so, we aimed to carry out a comparative study and to establish the impact and benefits of videogame-like applications, compared to more traditional learning tools (Garris, Ahlers, & Driskell, 2002; Schwienhorst, 2009). Taking into consideration our target students' language proficiency, the prime goal of each of the aforementioned tools was to provide learners with meaningful and comprehensible vocabulary input rather than excessive grammar and form training. Given this, we selected one of the main topics from the curriculum planned within the A1.1 level. This was related to food and beverages. In part, both topics had previously been practiced in the classroom and were now being fostered and widened by each student using one of the aforementioned applications. All three learning tools were based on the same vocabulary that was introduced by means of texts, photos and audio-recordings. Nevertheless, they were embedded in two different VLEs. Whilst the 3-D videogame-like application (see Figure 1) was lodged in a virtual platform called VirtUAM (Virtual Worlds at the Universidad Autónoma de Madrid) (Berns, González-Pardo, & Camacho, 2012), the J-CLIC (see Figure 2) and the Paper-based materials (see Figure 3) were accessible through the Virtual

Campus (VLE of the University of Cádiz). Both learning environments permit students access on a 24 hour basis and allow teachers to trace their students' access and learning path.

Figure 1. Supermarket-game

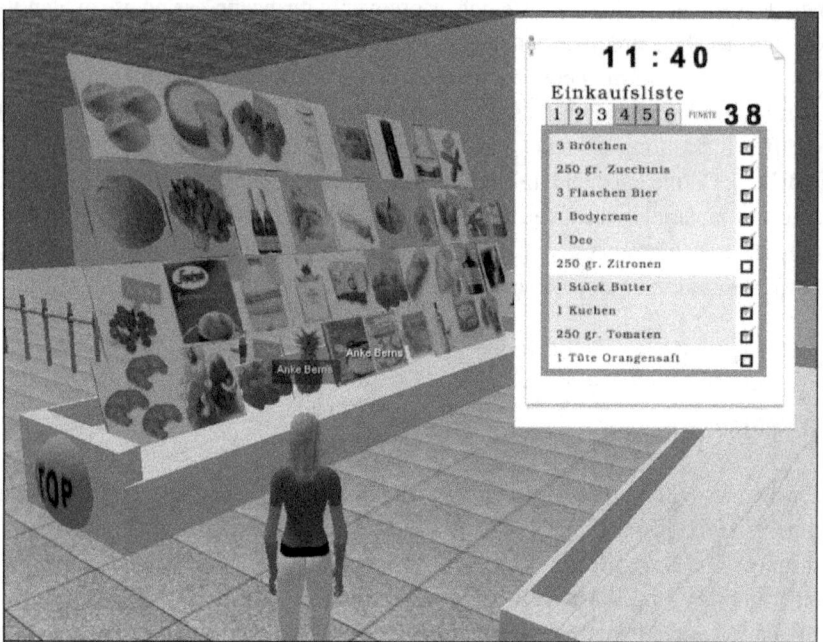

Figure 2. J-CLIC

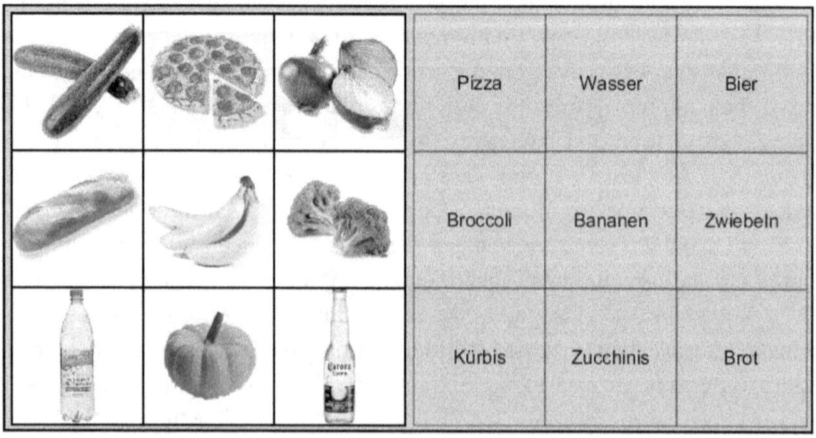

Figure 3. Paper-based material

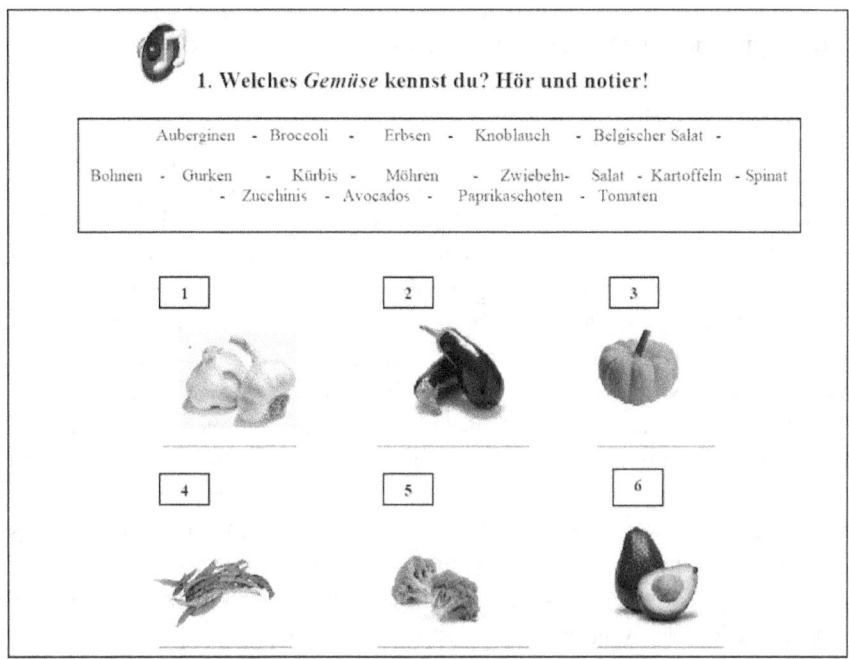

To analyze the videogame-like application's impact, a group of more than 60 students from the same German language course were randomly selected and were then arbitrarily placed into three different groups. In addition to this, each group was provided with a different learning tool. The first group was named Experimental Group (EXPG) and played the aforementioned Supermarket game. For a more detailed description of the game and the different activities designed within it we here refer to previous publications (Berns, González-Pardo, & Camacho, 2013). The second group was named Control Group One (CG1) and used the J-CLIC, whereas the third group, which was named Control Group Two (CG2), used the Paper-based materials. Each group was allowed to access only one of the online learning tools. The instructor had previously assigned each student a personal username and access code that would allow them to access only their respective VLE (VirtUAM or Virtual Campus) throughout the following two weeks. Whilst the study with both control groups (CG1 and CG2) was organized without a fixed schedule, as learners were free to enter the VLE as often and whenever they wanted, the study with the experimental group (EXPG) was structured into at least two sessions. During the first session the instructor met students within the VLE in order to familiarize them with the game-mechanism and tools they would need to use the game successfully. During the second as well as following sessions students worked mostly on their own, even though the instructor sometimes logged into the VLE to give individual support when students needed it.

## 2.2. Pre- and post-tests

In order to analyze the impact of each of the above mentioned learning tools on students' foreign language learning, we designed a four part pre- and post-test. Each part consisted of 15 questions which aimed to test the learning impact on students' receptive as well as productive language skills. Since the skills we wanted to train throughout the different learning tools were mainly listening, reading and writing, the pre- and post-tests focused on these skills. Parts 1, 2 and 3 were multiple choice tasks which focused on listening and reading. Students had to match different objects with their names (part 1), as well as several audio-recordings with their phonetic transcriptions (part 2) or with their corresponding visual concepts (part 3). Unlike this, part 4 focused on students' writing skills; students had to write the name of several categories of food and beverages. All participating groups were first asked to complete the same four-part pre-test online, following the same methodology. Whilst the pre-test had to be completed by all participants one day before starting the experiment, the post-test had to be repeated by each student twice: once immediately after using the assigned learning tool, and the second time two months later. By doing so we aimed to measure the impact of each on students' short and long-term memory.

## 3. Discussion

The results of post-test 1 show that the learners who played the videogame-like application (EXPG) got better marks in parts 1, 2 and 3, which focused on reading, listening and phonetic skills, than the students who used the J-CLIC (CG1) or Paper-based materials (CG2). However, there is a difference regarding the average marks obtained in part 4. Students who played the videogame got slightly lower marks when testing their writing skills compared to those obtained by students who had previously used the J-CLIC application. At the same time, it was conspicuous that in part 4 the videogame players got very similar results to the ones obtained by the students who used the Paper-based learning materials. In the case of the videogame this deviation might be explained by the fact that the game focuses more on reading and listening activities rather than on explicit writing tasks, whilst the J-CLIC application focuses on all three. However, with regard to the generally lower results of the Paper-based learning materials we believe that these can be related to their generally less motivational potential. Furthermore, the results of post-test 2 show that the videogame-like application had a higher impact on students' long-term memory than the J-CLIC and Paper-based learning materials did (see Table 1).

Table 1. Average marks of the three participating groups (EXPG, CG1 and CG2)

|        | Pre-test         |                 |                   | Post-test 1      |                 |                   | Post-test 2      |                 |                   |
|--------|------------------|-----------------|-------------------|------------------|-----------------|-------------------|------------------|-----------------|-------------------|
|        | V-Game (EXPG)    | J-CLIC (CG1)    | P-based (CG2)     | V-Game (EXPG)    | J-CLIC (CG1)    | P-based (CG2)     | V-Game (EXPG)    | J-CLIC (CG1)    | P-based (CG2)     |
| Part 1 | 3.15             | 3.25            | 3.25              | 8.15             | 7.91            | 7.30              | 7.98             | 6.73            | 6.56              |
| Part 2 | 5.32             | 5.18            | 5.43              | 7.80             | 7.58            | 6.65              | 7.67             | 6.57            | 6.40              |
| Part 3 | 3.94             | 3.89            | 3.53              | 7.80             | 7.58            | 6.65              | 7.67             | 6.57            | 6.40              |
| Part 4 | 1.02             | 1.04            | 0.89              | 3.76             | 4.20            | 3.75              | 3.61             | 3.45            | 3.26              |

The aforementioned results, together with the feedback information we got from the questionnaire, leads us to the hypothesis that videogame-like applications certainly hold great potential to enhance foreign language learning, but they need to be designed very carefully and according to students' specific weaknesses and needs. Some of our students' weaknesses refer to their writing skills since they are usually enrolled in language courses with very large size classes, which include a lot of oral input but few opportunities to focus on learners' individual writing skills. Furthermore, by tracing back students' logs and use of the different VLEs we were able to gain an insight into the appropriateness of each to engage students in autonomous learning. From the analysis of students' logs it seems that the students who were asked to play the videogame felt much more motivated to access the learning environment and to practice their language skills than the students of both control groups did. This was equally confirmed by the personal feedback we got from the participating students and their interest in using one or another learning tool.

## 4. Conclusions

Some final conclusions can be drawn from the results obtained as well as students' observations during the current pilot study. Videogame-like applications make foreign language learning in many cases more engaging and efficient since they are more entertaining and fun than many traditional online learning tools (in this case the J-CLIC and the Paper-based materials). One of the reasons is the fact that videogame-like applications provide highly immersive and interactive environments, in which language is presented in context and through game-based activities. In addition to this, videogame-like applications offer many opportunities for multidirectional interaction in the target language, thereby providing students not only with much valued foreign language input, but also with meaningful opportunities for foreign language output (Berns, Palomo Duarte, & Camacho, 2012; Berns, Palomo Duarte, Dodero Beardo, & Valero-Franco, in press). By combining both, the target language can be practised on a receptive as well as a productive level. However, a deeper statistical analysis on a greater data set is necessary to find reasonable evidence in favour of the videogame-like learning experience.

**Acknowledgements.** This research was partially supported by the following projects: (PI_13_011) Fortalecimiento de la comprensión escrita en LE mediante el uso de videojuegos, (AAA_53) El empleo de videojuegos para el apoyo al aprendizaje de lenguas extranjeras aplicado al alemàn, OpenDiscoverySpace (CIP-ICT-PSP-2011-5), ABANT (TIN2010-19872/TSI) and UbiCamp (526843-LLP1-2012-ES-ERASMUS-ESMO).

# References

Berns, A., González-Pardo, A., & Camacho, D. (2012). Implementing the use of virtual worlds in the teaching of foreign languages (level A1). In S. Czepielewski (Ed.), *Learning a language in virtual worlds: A review of innovation and ICT in language teaching methodology* (pp. 33-40). Warsow: Warsaw Academy of Computer Science, Management and Administration. Retrieved from http://www.v-langconference.eu/docs/V_Lang_International_Conference.pdf

Berns, A., Palomo Duarte, M., & Camacho, D. (2012). Designing interactive and collaborative learning tasks in a 3-D virtual environment. In L. Bradley & S. Thouësny (Eds.), *CALL: Using, Learning, Knowing, EUROCALL Conference, Gothenburg, Sweden, 22-25 August 2012, Proceedings* (pp. 20-25). Dublin: Research-publishing.net. Retrieved from http://research-publishing.net/publications/2012-eurocall-proceedings/

Berns, A., González-Pardo, A., & Camacho, D. (2013). Game-like learning in 3-D virtual environments. *Computers & Education, 60*, 210-220. doi: 10.1016/j.compedu.2012.07.001

Berns, A., Palomo Duarte, P., Dodero Beardo, J., & Valero-Franco, C. (in press). Using a 3D online game to assess students' foreign language acquisition and communicative competence. *Conference Proceedings of ECTEL 2013*. Springer.

Garris, R., Ahlers, R., & Driskell, J. E. (2002). Games, motivation and learning: a research and practice model. *Simulation & Gaming, 33*(4), 441-467. doi: 10.1177/1046878102238607

Schwienhorst, K. (2009). Learning a second language in three dimensions: potential benefits and the evidence so far. *Themes in Science and Technology Education, 2*(1-2), 153-164. Retrieved from http://earthlab.uoi.gr/theste/index.php/theste/article/view/30/21

# A Constructionist Approach to Student Modelling: Tracing a Student's Constructions Through an Agent-based Tutoring Architecture

## Katrien Beuls[1]

**Abstract**. Construction Grammar (CxG) is a well-established linguistic theory that takes the notion of a construction as the basic unit of language. Yet, because the potential of this theory for language teaching or SLA has largely remained ignored, this paper demonstrates the benefits of adopting the CxG approach for modelling a student's linguistic knowledge and skills in a language tutoring application. I propose a tutoring architecture for (adult) second language learning that relies on a student model that tracks a student's constructional knowledge. This model is embodied in a fully operational student agent, which has a construction inventory, a grammar engine (to process constructions) and learning strategies (to update constructions after learning). Through linguistic interactions between a language learner and the tutoring system, the student agent is enabled to model the behavior of the real student and tries to predict his input. The student construction inventory is aligned to the real student's input after every interaction. This innovative architecture, implemented in Fluid Construction Grammar, is demonstrated here for the use case of Spanish past tense expressions, which remains a complex task even for the most advanced learners of Spanish.

**Keywords**: construction grammar, student modeling, agent-based tutoring system, Spanish past tense.

---

1. Artificial Intelligence Lab, Vrije Universiteit Brussel, Brussels, Belgium; katrien@ai.vub.ac.be

**How to cite this article**: Beuls, K. (2013). A Constructionist Approach to Student Modelling: Tracing a Student's Constructions Through an Agent-based Tutoring Architecture. In L. Bradley & S. Thouësny (Eds.), *20 Years of EUROCALL: Learning from the Past, Looking to the Future. Proceedings of the 2013 EUROCALL Conference, Évora, Portugal* (pp. 45-50). Dublin/Voillans: © Research-publishing.net.

## 1. Introduction

Learning a new language from a native speaker is usually more successful than learning from an L2 teacher who does not fully master the target language and knows little more than the phrases in study books. The same argument applies to computer-based language tutors: a good model of the target language should be flexible enough to understand and produce utterances that are beyond those found in exercises. Moreover, apart from modeling the expert speaker, a good tutor also keeps a model of the student that he is tutoring, to estimate his proficiency level and the difficulties that he encounters. Once a tutor has full control over these two models, he can apply a range of tutoring strategies to best guide the student through a set of exercises. Yet, the structure and implementation of the underlying expert and learner models needs to be flexible enough to allow tutoring strategies to do their work. This paper demonstrates the benefits of using a Construction Grammar (CxG) approach as the basis for the expert and student model and shows how constructions can be learned and adapted over time.

I have used the bi-directional construction-grammar framework Fluid Construction Grammar (Steels, 2011, 2012) to test this innovative architecture for the use case of Spanish verb conjugation, which remains a complex task even for the most advanced learners of Spanish. Through the use of carefully designed diagnostics and repairs, the student construction inventory can be updated to maximally approach the real student's linguistic knowledge of the target domain. This paper first explains the basic architecture of the CxG-based tutor in Section 2 and further discusses the first results of the use of a student agent for Spanish verb learning in Section 3.

## 2. Method

The CxG-based language tutoring system advocates the use of deep language processing and agent-based modeling to construct a language tutoring system for second language (L2) learners. It demonstrates the benefits of keeping an active and predictive student model that takes the form of an autonomous learning agent. The system consists of three main elements that are explored in this section:

- Because domain knowledge is a crucial prerequisite to construct a personalized language tutor it is necessary to have a fully operational **language agent** that can function as a competent language user.

- A **predictive student model** in the form of a student agent with a structure that is identical to the language agent can be dynamically aligned to fit the real student's progress.

- A language agent can take up the role of the tutor if he is endowed with a set of **tutoring strategies**, which make use of the student model as well as a more general student profile module.

### 2.1. Language agent

The language agent that is presented here consists of three main components: a construction inventory, a grammar engine and a set of flexibility strategies (Figure 1). The first component, the construction inventory, is a catalogue of all the grammatical constructions that a language user typically uses. It can contain lexical constructions, phrasal constructions, morphological constructions, etc. that are each responsible for a small part in the processing of an utterance. The construction inventory can be organised according to different principles that are either driven by the implementation and processing perspective or by the psycholinguistic relevance of grammar organisation.

Figure 1. The language agent and the student agent share the same architecture; a full tutor agent that interacts with a student has three types of strategies that are distributed across its sub-agent components

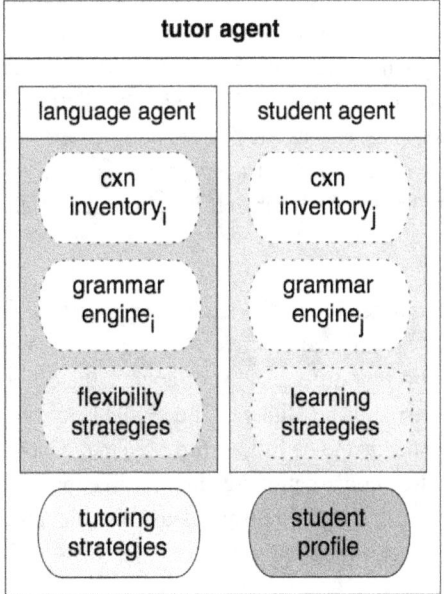

The second main component is the grammar engine. This is the component that is responsible for the actual linguistic processing of the constructions that are collected in the construction inventory. This processing involves a search through the inventory to retrieve the constructions that are required to build or interpret a particular utterance. The grammar engine should allow for bi-directional processing so that the same constructions can be used in production and parsing. This bi-directionality is a crucial feature if we want to enable flexible processing, which implies that the tutor can try to reproduce the student's utterance to reconstruct the constructions that he accessed and the possible search path that was taken.

Finally, an expert language agent also has a set of flexibility strategies that allow for robust processing of the learner's utterances, especially when they contain mistakes. These strategies allow to always retrieve a solution when an erroneous utterance is parsed and to come up with a correction as well as the source of the error. A flexibility strategy contains diagnostics and repairs that identify the irregularity and find a solution to solve it. They are constantly active in a linguistic meta-layer that runs on top of regular processing so that they can catch every small deviation of regular construction processing (Beuls, van Trijp, & Wellens, 2012; Maes & Nardi, 1988).

## 2.2. Student agent

A good teacher naturally constructs a model of his student that represents the student's skills and knowledge as a function over time. It is a kind of model that could mimic typical student utterances that are illustrative of the student's proficiency level. In order to operationalize such a predictive model it is convenient to reuse the three-component language agent architecture. This student model is thus implemented as a fully-fledged agent, who can actively participate in the linguistic community that he finds himself in. This agent is also further referred to as a student agent.

Because the language agent's and the student agent's architectures are identical (Figure 1), it becomes very cost-efficient to construct a student model from scratch. The most important difference is, of course, the difference in competence level between the tutor and the student. The student does not yet master all the constructions that are needed to be fully expressive in the language that he or she is learning. Gradually, their construction inventory will expand and mold towards the target language. It might take different paths to construct an L2 language, so that different learning strategies are required.

Instead of flexibility strategies, a student agent has a set of learning strategies that are in charge of the continuous expansion and adaptation of the agent's constructions, which in turn is based on information that is gathered during processing. Learning strategies encode personal tactics on how to solve a particular problem and they can thus differ greatly between students. For instance, one learning strategy for learning Catalan would be to first conjugate all the verbs in their first person singular form. Another strategy would imply that you construct your sentences in Spanish (in case you master this language) and replace some of the words by their Catalan counterparts.

### 2.3. Tutoring strategies

Apart from making a dynamic model of the students, a human teacher typically also applies a range of tutoring strategies to assist students in their problem-solving tasks. A tutoring strategy is a dynamic plan of action that stipulates future interactions with the student. To create or adapt a tutoring strategy, a teacher does not only depend on the information that is kept in the student model but also makes use of a more general record of the student's strengths and challenges in learning.

The language tutoring system that is proposed here therefore hosts an artificial tutor that simulates these typical teacher tactics. As a result, the original language agent architecture needs to be extended so that this agent can also function as a tutor (Figure 1). Such a revision implies two new components as parts of a tutor agent, apart from having direct access to the student agent: a tutoring strategies component and a student profile component. These components are vital elements of a personalized tutoring approach because they provide meta-information about the tutoring process, for instance to decide which type of exercise to repeat or where to challenge the student further.

### 3. Results

The first case study with the CxG-based tutoring system focuses on the language system of Spanish tense, aspect and mood. After the development of a Spanish language agent with flexibility strategies needed to effortlessly parse erroneous sentences and correct them (Beuls, 2012), a student agent with learning strategies can be "cloned" cost efficiently with empty construction inventory and default grammar engine settings, completed with a set of learning strategies and designed for the target language system. A set of 10 diagnostics and 12 repairs is needed to fully operationalize the acquisition process of the Spanish verb system from contrastive situations such as "cantaba/cantía una canción", *he sang (perfective/*

*imperfective) a song*. First results have shown that the student agent learns more quickly and more efficiently when he can also speak and not only listen.

## 4. Conclusions

The architecture presented in this paper allows building a tutoring system for a specific subpart of a language for which the grammar engineer can develop all elements of the language agent. Once these elements are provided, the meta-level runs through all components of the tutoring system by means of flexibility, learning and tutoring strategies. The agent-based model of the real student tracks the performance of the student and has the capability to predict future utterances, which can in turn be used to select appropriate exercises for the skill level of the student.

**Acknowledgements**. This research was funded by the Flemish Agency for Science and Technology. I want to thank my supervisor Luc Steels for creating excellent opportunities for scientific exploration into the field of computational linguistics, language evolution and so much more.

## References

Beuls, K. (2012). Grammatical error diagnosis in Fluid Construction Grammar: a case study in L2 Spanish verb morphology. *Computer Assisted Language Learning*, 1-15. doi: 10.1080/09588221.2012.724426

Beuls, K., van Trijp, R., & Wellens, P. (2012). Diagnostics and Repairs in Fluid Construction Grammar. In L. Steels & M. Hild (Eds.), *Language Grounding in Robots* (pp. 195-214). Berlin/Heidelberg: Springer.

Maes, P., & Nardi, D. (Eds.). (1988). *Meta-Level Architectures and Reflection*. New York, NY, USA: Elsevier Science Inc.

Steels, L. (Ed.). (2011). *Design Patterns in Fluid Construction Grammar*. Amsterdam: John Benjamins.

Steels, L. (Ed.). (2012). *Computational Issues in Fluid Construction Grammar*. Berlin: Springer Verlag.

# Separating Fact and Fiction: The Real Story of Corpus Use in Language Teaching

## Alex Boulton[1]

**Abstract**. This paper investigates uses of corpora in language learning ('data-driven learning') through analysis of a 600K-word corpus of empirical research papers in the field. The corpus can tell us much – the authors and the countries the studies are conducted in, the types of publication, and so on. The corpus investigation itself starts with frequency lists of words and clusters to detect initial themes, which are then extended (via distribution plots, collocates, concordances, etc.) to look at specific items: the researchers cited, the theoretical constructs and concepts investigated and how they are treated, and so on. The paper ends by dividing the corpus into early and more recent papers to compare evolution over time. This reveals keywords that were prevalent in earlier days as a snapshot of the past, and keywords today which may give an idea of future directions.

**Keywords**: corpora, language learning, DDL, data-driven learning, aboutness, empirical research.

## 1. Introduction

Language corpora and the tools used to investigate them are amenable to a tremendous variety of applications in many different fields. Even in language learning, there is "considerable variety in the pedagogical approaches adopted" (Johns & King, 1991, p. iii). This heterogeneity can make it rather difficult to make sense of what is really going on. Various attempts have been made elsewhere to analyse the results of empirical studies, especially in the form of a narrative synthesis (e.g. Boulton, 2010), but also more recently in a meta-analysis (Cobb & Boulton, in preparation). The aim of the present paper is not to analyse the

---

1. Crapel – ATILF, CNRS & University of Lorraine, Nancy, France; alex.boulton@univ-lorraine.fr

**How to cite this article**: Boulton, A. (2013). Separating Fact and Fiction: The Real Story of Corpus Use in Language Teaching. In L. Bradley & S. Thouësny (Eds.), *20 Years of EUROCALL: Learning from the Past, Looking to the Future. Proceedings of the 2013 EUROCALL Conference, Évora, Portugal* (pp. 51-56). Dublin/Voillans: © Research-publishing.net.

outcomes of empirical studies, but rather to identify typical themes and how they develop over time. To try to find core and peripheral areas of study, this paper investigates a corpus of published research papers in the field.

## 2. Methods

Given the many hundreds of papers that discuss various uses and applications of corpora in language teaching and learning, for present purposes it was decided to limit the study to published research papers which evaluate some aspect of corpus use in language learning and teaching, thus allowing a near-exhaustive collection rather than a sample. It further excludes papers in languages other than English (though only a handful of these had been identified), PhDs (which would have skewed the results given their length), duplicate papers which report the same study twice (if sometimes from different angles), and unpublished papers (e.g. conference presentations), though it did include proceedings papers (cf. the debate about including 'fugitive literature' for meta-analysis; e.g. Norris & Ortega, 2006). The final corpus comprises 110 papers dating from 1989 to 2012, with over half appearing in the last 6 years, which suggests a healthy growth in empirical studies in this area. Nearly half were published in Europe (52), which is perhaps unsurprising as much of the primary interest came from the UK in the work of Johns (e.g. 1986) in Birmingham, as well as from Europe through the TaLC conference series. Asia is also well represented (37), with 17 studies in Taiwan alone; the rest of the world (21) consists primarily of English-speaking countries. Most papers appeared in journals (68), notably *CALL* (14), *LL&T* (9) and *ReCALL* (8); a further 31 were book chapters, and 11 were in conference proceedings.

Some texts were available in electronic format, while others had to be scanned. All were then converted to plain text format (UTF8), which had to be manually checked for various conversion and other problems, a not inconsiderable task given the need to work with a suitably 'clean' corpus. As the main interest was in the authors' own text, further editing was required to exclude meta-data and abstracts, tables and figures, lists of examples and corpus data, long quotes, bibliographies and appendices. However, footnotes, endnotes, embedded examples and in-text citations were retained. The final corpus comprised 615,758 tokens (mean 5,597, varying from 1,631 to 15,029; $SD = 2,068.11$).

The aim of the present study is not so much to analyse *language* per se, but rather the ideas expressed through language to arrive at an understanding of the "aboutness" of the corpus as a whole (Scott & Tribble, 2006, p. 60), i.e. applying corpus linguistics tools as "a way of telling stories about texts" (Tribble, 2012, n.p.). The main software used was *AntConc* (Anthony, 2012), a free, simple, user-friendly, stable and reliable tool complete with on-line tutorials, help functions and discussion forums. *AntConc* is suitable for teachers and students (cf. Kaszubski, 2006), but also sufficiently flexible and powerful for research purposes (e.g. Charles, 2012).

## 3. Results and discussion

The first step was to compile a frequency list of the corpus as a whole. Inevitably, most of the high frequency items were grammar-function words (*the, of, too, and...*); though such "small words" are not without interest, they are of limited relevance for semantic purposes, so a stoplist[2] was applied to filter them out. The resulting list of lexical items, each with a frequency of over 1,000 occurrences per million words, allows a general overall picture to emerge of the prototypical study in this field. They can be recombined textually, if somewhat creatively, as:

> A *group* of *learners*, generally *students, using data* from *texts based* on *corpora* for *learning language* or *writing* through *concordancing*. According to their *level*, they can look at *both vocabulary* (*words*) or *grammar* to gain *information* from the *examples* of actual *use* given in a *concordance*, and *search* for *patterns* to improve their *knowledge* in their *English course*. This *teaching approach* is known as *DDL*, and each *research study* provides *analysis* of *results* from a *test*.

This intuitively corresponds to the picture generally projected of data-driven learning, but the corpus-based description provides a sounder empirical basis to build on here. Frequency lists of clusters were also produced, though the results did not contribute much semantically to the present research. For example, the top three tri-grams were *the use of, of the students* and *in order to*.

Case sensitive searches enabled the compilation of a list of researchers referred to in the texts. Unsurprisingly, Tim *Johns* was the most frequently cited with 317 occurrences, followed by Tom *Cobb* (210), Angela *Chambers* (145) and Guy *Aston* (122), all tremendously influential in the field. From an analysis of authors cited at least 20 times, it is apparent that most of the 65 individuals are originally specialists in language learning and teaching who have adopted corpus linguistics techniques in their research and teaching, rather than corpus linguists moving towards language pedagogy. The implications of this require further exploration.

---

2. http://nlp.cs.nyu.edu/GMA_files/resources/english.stoplist

Firstly, 31% of papers make no mention of Johns at all; this may be because the authors prefer more recent references, or are simply unaware of older research. However, it might be that some researchers do not consider what they are doing to be 'data-driven learning', the term coined by Johns. Nonetheless, *DDL* and *data-driven learning* (± hyphen) together appear 1,106 times in 69 papers. Following up on this, the term *corpus-driven* occurred 64 times in 11 papers, compared to *corpus-based* 367 times in 70 papers (± hyphens). Given the debate about the differences between the two terms (cf. Tognini-Bonelli, 2001), it is interesting to note that only 3 of the 110 papers use both, and only 2 make an explicit distinction. However, the differences become apparent from the collocates: *corpus-driven* tends to co-occur with *research* and *study/studies*, while *corpus-based* collocates most strongly with *learning, activity/activities* and *approach*. Again, this seems to reflect the preoccupations among these researchers, i.e. language teaching/learning which uses corpus linguistics rather than the other way round.

The next question is to identify exactly what pedagogical aspects are developed most. A list was drawn up of likely key terms, especially the advantages frequently attributed to the approach, leading to individual analyses of 30 separate families of items. The list was topped by *context\**, which occurred 1,133 times in 105 papers, and at least 10 times in 44 papers. Other items occurring at least 500 times and at least 10 times in 10 separate papers are *task\*, pattern\*, skill\** and *exercise\**. The bottom end of the scale is also revealing, with less than 20 occurrences of *constructiv\** or *individuali\** (for *individualisation, individualized*, etc.) for example. Even such items as *cogniti\** and *autonom\** are relatively infrequent: fewer than 5 papers mention them more than 10 times, suggesting they have not been the overt focus of much research. No papers feature even 10 occurrences of *collaborat\** or *creativ\**, again suggesting a need for further explicit work in these areas.

Pursuing the theme of this year's EUROCALL conference (*20 years of EUROCALL: learning from the past, looking to the future*), a final stage was to divide the corpus into two roughly equal components (by publication date, with the cut-off point at 2006/2007) to compare early and more recent themes. This is achieved by a keywords analysis, which counts all items in the two sub-corpora to arrive at a measure of statistical significance (log-likelihood), and ranks them according to their positive or negative keyness (Scott & Tribble, 2006). Keywords in the earlier papers include *concordancing, vocabulary* and *word*, as well as specific corpora such as the *Bank (of English)*. Keywords in more recent work include *writing* (with corpora being used as reference resources as well as learning tools) and *Google* (as the internet has become ever more present for professional and study purposes as well as in everyday life). Less significant items need careful interpretation in a corpus of this size, however, as the procedure used does not take account of distribution; so an item such as *stance*, for example, is considered key since it occurs 119 times in recent studies vs. only 2 in older ones, but 117 of these are from just one paper.

## 4. Conclusions

Corpus linguistics is not just for corpus linguists. The availability of high-quality yet free and simple tools opens up the methodology to teachers and learners for a tremendous variety of purposes, including language learning and teaching. In this paper, a large collection of empirical DDL-like studies was compiled and subjected to corpus analysis, revealing a picture of prototypical work in this area and suggesting themes requiring further work – especially on some of the advantages frequently attributed to a DDL approach but for which there is as yet little empirical backing. Future predictions are always delicate, but deriving them from real facts in a corpus puts them on a firmer footing than some more subjective approaches. Based on the corpus presented here, one might expect the future to hold a greater synthesis between researchers in language teaching/learning and in corpus linguistics, the continued development of corpus use as a reference tool as well as a learning aid, a bottom-up expansion from lexis to include more work at the level of text or discourse, and increasing use of the web-as-corpus and Google-as-concordancer.

## References

Anthony, L. (2012). *AntConc v3.2.4w/m*. Tokyo: Waseda University. Retrieved from http://www.antlab.sci.waseda.ac.jp

Boulton, A. (2010). Learning outcomes from corpus consultation. In M. Moreno Jaén, F. Serrano Valverde, & M. Calzada Pérez (Eds.), *Exploring new paths in language pedagogy: Lexis and corpus-based language teaching* (pp. 129-144). London: Equinox. [Electronic supplement available at http://bit.ly/STZegS]

Charles, M. (2012). 'Proper vocabulary and juicy collocations': EAP students evaluate do-it-yourself corpus-building. *English for Specific Purposes, 31*(2), 93-102. doi: 10.1016/j.esp.2011.12.003

Cobb, T., & Boulton, A. (In preparation). Classroom applications of corpus analysis. In D. Biber & R. Reppen (Eds.), *Cambridge handbook of corpus linguistics*. Cambridge: Cambridge University Press.

Johns, T. (1986). Micro-Concord: A language learner's research tool. *System, 14*(2), 151-162. doi: 10.1016/0346-251X(86)90004-7

Johns, T., & King, P. (Eds.). (1991). Classroom concordancing. *English Language Research Journal, 4*. University of Birmingham: Centre for English Language Studies.

Kaszubski, P. (2006). Web-based concordancing and ESAP writing. *Poznan Studies in Contemporary Linguistics, 41*, 161-193.

Norris, J. M., & Ortega, L. (Eds.). (2006). *Synthesizing research on language learning and teaching*. Amsterdam: John Benjamins.

Scott, M., & Tribble, C. (2006). *Textual patterns: Key words and corpus analysis in language education*. Amsterdam: John Benjamins.

Tognini-Bonelli, E. (2001). *Corpus linguistics at work*. Amsterdam: John Benjamins.

Tribble, C. (2012). Teaching and language corpora: Quo vadis? *10th Teaching and Language Corpora (TaLC) international conference*. Warsaw: Uniwersytet Warszawski, 11-14 July.

# German-French Case Study: Using Multi-Online Tools to Collaborate Across Borders

## Regina Brautlacht[1] and Csilla Ducrocq[2]

**Abstract.** This paper examines how students learn to collaborate in English by participating in an intercultural project that focuses on teaching students to work together on a digital writing project using various online tools, and documents their reflections working in an intercultural context. Students from Université Paris Sud Orsay and Bonn Rhein-Sieg-University of Applied Sciences participated in this digital collaboration project. Mixed groups of students, two French and two German, used several synchronous and asynchronous tools to communicate with their counterparts (Facebook, WordPress blog, WIMS e-learning platform, email, videoconferencing). Students had to produce an article together, comparing French and German attitudes about a topic they negotiated freely in their groups. Before publishing their post, students were expected to peer-review the article written by their group. Once published, the posts were commented on by the other participants of the project. The final stage consisted of voting for the best posts on the e-learning platform, WIMS. A videoconference was also organized to create cohesion between the participants. The result of the student evaluations, together with the administrative, technical and intercultural difficulties encountered during the collaboration between two vastly differing university setups is presented.

**Keywords**: online collaboration, e-learning, writing, speaking, intercultural comparisons.

---

1. Bonn-Rhine-Sieg University, Sankt Augustin, Germany; regina.brautlacht@h-brs.de
2. Université Paris Sud, Orsay, France; csilla.ducrocq@u-psud.fr

**How to cite this article**: Brautlacht, R., & Ducrocq, C. (2013). German-French Case Study: Using Multi-Online Tools to Collaborate Across Borders. In L. Bradley & S. Thouësny (Eds.), *20 Years of EUROCALL: Learning from the Past, Looking to the Future. Proceedings of the 2013 EUROCALL Conference, Évora, Portugal* (pp. 57-63). Dublin/Voillans: © Research-publishing.net.

## 1. Introduction

The aim of this collaborative project between students from Bonn Rhein-Sieg-University of Applied Sciences, Germany and Université Paris Sud, Faculté des Sciences, Orsay, France was to: (a) learn how to collaborate in an international environment using various web 2.0 tools; (b) find out how the other side feels about certain issues and compare opinions; (c) practice writing for an international audience using digital technologies; (d) become more autonomous in checking one's writing using the Internet or other tools such as the British National Corpus[3] and also learning how to proofread others' pieces of writing.

Four student groups (two German, two French) were assigned to each virtual team. Students freely chose a topic they wished to discuss and write about. Afterwards, the group members jointly wrote an article, which they published on a blog[4] set up for this purpose. A Facebook group was created to offer a joint platform to communicate with all group members of the project. The pilot project was first carried out in 2011, slightly modified after taking both students' and teachers' observations into account. In this paper we present the 4-month project as it was run in 2012.

## 2. Method

### 2.1. Introduction

The action research investigates which online tools students use to collaborate, which tools they prefer and how they perceive collaboration using online tools. We identified the experience students had in collaborating online using different tools prior to the project and designed the program accordingly. This is a small scale investigation with 19 undergraduate and graduate students from Germany and 19 university graduate students from France.

### 2.2. Background information (participants)

The research was conducted during the winter term 2012. Over a four-month period 38 students worked in 10 groups (9 groups of four with two German and two French students, 1 group of 2: one German and one French student) together.

---

3. http://corpus.byu.edu/bnc/

4. http://hebergement.u-psud.fr/blog-langues/wordpress/

Each group wrote a joint article, which they posted on a blog[5] set up for this purpose. The majority of German students were undergraduate, studying Business Administration (B.Sc.) and three were graduate students of IT. The French students were all graduate students of Primary Education.

## 2.3. Data collection

The perceptions of working collaboratively were analyzed by using an online questionnaire based on questions used in research conducted by Hughes and Narayan (2009) and Ducate, Anderson, and Moreno (2011). The questionnaire was offered online on the Web Interactive Multi-Purpose Platform (WIMS: open source platform)[6] and offered both quantitative and qualitative data. First, general demographic data and the previous experience of working online were gathered. Then, the program was designed and the act of collaboration was analyzed by asking students how they worked together online and how frequently they communicated. Furthermore, the students were asked to comment on their writing and proofreading skills. Finally, the students' perception of the project was examined.

There were 40 questions grouped into six categories:

- general information about the participant (age, gender, studies);

- prior experience in use of online collaborative tools;

- collaboration in virtual teams (type of online tools used, frequency of communication);

- writing skills (skills learned, proofreading, etc.);

- perceptions of the project (ease of communication and usefulness of the project);

- recommendations to future participants.

25 (13 Germans and 12 French) out of 38 students answered the questionnaire that was intended to evaluate the collaborative writing project. We did not have the means to analyze the progression in writing skills and media literacy.

---

5. http://hebergement.u-psud.fr/blog-langues/wordpress/

6. http://wims.u-psud.fr/wims

## 3. Results

### 3.1. Prior online experience

Except for one German student, all participants had a Facebook account prior to the project. The majority of students had never blogged before and only 4 French and 2 German students had blogged in English. While all the French respondents had never participated in a collaboration project in either French or English, 2 Germans had prior experience in collaborating in English.

### 3.2. Collaboration

The frequency of communication and the use of tools were examined to offer a basis to analyze collaboration. All students preferred to communicate via e-mail and Facebook and did not choose any other online tool to communicate (e.g. Skype). During the project 17 of 25 respondents communicated more than six times with their partners. 7 students corresponded 4 to 6 times.

### 3.3. Writing skills

Except for one French student, all proofread their own writing and those of their group. Concerning frequency of proofreading, a difference can be observed: 8 out of 13 Germans proofread their writing more than twice, whereas only 4 French students did so; 5 German and 7 French students proofread their writing once or twice and 1 French student never did any proofreading.

### 3.4. Perceptions of the project

Everyone thought the project was useful training for international collaborative work, and all the students enjoyed it on the whole. The comments made by the students show that most students enjoyed the opportunity to work in an international environment and to compare points of view. They appreciated the liberty they were given to negotiate the content of their writing[7]. Below are some selected comments:

---

7. A total of 10 articles and 102 comments were posted on the course blog: 1. How football became a business model in Germany and France; 2. German and French prejudice; 3. Energies; 4. Social networks; 5. French and German cinema; 6. Going abroad while studying; 7.The impact of the Internet on art; 8. Doping in cycling; 9. How to get abroad; 10. Student housing in Germany and France.

German student: "I liked the idea of working together with students from a foreign university compared to the tasks which we would have had to do otherwise".

German student: "A complete new experience…".

French student: "It was interesting to discover the less academic approach to writing of the Germans".

French student: "It was interesting to observe the way the Germans worked and to compare whether there were any differences with our way of working".

French student: "…the Germans were very nice and tolerant despite our lower level of English".

### 3.5. Recommendations to future participants

All except for one German student would recommend this project to other students. Most students urged frequent and regular communication, not only about the topic they had chosen but about themselves, and giving the project plenty of time because the topic had to be researched thoroughly and for success creating a rapport with team members was essential. The French recommended assigning clear roles to all the members of the team for more efficiency. They also advised future students about the need to impose the "legendary German rigor" throughout the collaboration and the need to answer e-mails without delay.

## 4. Discussion

In the analysis of the data presented, it is necessary to consider the different university set ups. The French students had no English classes throughout the project. Moreover, halfway through the project, the French students were informed that due to changes in the state curriculum no credits could be provided for their involvement in the online English project. Despite this the French students continued the project and were intrinsically motivated.

After a first kick-off meeting the language instructor communicated with the French students via Facebook or the WIMS platform. This may explain the French apprehension of oral encounters with the German students, i.e. reluctance to participate in the video conference or not choosing online tools for oral communication (e.g. Skype). Not having an English class could explain why most

French students had not felt their writing skills had improved, whereas the majority of German students felt that they had made progress in writing.

The German students had a three-hour English class each week where the language instructor could address issues and provide language guidance to the students. In addition, several online activities were done directly in class.

As seen in this case study, students learned from each other and spent time writing a collaborative article as well as meeting in synchronous situations. Some frustration was voiced by the French students who were unable to express their ideas in English during the video conference, whereas this was not an issue for the written assignment as they had time to look up words and formulate ideas. The use of multiple tools offers new forms of learning both linguistically and socially for language learners. Furthermore, it offers opportunities to communicate with other non-native speakers using English as *lingua franca*. It is important to point out that the language proficiency differed. In Germany the class was a level B2-C1, while in France the levels were lower: A2-B1.

Despite these differences the project had an overall positive outcome: some French students highlighted the tolerance and the pleasantness of their German counterparts and suggested enjoying the communication instead of focusing on language difficulties. Scaffolding offered by more experienced learners, as described in the Zone of Proximal Development (ZPD) from Vygotsky (1978) is an important element in social interaction. Blake (2011) points out recent trends in online learning have triggered a number of issues in language learning from traditional face-to-face instruction, newer hybrid learning scenarios or distant learning. The most important benefit from learning with online tools is that students are more involved, and social computing CALL offers new opportunities for students to learn from each other in an international setting.

Li (2012) points out that empirical research has found that each writing task and writing instruction needs to be designed for a specific purpose. As such, the instructor's role is an important aspect in each collaborative project. Providing feedback on collaborative work, offering scaffolding and participating within the collaborative environment is also essential. For future projects the question is what strategies and tools can be used to prepare students for spontaneous oral scenarios, and to offer more scaffolding for written and oral assignments. In addition, the coordinators/instructors' perceptions need to be included in a more detailed analysis. Furthermore, assessing the knowledge gained from the sociocultural perspective needs to be examined in more detail.

## 5. Conclusions

Despite different university set ups (undergraduate/graduate level, distance course versus regular language classes), language proficiency (B2-C1 versus A2-B1 levels) and assessment requirements, it is possible to run an international collaborative project online.

Student awareness of cultural differences and tolerance play an important role in such a project. It is also essential to provide clear objectives and detailed instructions to the participants to reduce stress. Close, constant collaboration between country coordinators is a necessary prerequisite for completing a successful project.

In the future, more guidance and practice in writing (e.g. using formal style) and speaking (e.g. strategies for reformulation, asking for clarification, paraphrasing) should be provided.

## References

Blake, R. J. (2011). Current Trends in Online Language Learning. *Annual Review of Applied Linguistics, 31*, 19-35. doi: 10.1017/S026719051100002X

Ducate, L. C., Anderson, L. L., & Moreno N. (2011). Wading Through the World of Wikis: An Analysis of Three Wiki Projects. *Foreign Language Annals, 44*(3), 495-524. doi: 10.1111/j.1944-9720.2011.01144.x

Hughes, J. E., & Narayan, R. (2009). Collaboration and Learning with Wikis in Post-Secondary Classrooms. *Journal of Interactive Online Learning, 8*(1). Retrieved from http://www.ncolr.org/jiol/issues/pdf/8.1.4.pdf

Li, M. (2012). Use of Wikis in Second/Foreign Language Classes: A Literature Review. *CALL-EJ, 13*(1), 17-35. Retrieved from http://callej.org/journal/13-1/Li_2012.pdf

Vygotsky, L. S. (1978). *Mind in society: The development of higher psychological processes*. Cambridge: Harvard University Press.

# Online Role-plays: Combining Situational and Interactional Authenticity in Foreign Language Learning

## Maria de Lurdes Correia Martins[1], Gillian Moreira[2], and António Moreira[3]

**Abstract**. Role-plays have been almost ubiquitous in foreign language classes and their potential has been widely recognised. In the last decade, the dissemination of Web 2.0 has created a wide range of possibilities for this type of activity, including conducting online role-plays between institutions, the opportunity to combine synchronous and asynchronous communication tools and also articulate online with face-to-face interactions. Online role-plays are first and foremost a social process in which knowledge is emergent resulting from interactions between participants. It is also an activity that mirrors contextualised everyday situations and students are faced with new information, promoting research and reflection, thus enhancing autonomy. Within a dialogical and dialectical perspective of English language learning, the following research question was developed: how can online role-plays in English language learning in higher education be integrated in order to enhance the development of communicative competence? In order to answer the research question, an action research project was carried out, according to the model proposed by Stringer (2007), and an online role-play was implemented over six weeks in the English II course unit from the degree in Tourism at the Polytechnic Institute of Viseu, Portugal.

**Keywords**: EFL, interactional authenticity, online role-play, situational authenticity.

---

1. Polytechnic Institute of Viseu, Viseu, Portugal; lurdesmartins@estv.ipv.pt
2. University of Aveiro, Campus Universitário de Santiago, Aveiro, Portugal
3. University of Aveiro, Campus Universitário de Santiago, Aveiro, Portugal

**How to cite this article**: Correia Martins, M. D. L., Moreira, G., & Moreira, A. (2013). Online Role-plays: Combining Situational and Interactional Authenticity in Foreign Language Learning. In L. Bradley & S. Thouësny (Eds.), *20 Years of EUROCALL: Learning from the Past, Looking to the Future. Proceedings of the 2013 EUROCALL Conference, Évora, Portugal* (pp. 64-70). Dublin/Voillans: © Research-publishing.net.

## 1. Introduction

Role-plays have been very popular in the foreign language classroom in order to simulate situations from the real world. Web 2.0 technologies have meant a lot of opportunities for expanding and enriching traditional role-plays, since they provide a scenario that enhances dialogue between participants assuming specific roles who will have to negotiate and discuss different perspectives in order to collaboratively create a common output. According to Wills, Leigh and Ip (2011):

> "Role plays are situations in which learners take on the role profiles of specific characters or representatives of organisations in a contrived setting. Role play is designed primarily to build first person experience in a safe and supportive environment. Much of the learning occurs because the learning design requires learners to explore and articulate viewpoints that may not be their own" (p. 2).

We can then say that online role-plays enhance discussion, dialogue and negotiation between participants, who assume specific roles with the ultimate goal of collaboratively creating something new. Recently, the EnROLE Project (Wills, Rosser, Devonshire, Leigh, Russel, & Shephard, 2009), which was developed in Australia with the intention of promoting the use of online role-plays in higher education, highlighted the following aspects:

- online role-plays are designed to increase understanding of real-life interaction and dynamics;
- participants assume the role of someone in a specific situation;
- participants undertake authentic activities in authentic contexts;
- tasks involve in-role interaction and negotiation with other participants/ roles;
- interaction between participants is mostly conducted in an online environment;
- final outputs should create opportunities for reflection.

Designing an online role-play is, undoubtedly, a complex and challenging task and encompasses three main elements from the learner's perspective: tasks to be done; resources, namely the adopted scenario, role descriptions and background readings; and support processes, that might involve scaffolding for team work, access to real world professionals and a moderator.

As far as tasks are concerned, Wills et al. (2011) distinguish between six complementary stages, known as the "6 Rs":

- enRole – students familiarise themselves with their role;

- Research – students gather information about their role and its social entourage;

- wRite – students share their role written profile;

- React – students share and discuss different viewpoints by interacting with other roles;

- Resolve – students attempt to reach a shared resolution to the proposed task;

- Reflection – students debrief about what has occurred and about what they have learned.

Regarding materials, students might be assigned some additional reading or encouraged to explore different links in order to put themselves in someone else's shoes. Wills et al. (2011) state that:

> "Materials need to support not only the content of the role play but also its process. They must also provide multiple perspectives supporting different possible solutions […]. Learners must be provided with more materials than they need, to force reliance on choices based on assessment of relevance" (p. 77).

The planning and design of rules and roles should be carefully considered by the moderator, who will need to consider aspects such as the distribution and use of power, the division of labour amongst participants, the relationship between the different roles and decision making. The role and functions of the moderator depend mainly on the learning objectives and the scope and design of the role-play. In line with this, Leigh and Rosser (2008) highlighted a need to adjust monitoring to the different phases of the role-play. The authors distinguish between four phases:

- Pre-play phase – at this stage it is crucial to be able to engage and motivate students, familiarising them with the online environment that will support the activity. It is also important to announce the start point and define the final outcome.

- Early stage – understanding roles and ensuring a fair distribution of work among participants is crucial for the success of the role-play. The moderator should make sure that the scenario, environment and functions have been fully understood.

- Development stage – will be the backbone of the role-play and, at this stage, the moderator should make sure students pursue the role-play agenda. It might be necessary to encourage participation or maintain focus.

- Final stage – it is a moment of reflection, disengagement and assessment, sharing experiences and evaluating the degree of achievement of objectives.

## 2. Method

The methodological approach adopted for this study consisted of an action research project over six weeks, adapted from Stringer (2007), in the English II course unit from the degree course in Tourism at the School of Technology and Management, Polytechnic Institute of Viseu. This study seeks to provide an answer to the following question: how to use online role-plays in English language learning in higher education in order to enhance the development of communicative competence?

Stemming from this question, there are two main objectives:

- Harnessing the potential of online role-plays in the teaching and learning of English in higher education.

- Identifying the strengths and weaknesses of using online role-plays in English language learning for the collaborative construction of knowledge in higher education.

Students organised into groups and assuming specific roles had to organise a visit to London for a group of 25 students. Table 1 presents a general overview of the activity.

Table 1. Overview of the role-play "A Trip to London"

| | |
|---|---|
| Roles | 19 roles (managed by 8 groups: 2 travel agencies; 3 airline companies; a students' representative; an events planning company; Word Travel Market) <br> The moderator allocated students to the different groups <br> Assignment of roles within each group made by students <br> Generic role (job / function) <br> Pair work (crucial to pull into the action) <br> Collaborative work (essential for communication between roles) |
| Learning goals | Develop proposals related to different aspects of organising a trip to London <br> Develop capabilities for planning a trip with Web tools and services <br> Develop connections with different roles and nodes to ensure effective collaboration to achieve specific goals |
| Moderator's role | Moderator (according to Leigh & Spindler, 2003): <br> Process planning <br> Orchestrating action, assigning weekly tasks to the different groups <br> Monitoring action <br> Drawing out main learning points |
| Students involved | 33 students (2 shifts) |
| Duration | 6 weeks (April 26th to June 1st). <br> Blended learning: <br> Tasks started on Tuesday in class and students continued online till the following Monday. |
| Virtual environment | Grouply, a social network that allows the construction of virtual learning communities. From the tools available, it was expected that students used the following: <br> News - for communication within groups <br> Events - used by the moderator to publicise the weekly task <br> Chat - for communication within groups. <br> Forum - for inquiries and submission of weekly reflections. <br> Blog - for proposals within the working group and the discussion on the role of students <br> Subgroups - for managing the personal space of each group as well as the information received from the different roles <br> Photos, videos and files - for information management |
| Output | Detailed travel plan of a trip to London for the entire class, including a visit to the World Travel Market |
| Data collection tools | Weekly reflections from students <br> Focus group <br> Direct observation <br> Linguistic analysis of written productions |

## 3. Discussion

Although the participation of different groups was not homogeneous, all accomplished at least part of the tasks they had been assigned. However, it should be noted that the activity took place almost exclusively face-to-face, since, whenever a group did not finish the task in class, the work was not completed until next class. Another fact worth mentioning is that in addition to the tasks issued by the researcher, roles took the initiative to establish additional contacts with other stakeholders in the role-play, in particular to thank, make complaints, or even to accelerate the process of sending information.

In their weekly reflections, students stressed the fact that this activity allowed them to get to know more about English culture and also the situational authenticity that enhanced research and, consequently, reading in English. On the other hand, reading comprehension and selecting information were reported as the main difficulties.

A thorough analysis of the 42 emails produced during the role-play reveal that most emails include a wide range of words and expressions related to the tourism industry (flights, accommodation, luggage policy, tourist attractions). However, regarding vocabulary control, it can be said that there were problems regarding word choice (in most cases influenced by their native language), but which did not hinder communication. About grammatical accuracy, some mistakes occurred, mostly associated with orthography and punctuation. The majority of the emails show concern about the use of linguistic markers of social conventions and also about politeness conventions. Students were also able to adapt their discourse to different types of communicative functions (inform, enquire, complain) and got familiar with email writing structures and conventions.

In the final focus group interviews students mentioned the quality of the output, which was only possible because each role focused on a specific part of the whole. They also reported the likelihood of the activity, which anticipated their working life, thus enhancing commitment and motivation. Moreover, students were more concerned with the appropriateness and accuracy of their written productions. The use of online translation tools was the main strategy used to overcome written comprehension and production problems. It should be mentioned that students lacked strategic competence to use these tools and, mostly in written production, students wrote emails in Portuguese first and then acritically simply copied the result of the translation.

## 4. Conclusions

The use of online role-plays in foreign language learning proved to be very positive because, in addition to increasing motivation, it also allowed students to get in contact with a rich and varied input in English, stimulating reading and autonomous exploration of these resources and improving their communicative competence. Students also felt the need to engage themselves, conducting research in the English language in order to be able to respond to the challenges posed, implying research, critical analysis and selection of information skills. These capabilities are of utmost importance in the current educational context. Contact with authentic materials also contributed to the development of a critical cultural awareness, including familiarisation with patterns, routines, behaviours and customs of a given community, a key aspect to building a democratic society.

## References

Leigh, E., & Rosser, E. (2008). Loosing Control... A strategy for maximising organisational benefits of learning through simulation. In *Simulation - Maximising Organisational Benefits, SimTecT 2008 Simulation Conference Proceedings, Melbourne.*

Leigh, E., & Spindler, L. (2003). *Congruent facilitation of simulations and games.* Retrieved from http://hdl.handle.net/10453/12756

Stringer, E. T. (2007). *Action research: A handbook for practitioners.* Thousand Oaks, CA: Sage.

Wills, S., Leigh, E., & Ip, A. (2011). *The power of role-based e-learning.* London: Routledge.

Wills, S., Rosser, E., Devonshire, E., Leigh, E., Russel, C., & Shepherd, J. (2009). *Encouraging role based online learning environments by building, linking, understanding, extending: The BLUE report.* Australian Teaching and Learning Council. Retrieved from http://ro.uow.edu.au/cgi/viewcontent.cgi?article=1114&context=asdpapers

# Discourse Markers in Italian as L2 in Face to Face vs. Computer Mediated Settings

## Anna De Marco[1] and Paola Leone[2]

**Abstract**. This pilot study aims to highlight a) differences in pragmatic function and distribution of discourse markers (DMs) in computer mediated and face to face (FtF) settings and b) any correlation of DM uses and language competence. The data have been collected by video-recording and analysing three speakers of Italian L2 (language level competence: A2, B2) talking with an Italian native speaker face to face and through computer mediated video calls. A pragmatic functional approach has been applied for analysing data. Our investigation shows that the difference between face to face and computer mediated environments is worth noting only in less expert L2 speakers' discourse (i.e. A2 level). In fact, less advanced learners show a tendency to use more discourse markers with an interactional function (specifically addressee oriented) in face to face than in virtual environments. Conversely, there is no remarkable difference in the use of discourse markers by the two more expert speakers.

**Keywords**: discourse markers, computer mediated communication, face to face communication, Italian, second language.

## 1. Introduction

The focus of the current study is justified by discourse markers' relevance as cohesion and interactional devices. Until now, different DMs in Italian L1 have been investigated (e.g. *ma, diciamo, bene*), but in Italian L2 the body of research is more reduced. As far as we know, little attention has been devoted to the use

---

1. Università della Calabria, Arcavata, Rende, Italy; demarco.anna@gmail.com
2. University of Salento, Lecce, Italy; paola.leone@unisalento.it

**How to cite this article**: De Marco, A., & Leone, P. (2013). Discourse Markers in Italian as L2 in Face to Face vs. Computer Mediated Settings. In L. Bradley & S. Thouësny (Eds.), *20 Years of EUROCALL: Learning from the Past, Looking to the Future. Proceedings of the 2013 EUROCALL Conference, Évora, Portugal* (pp. 71-77). Dublin/Voillans: © Research-publishing.net.

of DMs during multimodal communication mediated by Voice Internet Protocol software, apart from De Marco and Leone (2012).

Most studies on computer mediated oral discourse aims to understand whether when we practice computer mediated communication (CMC) we are practicing aspects of face to face communication. Differently, our perspective has overcome the position for which we need to justify the use of CMC for developing face to face interaction abilities. Our aim is to see if there are any differences between the two communication modalities that describe CMC, a widespread communication practice.

## 2. Method

### 2.1. Theoretical framework

The growing body of research on the use of DMs in L1 and L2 speakers' discourse of the last three decades reflect different theoretical perspectives discussed in Fischer (2000). For the purposes of the current research, the theoretical approach claimed by Bazzanella (2006), Moseegaard Hansen (2006) and Pons Bordería (2006) will be followed.

DMs are characterised by syntactic independence, i.e. if they are erased the sentence structure does not change. They constitute a functional class (Bazzanella, 2006) meaning that they are not identifiable either on their formal properties or on their grammatical class they belong to but on their property of establishing a "relationship between two units" (Pons Bordería, 2006, p. 82). As Moseegaard Hansen (2006) points out the two units that DMs link are not necessarily linguistic but they can be situational and cognitive, thus pertaining "to relations between the host utterance and its context in this wide non linguistic sense" (p. 25).

DMs are polyfunctional both at a paradigmatic and a syntagmatic level. At a paradigmatic level, the same form of DM can have different functions in relation to the distribution, the intonation and the voice volume and other elements of the cotext (Bazzanella, 1995; e.g. *diciamo*). At a syntagmatic level, the same DM can have different functions in the same utterance (Bazzanella, 1995).

The following parameters contribute to identify the DM function:

- at the cotext level: textual, paralinguistic components and gestures;

- at the contextual level: space, time, social roles and identity, age, textual genre, goal of interaction, ethnicity and also the channel such as oral, written or mediated by computer.

As Bazzanella (2006) points out DMs can have three macrofunctions, each of which include different microfunctions:

- cognitive which include procedural, epistemic markers and modulation devices;

- interactional which are distinguished on the speaker's and on the addressee's side. On the speaker's side, for instance, DMs can be used as turn-taking, phatic devices or for checking comprehension. On the addressee's side they also comprehend the so called listener perception (e.g. Eng.: *hm, huh*; in Italian (It.): *sì, mhm*; Yngve, 1970) and reactive expressions (Clancy, Thompson, Suzuki, & Tao, 1996), also named agreement/assessment signals (e.g. Eng.: *oh really/really*, It.: *bene, ok*) by which the listener wants to align to what has been previously said, also showing surprise (e.g. Eng.: *yeah, wow, gosh*);

- metatextual function used as textual markers (e.g. to signal transition and digression), focusing device and reformulation markers.

Concerning the use of DMs by L2 speakers, studies show that:

- even low proficient L2 learners use DMs, mostly non-lexical units;

- upper-intermediate Italian L2 speakers use a large variety of lexical and non-lexical DMs, in particular assessment and acknowledgement signals which are DMs with an interactional function (see above; Hellermann & Vergun, 2007; Lee, 1999; Pellet, 2005);

- advanced learners of Italian as L2 use different DMs such as fillers, and turn taking signals;

- most frequent non-lexical DMs (e.g. *eh, hm, mhm*) are produced either in turn-initial positions or for keeping the turn, thus showing difficulties in discourse planning. Furthermore, they are used for request clarification and to show attention (Bardel, 2004) and agreement/assessment and as mitigating devices in more advanced learners (Nigoević & Sučić, 2011).

## 2.2. Research questions and design

Research questions are:

- Which function and distribution do most frequent DMs have in CMC and FtF settings? Is there any difference?

- Is there any significant relationship between L2 proficiency and the use of DMs in FtF and in CMC?

Three pairs (PAIR1, PAIR2, PAIR3) have been recorded. All L2 speakers were university students (age 20-27). Different native and non-native speakers joined each pair. PAIR 1 was composed by two female participants. The L2 speaker, Mary, showed to be a A2-B1. PAIR2 was composed by two male participants. Tom, the L2 speaker was a B2 in Italian. Mary and Tom were both English native speakers. PAIR 3 was composed by a female Italian native speaker and by a male Russian native speaker, whose name was Andrej. This latter informant's L2 competence was B2 although during conversation he showed to be more fluent than Tom. To guarantee anonymity, participants' names have been replaced.

For the current research, the independent variable was channel setting, i.e. face to face and computer mediated communication. Dependent variables were distribution and function of DMs. Since the use of DMs is individual (Bazzanella, 1995), the data were analysed by comparing the use of DMs of the same pair in the two settings (control variable: individual differences).

All L2 participants talked for 10 minutes FtF and 10 minutes via Voice Over Internet Protocol with a native speaker. The topic choice for conversations was agreed with each L2 speaker and it was different for each task. The discourse type was either an interview or a discussion.

PAIR 1 and PAIR 3 were first recorded during FtF then during CMC conversation. To avoid practice effect on each task, the order of communication practice was reversed for one of participants' pair (i.e. PAIR2).

## 3. Discussion

In L2 speakers' discourse data, DMs entail various functions and occupy different positions. Mary, the less proficient L2 speaker, mostly uses non lexical DMs (e.g. *uhm*) as a turn taking device in initial positions and as a procedural device in middle turns. For the lexical unit, *sì* and *sì sì* are used, overlapping previous speaker's discourse to indicate reception and comprehension as well as for, in some cases, showing agreement. As regards FtF communication, *sì* is also used in final positions performing a metatestual function of focusing device (e.g. *e abita con i suoi genitori sì*, Eng.: and lives with his parents yes). In this latter setting *sì* as a DM is more frequent.

In FtF, Tom uses lexical DMs in the initial position as a turn-taking device (e.g. *sì sì sì, no però, però*) and to show agreement and "partial agreement". In middle turn positions there are DMs with a function of reception/agreement signals (i.e. *sì, sì sì sì, ah ok, uhm sì*). The lexical DM *sì* is also used in a final position, as a focusing and turn transition device (e.g. *qualcosa di molto diverso sì*, Eng.: something very different yes).

Andrej produces a consistent number of lexical DMs in FtF communication. The function of agreement is realised by the DM *sì* which is used in initial position to agree or to answer to a question stated by the listener.

*Penso* (Eng.: I think) is another DM the learner uses in the medial position with a cognitive function expressing a general modulating device or in the final position as a turn closing device. In Andrej's production, DMs are also used to confirm one's own beliefs (e.g. *certo, certamente*, Eng.: sure, certainly; *innanzitutto mi piace che l'Italia è il paese con la storia, certo capisco che Italia...* Eng[3].: First of all I like Italy is the country with the history, sure I understand that Italy), as prosecutor of the topic or topic shift (e.g. *quindi*, Eng.: then) as well as a memory support or a modulating device function (e.g. *ma, perché*, Eng.: but, why). For the two most competent L2 speakers, FtF and CMC interaction do not show differences in the use of DMs.

## 4. Conclusions

The study highlights differences in pragmatic function and distribution of DMs in CMC and FtF settings as well as correlation of DM uses and language competence.

The investigation reveals that the difference between the two interaction environments (i.e. FtF, CMC) is worth noting only in the less expert L2 speaker's discourse (i.e. Mary). In fact, the data show a tendency in less advanced learners

---

[3]. The word by word translation here is to give the general level of interlanguage as well as a sense of what is said in Italian.

to use more DMs with an interactional function in contact situations than in virtual environments. Specifically for what concerns Mary's production, it seems that she more frequently uses addressee oriented DMs (i.e. agreement signals) during FtF interaction. Conversely, there is no remarkable difference in the use of DMs by the two expert speakers (i.e. Tom and Andrej).

Concerning the relationship between L2 proficiency level and the use of DMs, the data confirm that:

- *sì* emerges in L2 less expert speakers, also showing the function of focusing device in final position;

- more advanced learners frequently use a variety of lexical DMs some of which entail metatestual functions.

- For the future, for better investigating different DMs distribution as well as function, a frequency count will be carried out. For better analysing structural properties, DMs' prosody will also be considered.

**Acknowledgements**. We would like to thank students and friends who allowed us to collect data for this study.

**Authors' comment**: The paper is the result of the joint work of the two authors. Particularly, De Marco is responsible for sections 1 and 3, and Leone for sections 2 and 4.

# References

Bardel, C. (2004). La pragmatica in italiano L2: l'uso dei segnali discorsivi. In F. Albano Leoni, F. Cutugno, M. Pettorino, & R. Savy (a cura di), *Il Parlato Italiano. Atti del Convegno Nazionale* (Napoli, 13-15 febbraio 2003). Napoli: D'Auria.

Bazzanella, C. (1995). I segnali discorsivi. In L. Renzi, G. Salvi, & A. Cardinaletti (a cura di), *Grande grammatica italiana di consultazione* (Vol. 3) (pp. 225-257). Bologna: il Mulino.

Bazzanella, C. (2006). Discourse markers in Italian: Towards a "compositional" meaning. In K. Fischer (Ed.), *Approaches to discourse particles* (pp. 449-464). Amsterdam: Elsevier.

Clancy, P. M., Thompson, S. A, Suzuki, R., & Tao, H. (1996). The conversational use of reactive tokens in English, Japanese, and Mandarin. *Journal of Pragmatics, 26*(3), 355-387. doi: 10.1016/0378-2166(95)00036-4

De Marco, A., & Leone, P. (2012). Computer mediated conversation for mutual learning: Acknowledgementand agreement/assessment signals in Italian as L2. In L. Bradley & S.

Thouësny (Eds.), *CALL: Using, Learning, Knowing. EUROCALL Conference, Gothenburg, Sweden 22-25 August 2012, Proceedings* (pp.70-75) Dublin, Ireland; Voillans, France: Research-publishing.net. Retrieved from http://research-publishing.net/publications/2012-eurocall-proceedings/

Fischer, K. (2000). Discourse particles, turn-taking, and the semantics-pragmatics interface. *Revue de Sémantique et Pragmatique, 8*, 111-137. Retrieved from http://nats-www.informatik.uni-hamburg.de/~fischer/rspfischer.pdf

Hellermann, J., & Vergun, A. (2007). Language which is not taught: The discourse marker use of beginning adult learners of English. *Journal of Pragmatics, 39*(1), 157-169. doi: 10.1016/j.pragma.2006.04.008

Lee, H. (1999). The acquisition of colloquial features by Korean Americans. *Journal of the Pan-Pacific Association of Applied Linguistics, 3*, 71-87.

Moseegaard Hansen, M-B. (2006). A dynamic approach to the lexical semantics of discourse markers (with an exemplary analysis of French toujours). In K. Fischer (Ed.), *Approaches to discourse particles* (pp. 21-40). Amsterdam: Elsevier.

Nigoević, M., & Sučić, P. (2011). Competenza pragmatica in italiano L2: l'uso dei segnali discorsivi da parte di apprendenti croati. *Italiano LinguaDue, 3*, 92-114. Retrieved from http://riviste.unimi.it/index.php/promoitals/article/view/1917/2170

Pellet, S. H. (2005). *The Development of Competence in French Interlanguage Pragmatics: The Case of the Discourse Marker 'donc'*. Doctoral dissertation. Austin: University of Texas at Austin. Retrieved from http://repositories.lib.utexas.edu/handle/2152/2351

Pons Bordería, S. (2006). A functional approach to the study of discourse markers. In K. Fischer (Ed.), *Approaches to discourse particles* (pp. 77-99). Amsterdam: Elsevier.

Yngve, V. H. (1970). On getting a word in edgewise. *Papers from the Sixth Regional Meeting of the Chicago Linguistic Society* (pp. 567-578). Chicago, IL : Chicago Linguistic Society.

# Developing Phonological Awareness in Blended-learning Language Courses

## Carmela Dell'Aria[1] and Laura Incalcaterra McLoughlin[2]

**Abstract.** This study is based on Second Language Acquisition through blended learning and explores the application of new educational technologies in the development of distance education. In particular, the paper focuses on ways to enhance oral, aural, and intercultural skills through learners' engagement, develop authentic social interaction and intercultural awareness in virtual environments and at the same time actively engage the students' powers of perception, communication and reasoning. A speech visualization technology is introduced, specifically tailored to pronunciation training. It provides relevant and comprehensible visual feedback of all three components of speech: prosody-intonation, stress and rhythm. In this paper we stress that the achievement of successful communication should be the main objective of a second language learner, whilst overcoming the foreign accent can be deemed as a secondary goal. A strong or incorrect placement of word stress may impair understanding – from the listener's point of view – of the word(s) being pronounced. On the other hand, acquiring correct timing of phonological units helps to overcome the impression of foreign accent, which may ensue from an incorrect distribution of stressed vs. unstressed stretches of linguistic units such as syllables or metric feet. For these reasons our study looks at how to improve a student's performance both in perception and production of spoken Italian prosodic features, which include the correct position of stress at word level, the alternation of stress and unstressed syllables, the correct position of sentence accent, the generation of the adequate rhythm from the interleaving of stress, accent, phonological rules, and the generation of adequate intonation patterns for each utterance related to communicative functions.

**Keywords**: speech analysis tools, interaction, Italian, blended learning, phonology.

---

1. Università degli Studi di Palermo, Italy; carmela.dellaria@unipa.it

2. National University of Ireland, Galway, Ireland

**How to cite this article**: Dell'Aria, C., & Incalcaterra McLoughlin, L. (2013). Developing Phonological Awareness in Blended-learning Language Courses. In L. Bradley & S. Thouësny (Eds.), *20 Years of EUROCALL: Learning from the Past, Looking to the Future. Proceedings of the 2013 EUROCALL Conference, Évora, Portugal* (pp. 78-85). Dublin/Voillans: © Research-publishing.net.

## 1. Introduction

The term phonological awareness refers to a general appreciation of the sound structure of spoken words. It is one component of a larger phonological processing system used for speaking and listening. It is developed through a variety of activities that expose foreign language (FL) students to the sound structure of the language and teach them to recognize, identify and manipulate it. Listening skills are an important foundation for the development of phonological awareness and they generally develop first. However, listening in itself is not enough. Therefore, different strategies must be implemented to aid students in becoming alert to sounds. Throughout this paper the expression phonological awareness is used to mean an awareness at all levels necessary to grasp the language system and progress from word and phrase level to sentence level.

This paper discusses aspects of foreign pronunciation in Italian which may affect intelligibility, and reviews a method for teaching prosody implemented experimentally at the National University of Ireland (NUI), Galway in 2012-13 and showing great potential for improving pronunciation practice. As such, it analyzes the intonation of 14 beginner students of Italian enrolled in an online course. Students worked with the assistance of computer technology which allowed them to see (graphically) as well as hear both out-of-context sentences and sentences which were part of coherent discourse-level intonation. We argue that this two-step procedure makes it possible for students to understand and learn how to apply intonation for their real communicative needs. Very often this technology is used to teach or enhance traditional sentence-level pronunciation, encouraging sentence level practice and even focusing on grammatical forms. We further argue that sentence-level practice is insufficient to teach how intonation is used in connected speech.

### 1.1. Theoretical framework

The prosodic system is a "suprasegmental"[3] feature of the "paralinguistic" system[4] and it is considered a basic element which characterizes the real meaning of communication. In current language teaching methodology, suprasegmentals are

---

3. This term refers to a phonological unit that lasts many segments and stays above them. This is the case of prosodic units such as stress, quantity, tone, syllable, junction, intonation and rhythm.

4. This expression indicates all the events which cannot be analyzed in themselves and are connected with the analysis of suprasegmental features (stress, rhythm, and intonation) and those ones concurrent to the pronunciation (voice volume, elocution speed, hesitation, speechless pauses).

given very high priority in the pronunciation curriculum (Chun, 1988; Dickerson, 1989; Gilbert, 1984, 1987; McNerney & Mendelson, 1987; Pennington & Richards, 1986) and are the subject of a branch of linguistics, called Phonology of Intonation.

According to Cruttenden (1986) the suprasegmentals provide the 'backbone' of utterances; they highlight the information that speakers regard as important (Bolinger, 1986). The intonation resistance to change (Liebermann, 1967) and the deep-rooted prosodic features of L1 are two important factors that impact negatively on the acquisition of intonation in a foreign language. For this reason FL learners are often not aware of any differences in intonation between L1 and L2.

Previous research proves that a prosodic approach can help learners to overcome these problems because it is based on the neural organization of linguistic perception (Gomez et al., 2008), which influences both perception and production of certain distinctions and characteristic of native speakers.

## 1.2. The present study

In this study we introduce multimedia web and speech analysis technology, which highlight the interrelatedness of various aspects of spoken Italian and provide relevant and comprehensible suprasegmental pronunciation training for non-native speakers (NNSs) of Italian. The project is underpinned by the basic principles for designing learning environments within Mayer's (2001) cognitive theory of multimedia learning and Fletcher and Tobias' (2005) argument in favour of visuals within multimedia learning environments: simultaneous involvement of the acoustic and the visual channel helps memory retention. It also takes into account Schmidt's (2001) noticing hypothesis: L2 learners should notice the input in order to transform it into intake for learning.

In our trials, students were not only watching and listening to the audio (visual) material, they also analyzed the "intonational contour" into the target language, noticed the language and provided contrastive association with the corresponding L1 item. We used PRAAT[5] software, which provides immediate visual feedback on intonation, thereby helping FL learners' apperception. For our experiment, five native (NS) Italian speakers and 14 NNSs (from the Republic of Ireland) served as subjects. The study was designed to obtain preliminary data on the differences in intonation patterns of some sentence types by NS and NNSs. Through the comparison of the NS and NNS sentences, the study aimed at getting evidence of

---

5. Freely downloadable from http://www.fon.hum.uva.nl/praat/

how the exposure to prosodic features through authentic audio (visual) material can affect foreign language prosodic retention.

## 2. Method

### 2.1. Experimental design

A pilot project, Inton.It@, was created by the researchers for fourteen NNSs with different levels of education and integrated as a blended learning experience in the first year of the *Diploma in Italian Online* (level 7). In the second semester the pilot received a grant from LLP - Grundtvig Visits and Exchanges and later the *Diploma in Italian Online* was awarded the European Language Label 2013 in Ireland.

The project followed a blended learning approach: material was delivered online in weekly packages; however, on-campus face-to-face meetings were also included. It was also based on a communicative and connectivist approach, and learners were encouraged to help each other in the construction of knowledge. Great emphasis was given to collaborative Web 2.0 tools. The methodology provided students with explicit descriptions of particular aspects of the language in the form of a rule-based intonation course to make them aware of the intonation structures of Italian and train them in listening analytically to pitch phenomena. During the first term students learnt how to use *speech analysis tools* for perception and production of Italian prosody and intonation. Students were first introduced to the communicative situation through a multimedia text comprising a specific intonation pattern and were asked to understand the global meaning of the multimedia text. In the discrimination stage there was a more accurate comprehension of both text and intonation pattern. Students were then guided towards a more independent use of certain expressions. The practice was realized through embedded tools in NUI Blackboard and with the support of other tools, online or desktop, among which some social networks and virtual learning environments.

### 2.2. The experiment

Each learning unit comprised two perception exercises about intonational pattern, pitch accents, boundary tones, and word stress. Students would then receive automatic feedback with evaluations and solutions to wrong answers.

In the first week of the unit, students practiced the target sentences with the support of PRAAT. They were provided with both visual and auditory prompts, consisting of digitized versions of sentences spoken by two adult males, NSs of Italian. The subjects were asked to repeat each sentence after hearing the entire sequence. Then, they listened again to the sentences, watched the intonation curve, and imitated the target sentence, while the example and its incitation could be compared visually. Finally, they recorded and digitized their repetitions.

Comparing the visual waveform representation of their speech with that of the NS helped students match their pitch and intonation contours with those of the model (Anderson-Hsieh, 1992). In the second semester, students were directed towards oral production in specific linguistic contexts, by listening and then recording dialogues. The unit started with a narrative text, introducing students to the communicative situation that would be rehearsed in the next dialogue. After listening and comprehension, students were guided (imitation) towards an autonomous use of authentic spoken language segments.

The class was split into two groups, experimental (Exg) and control group (Cg): the Exg practiced dialogue with NSs in a very credible context[6] and, playing the part of the dialogue's characters, re-used the previous sentences applying prosody and intonation while experiencing social interactions (Dell'Aria, 2013). In the Cg the dialogues were recorded separately: each learner submitted his/her part of the dialogue as an audio file. When files were joined, the resulting dialogues sounded "live", showing that training on phonological intonation helps to acquire the traits of real and meaningful communication acts.

### 2.3. Testing procedure

All participants made a pre-test two weeks before the experiment, in order to ensure that the target items were unknown. Immediate and delayed post-tests were administered after the treatment.

In group statistics the medians reveal that there is an improvement over time, although at the post-immediate point, scores were higher for the Exg than for the Cg. However, significantly, at the post-delayed point, scores were similar, proving that the effects of the activity were homogeneous in both groups. Therefore, comparing the results to pre-task performance, we can conclude that both conditions supported by speech analysis tools will result in retention of new prosodic schemes.

---

6. Some of these dialogues took place in the 3D virtual environment of Second Life. These sessions were done on a pilot basis with a small number of students who volunteered to take part.

Developing Phonological Awareness in Blended-learning Language Courses

The figures below compare the intonation patterns in one of the NS' productions of a salutation ('Buon giorno' Figure 1) with corresponding sentences produced by the NNS, before (Figure 2) and after audio-visual feedback (Figure 3).

Figure 1. NS' production

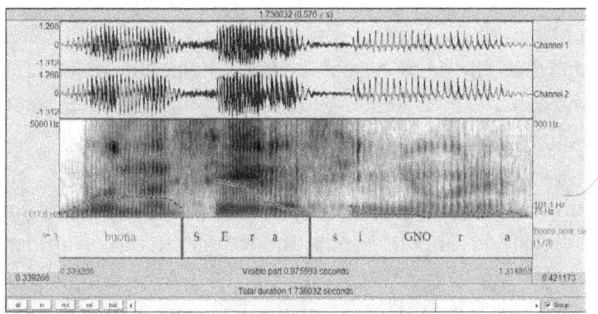

Figure 2. NNS' production

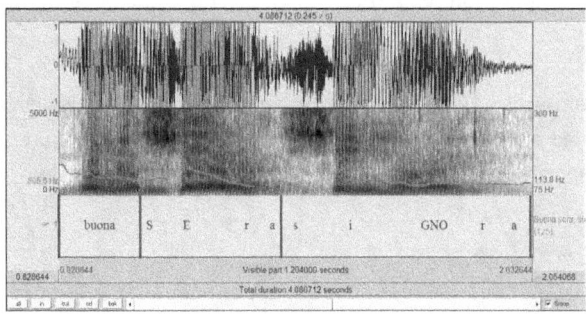

Figure 3. NNS' production

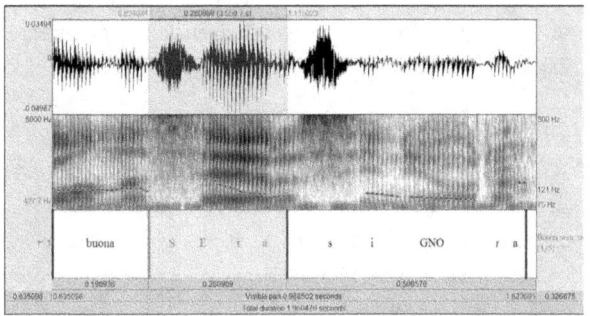

The figures reproduce the type of visualizations of the pitch patterns and sound waves of the speakers' utterances obtained with PRAAT.

## 3. Conclusions

The results of this small study indicate that using audio-visual feedback helps learners to improve their L2 productions and get closer to the target utterance with the help of an immediate and easy-to-read image of the differences existing between L1 and L2. The audio-visual feedback helps the NNSs to improve their Italian prosodic patterns considerably, to the point that the latter come to resemble closely those of the NS.

One of the difficulties that teachers face when adopting this method is the need to use clear and unambiguous phonetic material. Another problem is that the interpretation of the visual display must rely on teachers' knowledge of acoustic phonetics because most of the equipment on the market does not have these capabilities. This research supports the positive results obtained in similar studies which are being carried out on a variety of languages, indicating that speech-visualization technology is an effective pedagogical tool in the FL class.

**Authors' comment**: This paper is the result of the two researchers' shared reflections. The abstract and the paragraphs 1.1 and 2 are written by Dott.ssa Dell'Aria. The paragraphs 1, 1.2, and the conclusions are written by Dr Incalcaterra McLoughlin.

## References

Anderson-Hsieh, J. (1992). Using electronic visual feedback to teach suprasegmentals. *System, 20*(1), 51-62. doi: 10.1016/0346-251X(92)90007-P

Bolinger, D. (1986). *Intonation and its parts*. Palo Alto, CA: Stanford University Press.

Chun, D. M. (1988). The neglected role of intonation in communicative competence and language proficiency. *The Modern Language Journal, 72*(3), 295-303. doi: 10.1111/j.1540-4781.1988.tb04192.x

Cruttenden, A. (1986). *Intonation*. Cambridge: Cambridge University Press.

Dell'Aria, C. (2013). Integrating the Real and Virtual World for Academic Language Education in Second Life. In P. Pumilia-Gnarini, E. Favaron, E. Pacetti, J. Bishop, & L. Guerra (Eds.), *Handbook of Research on Didactic Strategies and Technologies for Education: Incorporating Advancements* (pp. 514-529). Hershey, PA: Information Science Reference. doi: 10.4018/978-1-4666-2122-0.ch045

Dickerson, W. B. (1989). *Stress in the stream of speech: The Rhythm of Spoken English/Teacher's Manual*. Urbana: University of Illinois Press.

Fletcher, J. D., & Tobias, S. (2005). The multimedia principle. In R. E. Mayer (Ed.), *The Cambridge handbook of multimedia learning* (pp. 117-134). New York: Cambridge University Press.

Gilbert, J. B. (1984). *Clear speech*. New York: Cambridge University Press.

Gilbert, J. B. (1987). Pronunciation and listening comprehension. In J. Morley (Ed.), *Current Perspectives on Pronunciation* (pp. 33-39). Washington, D. C.: Teachers of English to Speakers of Other Languages.

Gomez, P., Álvarez, A., Martínez, R., Bobadilla, J., Bernal, J., Rodellar,V., & Nieto, V. (2008). Applications of formant detection in language learning. In M. Holland & P. Fisher (Eds.), *The Path of Speech Technologies in Computer Assisted Language Learning*. New York: Routledge.

Lieberman, P. (1967). *Intonation, perception and language*. Cambridge, MIT Press.

Mayer, R. E. (2001). *Multimedia learning*. New York: Cambridge University Press.

McNerney, M., & Mendelson, D. (1987). Putting suprasegmentals in their place. *TESL Talk, 17*(1), 132-140.

Pennington, M. C., & Richards, J. C. (1986). Pronunciation revisited. *TESOL Quarterly, 20*(2), 207-225. doi: 10.2307/3586541

Schmidt, R. (2001). Attention. In P. Robinson (Ed.), *Cognition and Second Language Instruction* (pp. 3-32). Cambridge: Cambridge University Press.

# Written Corrective Feedback and Peer Review in the BYOD Classroom

## Daniel Ferreira[1]

**Abstract**. Error correction in the English as a Foreign Language (EFL) writing curriculum is a practice both teachers and students agree is important for writing proficiency development (Ferris, 2004; Van Beuningen, De Jong, & Kuiken, 2012; Vyatkina, 2010, 2011). Research suggests student dependency on teacher corrective feedback yields few long-term benefits for the developing writer (Bruton, 2009; Lee, 2004). Encouraging the learners to manage grammatical mistakes, as part of the learning process, must be followed up with post-writing activities that help them become more accountable and more autonomous in developing accurate rewrites. In this project, technological resources combined with peer group support and teacher assistance were used to scaffold the learner approach to error correction that showed positive knock-on effects for writing accuracy.

**Keywords**: written corrective feedback, EFL writing, grammar, peer correction, BYOD, iPad.

## 1. Introduction

The popular use of computer-based feedback systems for the writing curriculum has placed a greater demand for CALL environments that not all universities can meet. The bring your own device (BYOD) trend of blending mobile technologies into the traditional classroom may be one solution though understandably limited (Kharbach, 2013). Studies into learner willingness to use Mobile Assisted Language Learning in general do exist, such as Stockwell's (2012) work. However, this study was more concerned with the learner's preparedness and skill in using smartphone technology to access materials from cloud services. This project reports on the use of smartphone technology and the effect of a

---

1. International Christian University, Tokyo, Japan; ferreira@icu.ac.jp

**How to cite this article**: Ferreira, D. (2013). Written Corrective Feedback and Peer Review in the BYOD Classroom. In L. Bradley & S. Thouësny (Eds.), *20 Years of EUROCALL: Learning from the Past, Looking to the Future. Proceedings of the 2013 EUROCALL Conference, Évora, Portugal* (pp. 86-92). Dublin/Voillans: © Research-publishing.net.

written corrective feedback (WCF) approach on a process-oriented EFL writing program at a Japanese women's university.

Over the last few decades, research shows that many complex factors that go beyond the mere transfer of correct grammatical information from instructor to student affect the process of second language acquisition (Long, 1977; Truscott & Hsu, 2008). Some experts argue that written corrective feedback on grammar is ineffective for short-term grammatical accuracy (Krashen, 1984; Semke, 1984; Truscott, 1996). For example, the criticism of the article "Effects of the Red Pen" is that a complete canvassing of all errors is counterproductive and may even overwhelm or demotivate the learners from being open to a risk-taking attitude that is vital to the gradual improvement in accuracy in second/foreign language writing practices (Semke, 1984). Recent research suggests that a truly effective WCF system would have to incorporate different corrective feedback approaches for lexical, syntactic or morphological errors because each area represents a different cognitive process for correction (Ferris & Roberts, 2001; Truscott, 1996; Vyatkina, 2010).

Although students prefer explicit WCF comments, research shows that the indirect feedback method of using a coded WFC code sheet is better for accuracy in the long-term because it engages the learner to problem-solve and reflect on form. Successful students realize the benefits of the trial and error process (James, 1998; Lalande, 1982; Reid, 1998). There is evidence that direct feedback (i.e. writing the correct form over the mistake) has largely been proven to be ineffective for more accurate performance beyond the beginner level (Robb, Ross, & Shortreed, 1986).

Moreover, there is also the risk in direct feedback that the teacher may misinterpret the meaning intended by the writer (Ferris & Roberts, 2001). One way to minimize the WCF workload is to decide on error types that are in the students' ability to repair and to use a coded system effective for the learners to use.

This project aimed to address the following research questions:

- Which corrective feedback approach was most effective for grammatical accuracy from the students' point-of-view?

- Are learners prepared to use smartphones and cloud services as tools for learning in a writing program?

Daniel Ferreira

## 2. Method

### 2.1. Dropbox and the resources

For this project, 17 Japanese female students from an urban women's college with a group average of 437 on the TOEFL PBT[2] participated. Prior to the beginning of the term, the instructor set up and shared a class Dropbox folder. Within the folder were individual folders for each of the students and a class folder with all the resources. The resources included a PDF copy of the correction symbols sheet and scanned pages from a bilingual grammatical reference book entitled *An A-Z of Common English Errors for Japanese Learners* (Barker, 2008).

Figure 1. A sample of the student's corrected free writing text using numbers for the reference book pages

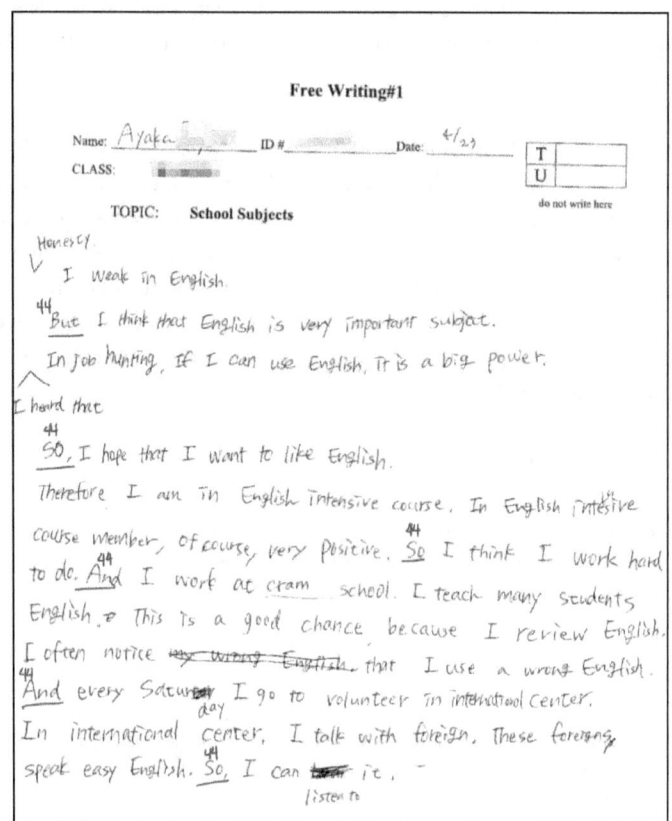

---

2. The Test of English as a Foreign Language Paper-based Test

On the first day of class, the students downloaded the Dropbox app from either Google Play or the App Store depending on the operating system of their smartphone. A brief explanation about the contents of the folders and how the app was going to be used throughout the course followed. For the first assignment on paragraph writing, the students generated ideas doing a 10-minute free writing exercise on a topic. At the end of class, the teachers collected the free writes that were later scanned into PDF format. The scanned free writes were corrected focusing only on the bilingual reference book. Using an iPad app called GoodReader[3], the errors on each student's free writing text were underlined and coded using only a number referring to a page in the reference book (see Figure 1 above). The corrected work was transferred directly into the respective student folders in Dropbox.

## 2.2. BYOD and peer review

In the next class, the teacher divided the students into pairs, and they received a worksheet (see Figure 2) that contained three examples of the most common errors from their free writes. The students were encouraged to work independently to try and find the errors. After a reasonable amount of time had elapsed, they shared their knowledge with their partners. The instructor circulated amongst the pairs facilitating the peer correction process. After peer correction had elapsed for some time, the learners were encouraged to look up the explanation to each error in the grammatical reference textbook. The page numbers are written next to each error on the worksheet. The teacher demonstrated how to access the reference book on an overhead projector using an iPad and Dropbox app. The students read the explanation in either English or Japanese, confirmed the correction of the errors on their worksheets with their partners. Using the GoodReader app and an iPad connected to the overhead projector, the teacher encouraged students to share their corrections with the whole class. At least one corrected passage was typed out for the rest of the class to see, but variations on the corrections were also discussed.

The free writes from the week before were returned to the students and they looked up the corrected PDF versions in their Dropbox folders. The teacher asked the students to use the returned free writing assignment and the grammatical resource to make the necessary grammatical changes for writing the first draft of the paragraph. The received first draft of the paragraph was corrected using the grammatical resource and the corrections symbols sheet (see Figure 3). Once the corrected work was returned to the students, a group email was sent out with instructions for students to look at their work. In the next class, students worked in

---

3. itunes.apple.com

groups of three and peer corrected their work. While moving from group to group, the teacher provided assistance, and gave advice on corrections. The second drafts were submitted online later that week.

Figure 2. A worksheet with three of the most common grammar mistakes from the students' free writes

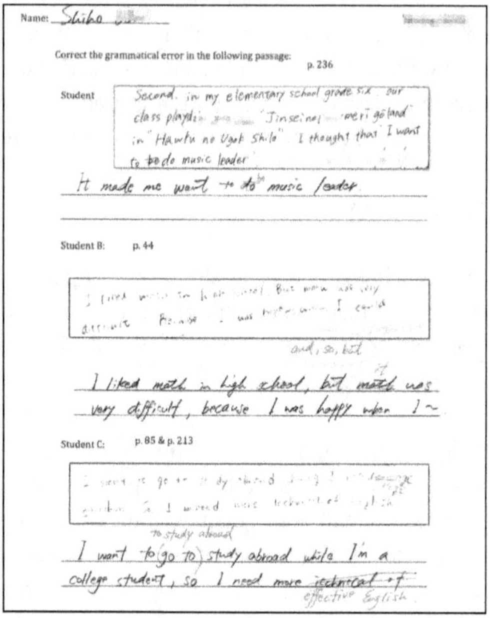
Name: Shiho

Correct the grammatical error in the following passage:

p. 236

Student

It made me want to be music leader.

Student B: p. 44

I liked math in high school, but math was very difficult, because I was happy when I ~

Student C: p. 85 & p. 213

I want to (go to) study abroad while I'm a college student, so I need more effective English

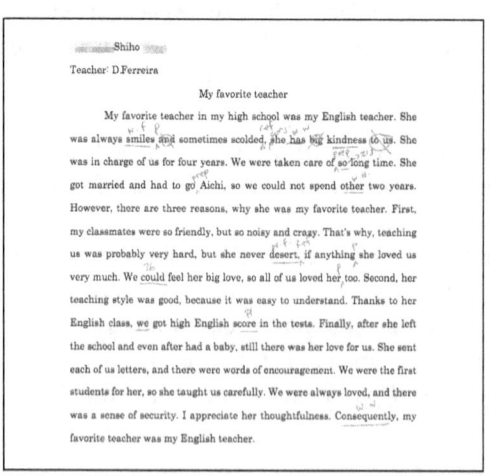

Figure 3. A sample of a first draft with corrections symbols

Shiho

Teacher: D.Ferreira

My favorite teacher

My favorite teacher in my high school was my English teacher. She was always smiles and sometimes scolded, she has big kindness to us. She was in charge of us for four years. We were taken care of so long time. She got married and had to go Aichi, so we could not spend other two years. However, there are three reasons, why she was my favorite teacher. First, my classmates were so friendly, but so noisy and crazy. That's why, teaching us was probably very hard, but she never desert, if anything she loved us very much. We could feel her big love, so all of us loved her too. Second, her teaching style was good, because it was easy to understand. Thanks to her English class, we got high English score in the tests. Finally, after she left the school and even after had a baby, still there was her love for us. She sent each of us letters, and there were words of encouragement. We were the first students for her, so she taught us carefully. We were always loved, and there was a sense of security. I appreciate her thoughtfulness. Consequently, my favorite teacher was my English teacher.

## 3. Discussion

There were some notable concerns regarding the use of smartphones and accessing cloud services. At the beginning of the term, the students complained that the display of their devices were too small. Encouraging users to change their viewing mode to landscape instead of the preferred portrait view rectified part of that problem. However, as the students became more and more dependent on accessing their Dropbox documents throughout the term, low battery power became a major obstacle. Late into the term, two students reported still having problems accessing corrected documents that the teacher returned to their folders. However, other students in the class were quick to assist and promptly rectified the situation.

Overall, the short-term benefits of post-writing activities that focused on accountability of grammar errors were apparent. The reappearance of the common errors that the instructor marked for correction significantly diminished in later free writes and paragraph writing assignments. Whenever a common error reappeared in later assignments, the learners easily accessed the grammatical reference, the correction symbols sheet or older assignments during the peer review process, thus freeing the teacher to focus on other writing features that needed more extensive explanations such as content or lexical choice.

## 4. Conclusions

Consistent with the findings of recent research on writing, combining the use of indirect WFC with peer review seemed to have some positive effects in the short-term (Ferris & Roberts, 2001; Robb et al., 1986; Vyatkina, 2010). Unfortunately, due to the limit of the scope of this research, it remains unclear whether the changes in grammatical accuracy would resist attrition in the long-term (Truscott & Hsu, 2008). Nevertheless, it is hoped that some of the ideas presented in this project will be of benefit to instructors who may have a similar teaching context.

## References

Barker, D. (2008). *An A–Z of Common English Errors for Japanese Learners*. Nagoya, Japan: BTB Press.

Bruton, A. (2009). Designing research into the effects of grammar correction in L2 writing: Not so straightforward. *Journal of Second Language Writing, 18*(2), 136-140. doi: 10.1016/j.jslw.2009.02.005

Ferris, D. R. (2004). The "Grammar Correction" Debate in L2 Writing: Where are we, and where do we go from here? (and what do we do in the meantime ...?). *Journal of Second Language Writing, 13*(1), 49-62. doi: 10.1016/j.jslw.2004.04.005

Ferris, D. R., & Roberts, B. (2001). Error feedback in L2 writing classes How explicit does it need to be? *Journal of Second Language Writing, 10*(3), 161-184. doi: 10.1016/S1060-3743(01)00039-X

James, C. (1998). *Errors in language learning and use*. London, New York: Longman.

Kharbach, M. (2013). What Teachers Need to Know about BYOD (Bring Your Own Device) Trend in Education. *Educational Technology and Mobile Learning* [Website]. Retrieved from http://www.educatorstechnology.com/2012/07/what-teachers-need-to-know-about-byod.html

Krashen, S. D. (1984). *Writing: Research, theory, and applications*. New York: Pergamon Institute of English.

Lalande, J. F. (1982). Reducing composition errors: An experiment. *The Modern Language Journal, 66*(2), 140-149. doi: 10.1111/j.1540-4781.1982.tb06973.x

Lee, I. (2004). Error correction in L2 secondary writing classrooms: The case of Hong Kong. *Journal of Second Language Writing, 13*(4), 285-312. doi: 10.1016/j.jslw.2004.08.001

Long, M. H. (1977). Teacher feedback on learner error: Mapping cognitions. In H. D. Brown, C. A. Yorio, & R. H. Crymes (Eds), *On TESOL, 77* (pp. 278-294). Washington, D.C.: TESOL.

Reid, J. M. (1998). Responding to ESL student language problems: Error analysis and revision plans. In P. Byrd & J. M. Reid (Eds), *Grammar in the composition classroom: Essays on teaching ESL for college-bound students* (pp. 118-137). Heinle ELT.

Robb, T., Ross, S., & Shortreed, I. (1986). Salience of feedback on error and its effect on EFL writing quality. *TESOL Quarterly, 20*(1), 83-96. doi: 10.2307/3586390

Semke, H. D. (1984). Effects of the red pen. *Foreign Language Annals, 17*(3), 195-202. doi: 10.1111/j.1944-9720.1984.tb01727.x

Stockwell, G. (2012). Investigating learner preparedness for and usage patterns of mobile. *ReCALL, 20*(3), 253-270. doi: 10.1017/S0958344008000232

Truscott, J. (1996). The Case Against Grammar Correction in L2 Writing Classes. *Language Learning, 46*(2), 327-369. doi: 10.1111/j.1467-1770.1996.tb01238.x

Truscott, J., & Hsu, A. Y.-P. (2008). Error correction, revision, and learning. *Journal of Second Language Writing, 17*(4), 292-305. doi: 10.1016/j.jslw.2008.05.003

Van Beuningen, C. G., De Jong, N. H., & Kuiken, F. (2012). Evidence on the Effectiveness of Comprehensive Error Correction in Second Language Writing. *Language Learning, 62*(1), 1-41. doi: 10.1111/j.1467-9922.2011.00674.x

Vyatkina, N. (2010). The Effectiveness of Written Corrective Feedback in Teaching Beginning German. *Foreign Language Annals, 43*(4), 671-689. doi: 10.1111/j.1944-9720.2010.01108.x

Vyatkina, N. (2011). Writing Instruction and Policies for Written Corrective Feedback in the Basic Language Sequence. *L2 Journal, 3*(1), 63-92. Retrieved from http://www.escholarship.org/uc/item/6jg9z585.pdf

# E-xperience Erasmus: Online Journaling as a Tool to Enhance Students' Learning Experience of their Study Visit Abroad

## Odette Gabaudan[1]

**Abstract**. Students on the BA International Business and Languages who spend a full academic year on a study visit abroad experience many new challenges such as a different culture, a new university, different academic practices, a foreign language, etc. The assessment methods for the year include the results of the modules taken in the partner universities, a language examination and the submission of a country notebook. This research is a pilot study that explores how the maintenance of an online journal via a blog/e-portfolio structure can support students in their new learning experiences, alert the home coordinator to any potential difficulty before it escalates, provide them with regular online feedback on their progress and enhance their final reflective paper submission. The cohort of students is small and limited to those who are currently in France, spread across five different locations. The research is framed within an interpretivist paradigm using case-study as a research design. Data is gathered through documentary evidence, field observations, questionnaires and interviews. The project's results are of interest to Erasmus coordinators and educational institutions whose programmes include a study visit or even a placement component. The research brings insights on how reflective thinking can augment students' learning by practicing regular online reflective writing. Rubrics are used as a powerful tool for online feedback and for the continuous formation of students' learning. The advantages and challenges of using an enhanced blog structure for the maintenance of an online journal are also reviewed.

**Keywords**: online journaling, reflective writing, language learning, study visit, Erasmus.

---

1. Dublin Institute of Technology, Dublin, Ireland; odette.gabaudan@dit.ie

**How to cite this article**: Gabaudan, O. (2013). E-xperience Erasmus: Online Journaling as a Tool to Enhance Students' Learning Experience of their Study Visit Abroad. In L. Bradley & S. Thouësny (Eds.), *20 Years of EUROCALL: Learning from the Past, Looking to the Future. Proceedings of the 2013 EUROCALL Conference, Évora, Portugal* (pp. 93-97). Dublin/Voillans: © Research-publishing.net.

## 1. Introduction

Undergraduate students who spend a full academic year on an Erasmus study visit experience many new challenges. They have to adapt to a different culture, a new university and different academic practices. They need to make new friends and they are often away from home for a period of time longer than a holiday. For many who go on an Erasmus study visit, one of the primary objectives is to become confident and comfortable with the foreign language that they have chosen as part of their course of study.

This paper is based on a pilot initiative with students who study French as their major language on the BA (Hons) International Business and Languages in the Dublin Institute of Technology (DIT) in Ireland. During their four-year programme, students are required to spend their third year on a study visit abroad. Students' performance over the course of the year is evaluated by a mix of assessment methods including results of modules taken in partner universities, a language examination upon their return to DIT and the submission of a country notebook. This research explored how the maintenance of an online journal, using a blog or e-portfolio format, can support students in their new learning experiences, foster regular communication with the home tutor, provide them with regular online feedback on their progress, enhance their final reflective paper submission, and facilitate peer learning and support.

The focus of this paper is on online journaling as a vehicle for supporting students' learning in particular in terms of reflective writing and language development.

## 2. Method

The research is framed within a phenomenological paradigm as it aims to gain insights into the contextualised processes, the subjective views and the multiple realities of the students who engage with their experience of the year abroad (Merriam, 2001). The enquiry seeks to explore not only the students' behaviour as seen from their own standpoint but also the researcher's interactions with the participants and overarching pedagogical objectives.

As a direct participant, the researcher brought her own pedagogical values and bias to the research. The methods now described are framed within an educational case study design. They were chosen in order to describe and reveal the meaning of the investigated social phenomena rather than to report on its frequency (Van Maanen, 1983, cited in Hussey & Hussey, 1997). Methods included documentary evidence (students' blog entries, researcher's field notes), observations (tracking of students' interactions with journal entries in terms of content, length, depth of analysis, media and language used), questionnaires (sent by email) and semi-structured interviews with a sample of students.

## 3. Discussion

### 3.1. Implementation

During their second year, students set up their blog on wordpress.com, a free blogging tool that incorporates many of the features recommended in the literature such as being user friendly, promoting a sense of ownership, providing options for customisation and sharing with others (Garrett, 2011; Jafari, Mcgee, & Carmean, 2006; Plaisir, Hachey, & Theilheimer, 2011). The coordinator also set up her blog as a means of communicating with the group on pedagogical matters linked to the online journal.

Activities designed to develop students' reflective writing skills and practice with the foreign language were posted on the coordinator's blog on a monthly basis. Feedback on students' reflective writing and language competence was also provided on a monthly basis, both individually and to the group. Individual written commentaries were posted on each student's blog. In addition, the researcher designed a rubric which she annotated and emailed to individual students on completion of their monthly activities.

### 3.2. Reflective writing

Each of the monthly activities focused on one of the learning outcomes set out in the programme documentation for the year abroad. One of the key aims for the monthly activities was to support students in their engagement with reflective writing. A reflective activity consists in making sense of one's world by standing back from the immediacy of reality, seeing reality from different perspectives, questioning assumptions and practices, analysing successes and failures, and reflecting on how to use previous experience for future action (Dalal, Hakel, Sliter, & Kirdendall, 2012; Moon, 2006).

As a means of guiding critical reflection, the researcher developed a rubric that included a number of criteria and four corresponding levels of performance. This rubric served as a formative assessment tool, helping students to frame their performance on each criterion within an overarching frame of different levels.

## 3.3. Learning of French

Reflective writing was a new activity for most students and none had previously engaged in reflective activity through French. Students always find the initial immersion into the French language and culture a challenge. They can feel overwhelmed by their new environment. In an attempt to reduce this sense of overload, students were initially given the option to post their entries in English. All three interviewees report having done their initial postings, at least partly, in English but, in hindsight, feel that it could have been of benefit to complete them in French from the outset. In spite of the added language difficulty and therefore time and effort required, "it is a French blog so it makes sense to write in French" as reported by one of the interviewees.

Students whose competency in the foreign language is lower find they have to try harder while students with a higher level of French enjoy the opportunity to express their thoughts in writing through French as this often remains the greatest challenge on their journey towards language acquisition. On completion of the reflective activity, a number of students report experiencing a sense of achievement. Such comments show that providing students with opportunities to build their confidence and develop their written fluency is as important as fostering reflective writing skills. Posting reflective activities in French is much appreciated by all students who engaged with the online journal as in many instances they do not get regular academic practice in composing in French nor do they get feedback on their actual language competence. Consequently, students particularly value the combination of practice and feedback.

## 4. Conclusions

While two thirds of the students fully engaged with the online journal, another third did not. The same third did not complete the questionnaire or participate in the interviews. It is the researcher's intention to investigate the underlying reasons for this lack of engagement with an initiative that has otherwise been considered very positive by all other participants.

Indeed, interviewees are unambiguous about the value of maintaining an online journal. They also unequivocally appreciate the tutor's feedback and feel that knowing the tutor will read their entries stimulates them to complete the tasks set out for them. Encouraging students and providing them with opportunities to develop a sense of achievement are key factors in sustaining students' engagement after their initial attempts at online journaling and reflective writing through French.

Reflective writing is a challenging activity for students and it requires considerable time and skill for tutors to provide useful and meaningful feedback. To that effect, rubrics are valuable tools that give students clear indications on areas to improve, particularly when face-to-face communication is not possible as is the case when students are abroad for a lengthy period of time.

The main constraint to online journaling as a form of pedagogical support is the time required to adequately guide students in their reflective writing and in their language development. Tutors should be given adequate allowances so they can invest the necessary time and effort, particularly for cohorts of students that are larger or that require a higher level of guidance and encouragement.

## References

Dalal, D. K., Hakel, M. D., Sliter, M. T., & Kirkendall, S. R. (2012). Analysis of a Rubric for Assessing Depth of Classroom Reflections. *International Journal of ePortfolio, 2*(1), 75-85. Retrieved from http://www.theijep.com/pdf/IJEP11.pdf

Garrett, N. (2011). An e-portfolio Design Supporting Ownership, Social Learning, and Ease of Use. *Educational Technology and Society, 14*(1), 187-202. Retrieved from http://www.ifets.info/journals/14_1/17.pdf

Hussey, J., & Hussey, R. (1997). *Business Research, a Practical Guide for Undergraduate and Postgraduate Students*. London: MacMillan Business.

Jafari, A., Mcgee, P., & Carmean, C. (2006). Managing Courses Defining Learning: What Faculty, Students, and Administrators Want. *EDUCAUSE Review, 41*(4), 50-70. Retrieved from http://net.educause.edu/ir/library/pdf/ERM0643.pdf

Merriam, S. B. (2001). *Qualitative Research and Case Study Applications in Education* (2nd ed.). San Francisco: Jossey-Bass Publishers.

Moon, J. A. (2006). *Learning Journals, a Handbook for Reflective Practice and Professional Development* (2nd ed.). Oxon: Routledge.

Plaisir, J. Y., Hachey, A. C., & Theilheimer, R. (2011). Their Portfolios, Our Role: Examining a Community College Teacher Education Digital Portfolio Program from the Student's Perspective. *Journal of Early Chidhood Teacher Education, 32*(2), 159-175. doi: 10.1080/10901027.2011.572231

Van Maanen, J. (1983). *Qualitative Methodology*. London: Sage

# A Facebook Project for Japanese University Students (2): Does It Really Enhance Student Interaction, Learner Autonomy, and English Abilities?

### Mayumi Hamada[1]

**Abstract**. Facebook is, in most countries, a very popular Social Network Service (SNS). Since the launch of its service in Japan in 2008, it has been growing rapidly. As a platform for a link to the world, Facebook can also be used effectively for language learning in English as a foreign language (EFL) environments. The purpose of this project was to investigate how Facebook can help Japanese university students to improve their English by integrating Facebook activities into English lessons, and examine whether it could facilitate student interaction and self-motivation for learning English. The Facebook project was conducted over the course of one academic year in two parts. A previous study reported on the results of the first semester (Hamada, 2012). In the second semester, the students were given an opportunity to exchange opinions with American university students. A writing task on Facebook was assigned to both Japanese and American students every week. In this study, I will present the results of the second semester based on a survey and feedback from the students. I will also discuss how the Facebook exchange with the American students can facilitate not only the language learning of the Japanese students, but also the interactions between students and inter-cultural understanding.

**Keywords**: social network, Facebook, learner autonomy, writing.

## 1. Introduction

The number of Facebook users in the world has exceeded 1.1 billion (Stotland, 2013). As a platform for a link to the world, it has great potential for language

---

1. University of Marketing and Distribution Sciences, Kobe, Japan; mayumi_hamada@red.umds.ac.jp

**How to cite this article**: Hamada, M. (2013). A Facebook Project for Japanese University Students (2): Does It Really Enhance Student Interaction, Learner Autonomy, and English Abilities? In L. Bradley & S. Thouësny (Eds.), *20 Years of EUROCALL: Learning from the Past, Looking to the Future. Proceedings of the 2013 EUROCALL Conference, Évora, Portugal* (pp. 98-105). Dublin/Voillans: © Research-publishing.net.

learning in EFL environments. By integrating Facebook activities into English lessons, the purpose of this study is to investigate how Facebook can help students improve their English. The study also examines whether or not it can facilitate student interaction and self-motivation for learning English.

The Facebook project was conducted over two semesters. In the first semester, the main goals were to familiarize the students with Facebook and help them get in the habit of writing regularly in English. It was found that the students' overall reaction to Facebook was positive and they became accustomed to writing English comments on Facebook. It was also indicated that the project could help to develop the students' English ability and facilitate learner autonomy to some extent. However, it was also found that most students were reluctant to make foreign friends on their own and their Facebook activities in English were quite limited (Hamada, 2012).

In the second semester, upon consideration of the results from the first semester, the Facebook exchange project was re-designed to further motivate the "reluctant" students. They were provided with an opportunity to exchange information and opinions with American university students and broaden their views about the outer world. This research investigates the following three questions:

- Does the Facebook project encourage student interaction?
- Does the Facebook project enhance learner autonomy for studying English?
- Does the Facebook project help to develop the students' English skills?

## 2. Methodology

The Facebook exchange project was conducted in the spring semester of 2012 with the collaboration of Portland State University (PSU). The Japanese participants from University of Marketing and Distribution Sciences (UMDS) consisted of 12 sophomores with an average Test of English for International Communication (TOEIC) score of around 420. The project was conducted as a homework assignment and was included in their grade. Ten PSU students in a first-year-Japanese class volunteered to participate in the project.

A closed group was formed on Facebook so that only designated student members were able to have access to the group. A writing task was assigned to both PSU and UMDS students every week, and all the students wrote about the same topic using at least four lines of text. The Facebook exchange project lasted throughout the semester and the students wrote about 15 topics.

As for correcting mistakes of the UMDS students, the teacher selected one grammatically incorrect sentence from each student's comment and made an "error correction" worksheet every week. At the beginning of each lesson, approximately 10 minutes of class time was devoted to allowing the students to correct their mistakes on their own. Afterwards, the teacher provided correct answers as well as explanations.

## 3. Results

A questionnaire was administered at the end of the semester in order to collect Japanese student feedback and investigate their views.

The first three questions were in the format of a five-level Likert scale: 1. Strongly disagree; 2. Disagree; 3. Neither agree nor disagree; 4. Agree; 5. Strongly agree. The formats of the other questions are displayed in Figures 4-8.

In response to Question 1, 75% of the students either strongly agreed or agreed (Figure 1). The average was 4.0, indicating that most of the students enjoyed the Facebook exchange project. They commented that they especially enjoyed learning cultural differences.

In the case of Question 2, 75% of the students either strongly agreed or agreed, with the average result of 3.92 (Figure 2). The result suggests that most of the students believed that the project was helpful to their English study. According to their feedback, they benefited most from the acquisition of new vocabulary.

In response to Question 3, the average result was 4.3. 83% of the students stated that the error correction helped them to improve their English ability (Figure 3).

Figure 1. Question 1

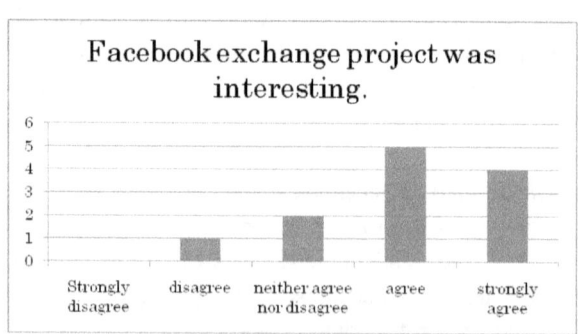

Figure 2. Question 2

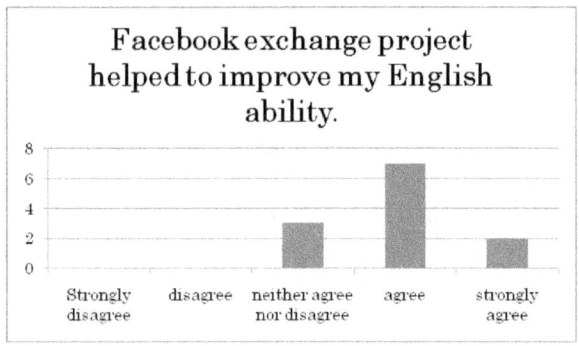

Figure 3. Question 3

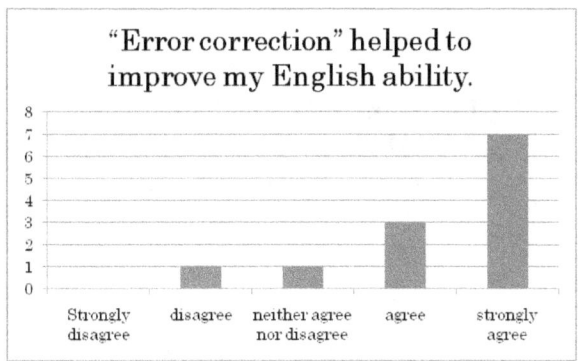

Concerning Question 4, 10 students out of 12 made at least one friend, indicating that they got more closely connected with the PSU students privately (Figure 4). As regards Question 5, whether the opportunity of using English on Facebook had increased, 8 students stated "Yes" while four students stated "No" (Figure 5). It seems that the students were divided into two groups: one motivated to use English on Facebook voluntarily, the other not. It was also found that the three major activities by the first group were socializing with the PSU students outside the group, making new foreign friends other than the PSU students, and getting information in English.

Questions 6 and 7 were given to the first group who answered "Yes" in Question 5. The two figures show that the students engaged in reading activities more than in writing comments (Figure 6 and Figure 7).

To Question 8, 75% of the students stated that they wanted to continue the Facebook exchange project, mainly for English study and staying connected with the PSU students (Figure 8). There was only one student who answered "No". The reason was that she did not like the SNS activities.

In addition to the data above, open-ended questions were given to the students. To the question, "Since you started to use Facebook, how has using it helped you with your English study, other than in the area of assignments?", the answers included getting information about other countries and the interests of people in those countries, as well as increasing their opportunities for using English.

To the question, "How do you want to use Facebook from now on?", several students commented that they wanted to make more foreign friends and broaden their world.

Figure 4. Question 4

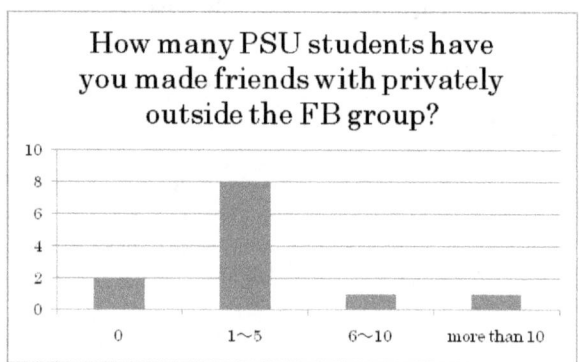

Figure 5. Question 5

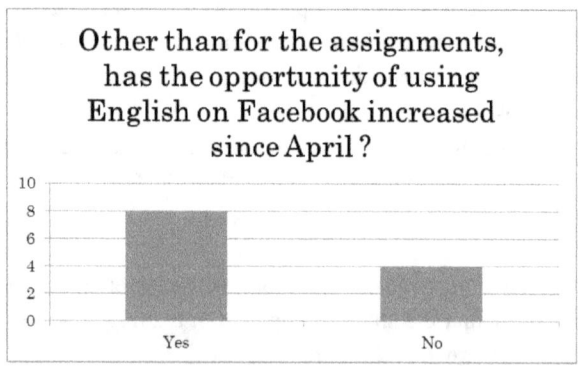

Figure 6. Question 6

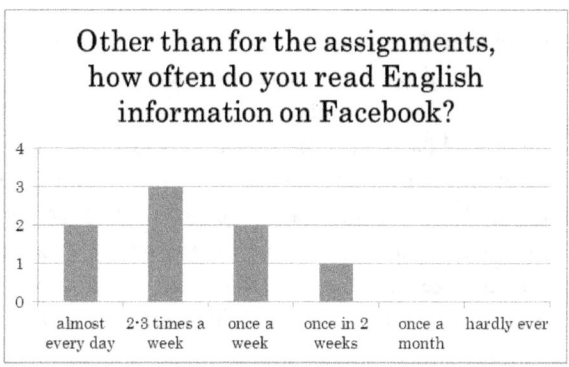

Figure 7. Question 7

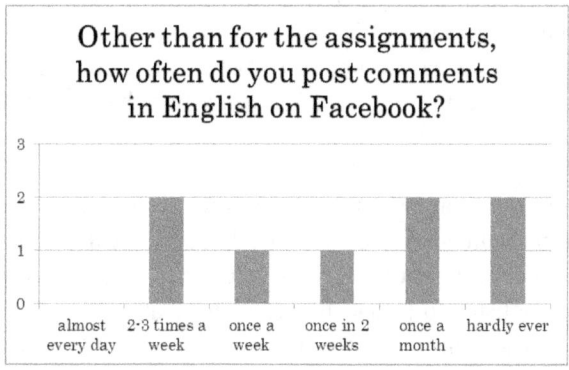

Figure 8. Question 8

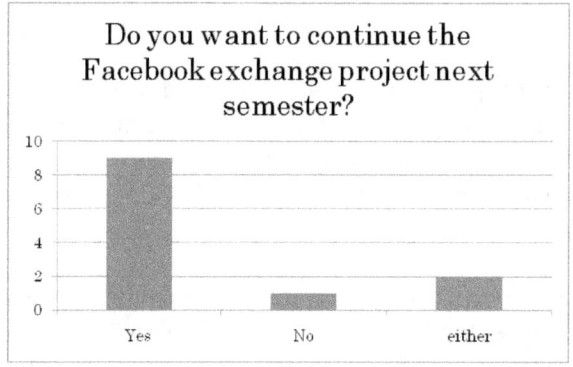

## 4. Discussion

The overall results indicate that the Facebook exchange project was very successful in that it stimulated the Japanese students' curiosity and their "intrinsic motivation" to communicate with the PSU students and learn more about their lives, culture, and ways of thinking. What they experienced was not anything "artificial" or "virtual" but communications with real people, which naturally motivated the Japanese students to learn the English language itself. This finding supports Gardner's (1985) claim that there is a close relationship between motivation and success of second language learning. The main focus in the second semester was on encouraging student interaction and enhancing learner autonomy.

Concerning research question one, it was observed that there was a lot of interactions between the UMDS and PSU students. They enjoyed not only reading posts but also actively commenting on these posts. It seems that the UMDS students especially enjoyed learning about cultural differences by interacting with the PSU students. The survey also showed that most of the UMDS students got connected with PSU students privately outside the group, indicating that the project did encourage student interaction.

As for research question two, the survey strongly suggests that the project enhanced learner autonomy. It was found that in addition to the weekly assignment, all of the Japanese students voluntarily used Facebook for getting information in English. Most students commented that they wanted to make more foreign friends, learn more about different cultures, and broaden their views. One student stated that she was now writing posts in English almost all the time. Another interesting finding, however, was that most of the students were engaged in reading activities more often than writing ones. This may support Schalow's (2011) view that Japanese students are rather passive learners or "inhibited learners" (p. 100).

As regards research question three, the findings indicate that the project helped them to improve their English ability. The two main skills the students felt were improved were vocabulary and grammar. Most of the students commented that they learned new expressions by reading the PSU students' posts. The error correction also helped the students with grammar and vocabulary.

It can thus be advocated that Facebook activities in English will help the students to become more independent learners, and that they can improve their English ability without making too much "effort" or feeling they are being made to "study".

## 5. Conclusion

This paper has presented the second part of the Facebook project to investigate how Facebook can enhance student interaction, English study, and learner autonomy. It was found that the project encouraged the students to become interested in learning about cultural differences and initiating interaction with others. The project also facilitated learner autonomy, motivating the students to spend more time voluntarily using English on Facebook. It was also indicated that the project helped to improve the students' English ability, especially in regard to grammar and vocabulary. It is unknown, however, how long and voluntarily the rather "passive" students will continue to be engaged in Facebook activities in English from now on, without any assignments. A follow-up study will be needed to further investigate the effect of Facebook for their language learning.

It is hoped that the students will continue to enjoy broadening their knowledge and views through Facebook, and to use English not only for learning English, but also for communicating with people throughout the world.

**Acknowledgements.** I am grateful to my colleague Thomas Schalow for his constructive comments.

## References

Hamada, M. (2012). A Facebook project for Japanese university students: does it really enhance student interaction, learner autonomy, and English abilities? In L. Bradley & S. Thouësny (Eds.), *CALL: Using, Learning, Knowing, EUROCALL Conference, Gothenburg, Sweden, 22-25 August 2012, Proceedings* (pp. 104-110). Dublin: Research-publishing.net. Retrieved from http://research-publishing.net/publications/2012-eurocall-proceedings/

Gardner, R. C. (1985). *Social psychology and second language learning: The role of attitudes and motivation.* London, UK: Edward Arnold.

Schalow, T. (2011). Building an online learning community in Japan: the challenge of distributed learning in a social network. In S. M. Thang, K. Pramela, F. F. Wong, L. K. Lin, M. Jamilah, & M. Marlyna (Eds), *Language and Cultural Diversity* (pp. 89-105). Serdang: Universiti Putra Malaysia Press.

Stotland, D. (2013, June 19). Facebook, Asia taiheiyo tantokanbu Stotlandshini kiku [Interview with Mr Stotland, manager of the Asian and Pacific region] (p. 13). *Nihon Keizai Shimbun.*

# A Chinese-French Case Study of English Language Learning via Wikispaces, Animoto and Skype

Laura M. Hartwell[1] and Bin Zou[2]

**Abstract**. This paper reports on the learning experience of Chinese and French students participating in a computer mediated communication (CMC) collaboration conducted in English and supported by Wikispaces, Animoto, and Skype. Several studies have investigated CMC contexts in which at least some participants were native speakers. Here, we address the linguistic and cultural challenges that students face when language code-switching is impossible. Twenty-five French students enrolled in their final semester of an undergraduate program in Sports Management and 40 Chinese students enrolled in their second year of undergraduate program in Business completed individual and group projects related to tourism in Europe based on information gathered through communication in English with their foreign partners. Data from students' written and oral productions were complemented by students' self-reflective evaluations. This study illustrates that mastering new technologies and interacting with an authentic audience motivated student learning. Some students also benefitted from the possibility of improving speaking skills through recording and listening to their own voices.

**Keywords**: computer mediated collaboration, oral skills, cross-cultural, audience, recording.

## 1. Introduction

This paper reports on the impact of technology and cross-cultural communication among Chinese and French students during a computer mediated communication (CMC) collaboration over a one semester course in English. Studies investigating

---

1. University Grenoble Alpes, UJF-LIDILEM, Grenoble, France; Hartwell@ujf-grenoble.fr

2. Xi'an Jiaotong-Liverpool University, China

How to cite this article: Hartwell, L. M., & Zou, B. (2013). A Chinese-French Case Study of English Language Learning via Wikispaces, Animoto and Skype. In L. Bradley & S. Thouësny (Eds.), *20 Years of EUROCALL: Learning from the Past, Looking to the Future. Proceedings of the 2013 EUROCALL Conference, Évora, Portugal* (pp. 106-111). Dublin/Voillans: © Research-publishing.net.

CMC contexts in which some students were native speakers of the target language have highlighted student involvement and motivation, as well as challenges of cross-cultural communication (Jauregi & Bañados, 2010; Mangenot & Tanaka, 2008), the importance of organizational considerations (Cloke, 2010; Fratter & Helm, 2010), cultural differences in giving feedback (Guth & Marini-Maio, 2010), and positive impact on social register use (Cunningham & Vyatkina, 2012). Here, we address the linguistic and cultural challenges that participants negotiate when language code-switching is impossible as neither group speaks the first language of their partners. Neither the Chinese nor the French students or instructors spoke the language or possessed an in-depth knowledge of the other community's culture. However, a desire to become better acquainted with the "other" culture and to participate in projects outside of the standard curriculum piqued the interest of the students.

The results of this study echo notions that can be found in other contexts related to second language production, such as first-language influence, a lack of an appropriate range of vocabulary and the preference of many students for written over oral communication. Here, we will specifically address issues related to the mediation by computers linking two historically distinct communities. These issues comprise technical considerations and the presence of an authentic public.

## 2. Context

### 2.1. Population

Between January and April 2013, 25 French students enrolled in their final year of an undergraduate program in Sports Management and 40 Chinese students enrolled in their second year of undergraduate program in Business communicated via a Wikispaces platform, which integrated technical tutorials and on-line resources, instructions on individual and group assignments, publication of those assignments for class viewing and written interaction. To ensure international inter-student contact, each of the 25 French students was assigned to two of the twelve sub-groups. Then, each of the 40 Chinese students joined one sub-group. Each of the twelve sub-groups had a dedicated page on the Wikispaces platform on to which all of the students posted a one-paragraph presentation of themselves. Many students illustrated their page with pictures of local scenery, sports events or maps.

### 2.2. Assignments

The first project was a group-constructed 30-second Animoto project about their country of origin incorporating both images of students' choice in the form of a slide show and an oral document. All French students began by uploading pictures found on the Internet before writing a text and then recording it using Audacity software. As the semester in China began four weeks after the French semester, the Animoto projects were produced in two waves. In contrast to the French projects, the Chinese students included many personal pictures of themselves visiting famous sites in China or participating in artistic or athletic events. The French students expressed their enthusiasm concerning what they interpreted as the Chinese students' overall outgoing and friendly manner. This positive reception became a continuing motivating factor for the French students over the semester.

For the second project, students were required to communicate via Skype in gathering information about the other culture. The Chinese students were to organize a trip within Europe originating in Liverpool and budgeted at 700 pounds. Many of these students were motivated by a possible year of study abroad in Liverpool the following year. The French students were to create a flyer and a corresponding oral document concerning a three-day, sport-oriented trip in France that would particularly target a Chinese audience.

### 2.3. Technology

The use of technology was supported by publicly-available and teacher-made on-line tutorials, both integrated into Wikispaces, Audacity, Animoto, Skype or Skype recordings. The Chinese instructor had Instructional Technology staff and students equipped with laptops, iPads or mobile telephones equipped with Skype. The French students worked in a computer lab with Internet connection, but had no technical assistance.

### 3. Method

The qualitative data for this study were collected from the students' work deposited on Wikispaces and from a French self-reflective assignment comprised of three open-ended questions in English related to participation, learning and challenges.

### 4. Results

Despite varied levels of English skills, all students actively participated in the different activities. The number of contributions per group page ranged from 41 to 162, with a mean of 90.9. Five of the 12 groups posted from one to 12 images on their page. Furthermore, the page for depositing and viewing the French flyers and oral documents recorded 45 comments from both Chinese and French students.

The comments appear to refer only to the flyers and not to the oral documents. The written expression was clearly addressed to the other students and often incorporated emoticons or comments such as "Hello and welcome to our place!", "Teamwork is the key of the success", "I'm glad to meet all of you" or "Sorry, I did not do it very well".

### 4.1. Skype

Students also participated in Skype communication either through written or oral modes. Many students either submitted copies of written Skype communication or commented on their oral communications. Although the Chinese students were accustomed to Skype, this was only true for about one-third of the French. Some French students used Google Translate simultaneously with Skype in order to verify meaning and prepare written answers. Class projects were generally discussed via written Skype, while more general topics such as driving, family life, vacations and food were discussed orally. On several occasions, Skype conferences of three or more students also took place. Students were more at ease with written communication when communicating cross-culturally. French students also used Skype to record discussions in English among themselves, which they then posted on Wikispaces.

### 4.2. Authentic audience

The context of an authentic audience motivated genuine conversation as noted in the self-reflective student reports. French students commented on the excellent level of English of the Chinese students, which motivated them to produce work at the upper limits of their capacities. One student commented "Correspondents were really friendly and always eager to speak to us, that made the task easier" and a second explained "The most stimulating aspects of this project were to be able to speak in English with foreigners and to be able to give them some information about our country and to help them to improve their trip". There were also clear indications of a *division of labor* among students, for example the creation of written rules to "keep this page clear and understandable" (See Blin, 2012 on Cultural Historical Activity Theory).

### 4.3. Listening to one's own speaking

Recording oral documents via Audacity and Skype permitted students to listen to each other despite the time lag. An unexpected outcome to these technical options was the capacity for students to listen to their own voice. For the recorded individual and group projects, students wrote out the script first while checking dictionaries for richer vocabulary or consulting the instructor about syntax. Students also took advantage of the capacity to record repeatedly and to edit using Audacity software. Some students preferred recording at home, either because of the noise level in class or out of shyness as they felt more at ease in a private setting. One student concluded "This may sound strange but I loved working on an oral recording"; this allows one to reflect on pronunciation and encourages self-correction.

## 5. Discussion

This study highlights the contrasting apprehensions that students bring to written and oral communication and how computer mediation offers new approaches to dealing with these apprehensions. The instructors implemented student projects that, with the integration of CMC, centered the attention towards student production in a positive socio-affective environment (see Develotte, 2009). The student productions incorporated images, voice and text, but moreover they incorporated the desire to communicate well with people at a distance. In other words, it was not the technology in itself that led to moments of tension or breakdown, but the occasional difficulty to contact a foreign partner due to time lag and conflicting schedules. Although technology was a central piece of this project, it was the human "presence" that drove the level of student participation.

Finally, the technology used in these projects allowed students to slow down the oral production process into a series of steps, a method of production more often associated with writing production. Here, the multiple steps of recording oral documents – brainstorming on content, pre-recording script preparation, evaluation of one's own pronunciation and prosody, comparison with other student projects, modification of the final product – permitted students to reflect on their oral production. This led to reduced anxiety and increased confidence over the semester, however, direct oral communication via Skype often remained a source of stress for some students.

**Acknowledgements**. We would like to thank the organisers of the Gothenburg 2012 EUROCALL conference where this project was conceived.

## Resources

Animoto: http://animoto.com/
Audacity: http://audacity.sourceforge.net/
Google Translate: http://translate.google.com/

Skype: http://www.skype.com/fr/download-skype/skype-for-computer/
Skype Record: http://www.skype-rec.com/
Wikispaces: https://www.wikispaces.com/

## References

Blin, F. (2012). Introducing cultural historical activity theory for researching CMC in foreign language education. In M. Dooly & R. O'Dowd (Eds.), *Researching online foreign language interaction and exchange: Theories, methods and challenges* (pp. 79-106). Oxford: Peter Lang.

Cloke, S. (2010). The Italia-Australia intercultural project. In S. Guth & F. Helm (Eds.), *Telecollaboration 2.0: Language, literacies and intercultural learning in the 21st century* (pp. 375-384). Bern: Peter Lang.

Cunningham, D. J., & Vyatkina, N. (2012). Telecollaboration for professional purposes: Towards developing a formal register in the German classroom. *Canadian Modern Language Review, 68*(4), 422-450. doi: 10.3138/cmlr.1279

Develotte, C. (2009). From face-to-face to distant learning: The on-line learner's emerging identity. In R. Goodfellow & M.-N. Lamy (Eds.), *Learning Cultures in Online Education* (pp. 71-92). London: Continuum International Publishing Group.

Fratter, I., & Helm, F. (2010). The intercultura project. In S. Guth, & F. Helm (Eds.), *Telecollaboration 2.0: Language, literacies and intercultural learning in the 21st century* (pp. 385-398). Bern: Peter Lang.

Guth, S., & Marini-Maio, N. (2010). Close encounters of a new kind: The use of Skype and wiki in telecollaboration. In S. Guth & F. Helm (Eds.), *Telecollaboration 2.0: Language, literacies and intercultural learning in the 21st century* (pp. 413-426). Bern: Peter Lang.

Jauregi, K., & Bañados, E. (2010). Case study: An intercontinental video-web communication project between Chile and the Netherlands. In S. Guth & F. Helm (Eds.), *Telecollaboration 2.0: Language, literacies and intercultural learning in the 21st century* (pp. 427-452). Bern: Peter Lang.

Mangenot, F., & Tanaka, S. (2008). Les coordonnateurs comme médiateurs entre deux cultures dans les interactions en ligne : le cas d'un échange franco-japonais. *ALSIC, Apprentissage des langues et systèmes d'information et de communication, 11*(1), 33-59. Retrieved from http://alsic.revues.org/472

# Listeners' Responses in Interaction Through Videoconferencing for Presentation Practices

## Atsushi Iino[1], Yukiko Yabuta[2], and Yoichi Nakamura[3]

**Abstract**. This study investigated the change of listeners' responses of Japanese learners of English over a semester of presentation training sessions. We were also concerned with the relationship between speaking ability and perceived use of listeners' responses. In this paper, the listeners' responses we focused on were: acknowledging signals, repetition of the teacher's utterances, and asking questions to the teacher. Therefore, the research questions were: (1) how did the learners' perceived use of listener's responses change over time?, and (2) what is the relationship between speaking ability and listeners' responses? The participants were 21 Japanese university students whose majors were in Economics. During the semester, the participants experienced five videoconferencing sessions in total. Each English teacher in charge of a group of three Japanese learners listened to three presentations during a 50-minute session. Speaking ability was assessed through an interview test following the format of STEP Eiken test for Japanese learners of English. To obtain the data of the listeners' responses, a questionnaire was provided after each session, asking how much they could actually put into practice from the three types of responses. The results indicated that as for RQ (1), three learners' responses changed to some extent over the sessions. Concerning RQ (2), there was only a significant relationship between speaking ability and repetition of the teacher's utterance. From these results it can be said that videoconferencing interaction, particularly after presentation, provided opportunities for the learners to increase output and interaction, which boosts their L2 performance development.

**Keywords**: listener's responses, speaking, interaction, videoconferencing, Japanese.

---

1. Hosei University Tokyo, Japan; iino@hosei.ac.jp
2. Seisen Jogakuin College, Nagano, Japan
3. Seisen Jogakuin College, Nagano, Japan

**How to cite this article**: Iino, A., Yabuta, Y., & Nakamura, Y. (2013). Listeners' Responses in Interaction Through Videoconferencing for Presentation Practices. In L. Bradley & S. Thouësny (Eds.), *20 Years of EUROCALL: Learning from the Past, Looking to the Future. Proceedings of the 2013 EUROCALL Conference, Évora, Portugal* (pp. 112-116). Dublin/Voillans: © Research-publishing.net.

## 1. Introduction

In Japan where English is taught as a foreign language, learners of English at university level have few chances of output and interaction in English as L2. While they have a fair amount of linguistic knowledge crammed for the competitive entrance examination, they have a weakness in applying their knowledge to performance. For example, the learners with a high score in a Test of English for International Communication (TOEIC) may not necessarily speak or write well enough in accordance with their listening and reading ability.

As a solution for such learners, we provided opportunities of videoconferencing sessions using Skype in order to further develop their spoken English performance. Concretely, they gave presentations to the English teachers and each one of the presenters had a chance to interact with the teacher about what they had presented after their presentation. That kind of interaction was a crucial opportunity of uncontrolled conversation which indicated the virtual spoken performance of the learners.

## 2. Review of literature

### 2.1. Use of videoconferencing for L2 learning

Among previous studies on the use of videoconferencing in L2 instruction, O'Dowd (2000) reported an exchange project between foreign language classes in Spain and the USA. The two groups integrated videoconferencing technology into a task based exchange. As a result, it was demonstrated that the students became more aware of how they viewed their own culture as well as the target cultures through intercultural communication.

Hampel and Stickler (2012) analysed written and spoken interaction in recorded videoconferencing sessions, examining some quantitative data to reveal participation patterns. They also demonstrated a way to use videoconferencing with its multiple modalities for language teaching, showing that new patterns of communication emerged in the process.

### 2.2. Use of videoconferencing and listeners' responses

A listeners' response, called 'reactive token' by Clancy, Thompson, Suzuki and Tao (1996), is defined as "a short utterance produced by an interlocutor who is playing a listener's role during the other interlocutor's speakership" (Clancy et al., 1996, p. 355). They classify reactive tokens into five types: backchannels, reactive expressions, collaborative finishes, repetitions, and resumptive openers. Among the categories, De Marco and Leone (2012) investigated backchannels and reactive expressions, which are in their terms, acknowledgement and agreement/ assessment signals. De Marco and Leone (2012) used the spoken data elicited from two videoconferencing conversations by a speaker learning Italian as L2 and a native speaker of Italian. Based on the transcribed data, they found that L2 subjects employed a great variety of acknowledgement and agreement listener responses depending on the situations such as the levels of involvement in the discourse and of acquaintance of the two speakers, and the task type.

Following the results of De Marco and Leone (2012), we tried to find the features of listeners' responses by Japanese university level learners of English and investigated the two following research questions:

- RQ1. How did the learners' use of listener's responses change over time?

- RQ2. What is the relationship between speaking ability and listeners' responses?

## 3. Method

### 3.1. Participants

The participants were twenty-one Japanese university students whose majors were in Economics. They were aged between 19 and 21, including 6 females and 15 males, and counted 11 sophomores and 10 seniors. Their proficiency level was, on average, 614 points out of 1000 points in the CASEC[4] test, which is roughly equivalent to 470 points in the TOEFL PBT[5].

### 3.2. Procedure

During one semester from April to July 2012, the participants experienced five videoconferencing sessions in total. The learners were asked to give a presentation in the videoconferencing session for approximately 10 minutes on the topic they chose. An English teacher was responsible for a group of three Japanese learners. She listened to three presentations during a 50 minute session.

---

4. Computerised Assessment System for English Communication.

5. Test of English as a Foreign Language Paper-based Test.

During this period, the teacher interacted with the presenter, asking questions and/or giving some comments.

### 3.3. Data collection procedure

After each session, learners were asked to respond to questionnaires on their preparation and the presentation itself. Most of the interactions were successfully recorded through an application program to record both sides of a videoconferencing interaction.

Speaking ability was assessed through an interview which follows the format of an STEP Eiken test for Japanese learners of English, which consists of reading aloud, picture narration and open-ended free Q&A. The presenter listened to the recorded data and rated each sub-test category with a 5 point scale.

## 4. Results

The results of the questionnaire between May and July indicated that acknowledgement signals such as "a-ha", "I see", "OK", etc. were perceived to be used constantly by around 80% of the learners ("Yes": May 78% -> June 83%), but did not change much over the sessions. Repetition of the teacher's utterances was not frequently used, though the ratio of its use rose over time (May 33% -> July 39%). Concerning asking questions to the teacher, the percentages of perceived use rose drastically over time (May 61% -> July 89%).

As for the speaking test, the average score was 18.41 out of 25 points ($N = 21$). The results of the correlational studies were as follows: between speaking test and the perceived listeners' responses, acknowledge signals showed the highest correlational coefficient .846 with 1% significant level. Neither repetition of the teacher's utterances nor asking questions to the teacher showed any significant correlational coefficients (.166 and .187, respectively).

## 5. Discussion

With reference to RQ (1), the answer was positive. From this result we could say that over time the learners could use listeners' responses more frequently. This could be interpreted in two different manners. Firstly, and in line with O'Dowd's (2000) findings, the presentation training program with videoconferencing generated more interest in intercultural communication for the learners. Secondly, using presentation as a source of videoconferencing may have caused more fruitful communications, leading to more active interactions with the teacher as listener. In order for the students to give successful presentations, they prepared written scripts and slides. This kind of multimodality in the project, as Hampel and Stickler (2012) hinted, may have stimulated active interactions after the presentations.

Regarding RQ (2), a strong relationship was found between speaking ability and repetition of the teacher's utterances. The reason might be that the more the learners and the teacher know each other, the more learners were likely to be able to control the conversation. These results seemed to follow De Marco and Leone (2012) in that the levels of acquaintance of the two speakers influenced L2 learner's employment of listeners' responses.

## 6.    Conclusion

Overall, we could conclude that videoconferencing interaction particularly after presentation provided opportunities for the learners to increase listeners' responses, in other words, to increase the amount of interactions. This was naturally supposed to boost their L2 development. We believe that this study contributes to the CALL discipline as a case of successful blended instruction of videoconferencing and face-to-face instruction.

## References

Clancy, P. M., Thompson, S. A., Suzuki, R., & Tao, H. (1996). The conversational use of reactive tokens in English, Japanese, and Mandarin. *Journal of Pragmatic, 26*(3), 355-387. doi: 10.1016/0378-2166(95)00036-4

De Marco, A., & Leone, P. (2012). Computer mediated conversation for mutual learning: acknowledgement and agreement/assessment signals in Italian as L2. In L. Bradley & S. Thouësny (Eds.), *CALL: Using, Learning, Knowing, EUROCALL Conference, Gothenburg, Sweden, 22-25 August 2012, Proceedings* (pp. 70-75). Dublin: Research-publishing.net. Retrieved from http://research-publishing.net/publications/2012-eurocall-proceedings/

Hampel, R., & Stickler, U. (2012).The use of videoconferencing to support multimodal interaction in an online language classroom. *ReCALL, 24*(2), 116-137. doi: 10.1017/S095834401200002X

O'Dowd, R. (2000). Intercultural learning via videoconferencing: a pilot exchange project. *ReCALL, 12*(1), 49-61.

# The Use of New Technologies for the Teaching of the Igbo Language in Schools: Challenges and Prospects

Modesta I. Iloene[1], George O. Iloene[2], Evelyn E. Mbah[3], and Boniface M. Mbah[4]

**Abstract.** This paper examines the experience of teachers in the use of new technologies to teach the Igbo language spoken in South East Nigeria. The study investigates the extent to which new technologies are available and accessible to Igbo teachers, the competence of the Igbo language teachers in the new technologies and the challenges they face that limit the use of the new technologies in the teaching of the Igbo language. Forty respondents from two Nigerian universities were used for the study. The instrument is made up of fifteen questions divided to generate answers to five research questions. The findings show that new technologies are both available and accessible to the Igbo language teachers, and most of them are very competent in use. Furthermore, they are positively disposed to the use of computers in teaching, but do not sufficiently use them for exercises because systems and application software are not available by default for Igbo. This creates the need to advocate some interventions to enhance the utility of the Igbo language as a vehicle for new technologies in language teaching. Comparisons of responses from the two universities also reveal some significant differences in the extent of access to and expertise in the new technologies as well as perception of the need for and challenges to these technologies.

**Keywords**: computer, internet, access, competence, challenges, Igbo language.

---

1. Department of Linguistics, Igbo and other Nigerian Languages, University of Nigeria, Nsukka; modesta.iloene@unn.edu.ng
2. Department of languages and Linguistics, Ebonyi State University, Abakaliki
3. Department of Linguistics, Igbo and other Nigerian Languages, University of Nigeria, Nsukka
4. Department of Linguistics, Igbo and other Nigerian Languages, University of Nigeria, Nsukka

**How to cite this article**: Iloene, M. I., Iloene, G. O., Mbah, E. E., & Mbah, B. M. (2013). The Use of New Technologies for the Teaching of the Igbo Language in Schools: Challenges and Prospects. In L. Bradley & S. Thouësny (Eds.), *20 Years of EUROCALL: Learning from the Past, Looking to the Future. Proceedings of the 2013 EUROCALL Conference, Évora, Portugal* (pp. 117-122). Dublin/Voillans: © Research-publishing.net.

## 1. Introduction

The world has become a global village, thanks to developments in computer and internet technologies. The life wire of these new technologies is language. In other words, it is only through the instrumentality of language that information in and about computers and related technologies are made available to the world. Thus, technologies have a dual relationship with language. First, it is driven by language, and second it is a catalyst for language propagation. Little wonder then that the dynamics of many fields of endeavor have been influenced by revolution brought about by new technologies, and practitioners in these fields have been making efforts to become relevant to the new order.

The field of language teaching is not left out of this great wind of change as many teachers make use of 'cutting edge' technologies in their bid to achieve the desired language instructional objectives. Yet we know that languages do not just acquire new technologies. In other words, language teachers do not just wake up one morning and boot the computer, for instance, for use in teaching, at least not for some less commonly taught languages, even if it is possible with the likes of English, French, etc. Therefore, while many languages effectively serve as both media and object of new technologies, many others are battling with teething problems associated with the new technologies.

The Igbo language spoken in South East Nigeria belongs to the latter category. Though a less commonly taught language (LCTL), the Igbo language is one of the three major Nigerian languages, and is fast developing. It is a medium of instruction in the junior primary schools in south east Nigeria and it is studied both as a first and alternate language in government secondary and tertiary institutions in the country. The age of globalisation requires that the teaching of Igbo be taken to another level. Shyamlee and Phil (2012) warn that if we neglect or ignore technological developments they will continue and perhaps we will never be able to catch up, irrespective of our discipline or branch. For this reason, many Igbo teachers especially in the higher institutions make efforts to infuse new technologies into their jobs not just to become relevant to the new age but also to post Igbo on the global village map. This explains why Shyamlee and Phil (2012) assert that "the new era assigns new challenges and duties on the modern teacher" (p. 150).

It is therefore imperative to assess the extent of use of the new technologies in the teaching of the Igbo language and ascertain the challenges that teachers most commonly face in order to seek interventions that will facilitate their response to this call to duty. In carrying out this major objective, the following research questions confront this study: To what extent are new technologies available to teachers? To what extent are new technologies accessible to the teachers? How competent are the teachers in the use of new technologies? Finally, what challenges confront the use of new technologies for teaching the Igbo language? Answers provided to these questions will lead to some suggestions of possible solutions.

## 2. Literature review

According to Zhao (2003), "technologies is an ill-defined concept that encompasses a wide range of tools, artifacts, and practices, from multimedia computers to the Internet, from videotapes to online chat rooms, from web pages to interactive audio conferencing" (p. 8). The onset of technologies in the past few decades has revolutionised various activities of man. Interaction and information dissemination has particularly been enhanced in most professions including teaching where language teaching has a considerable share. The use of technologies is not new in the teaching of many European languages like English, French and the like. Concerning English, for instance, Shyamlee and Phil (2012) assert that "as the number of English learners is increasing, different teaching methods have been implemented to test the effectiveness of the teaching process. Use of authentic materials in the form of films, radio, TV has been there for a long time" (p. 150). The high status enjoyed by English across the globe has earned it a principal position as both a subject and a medium for technologies, and these developments continue to advance its fortune. In Nigeria, for instance, the use of computers and Internet mainly depends on English.

The findings of reviewed studies on the use of new technologies in language teaching reveal that there is no limit to the advantages that accrue from it (Godwin-Jones, 2013; Tella, Tella, Toyobo, Adika, & Adeyinka, 2007; Xing, 2008; Zhao, 2003). Others reveal challenges associated with it especially in Africa and most developing countries (Anderson, 1997; Hennessy & Onguko, forthcoming; Winke, Goertler, & Amuzie, 2010; Uchechukwu, 2005).

The challenges of new technologies have been a major setback for Igbo teachers and this does not only dampen their morale but also limit the possibilities of the language as a vehicle for new technologies. This poses a serious survival problem for Igbo in a multilingual, multicultural world in which language maintenance and language learning aptitude have become very important. At a time when Computer Assisted Language Learning (CALL) has dominated language pedagogy, it will amount to language 'linguicide' not to create the necessary platform to launch Igbo into these new technologies. Hence, the need for this study.

## 3. Methodology

The research design adopted for this study is a descriptive survey. Questionnaires were distributed to 40 teachers of Igbo in two higher institutions (one federal and the other state) in South east Nigeria. 15 question items were constructed to elicit responses in line with the objectives set for the study. The questionnaire was studied and validated by experts in language and education. The statistical tools used in the analysis were percentage, mean, standard deviation and T-Test. In the analysis, mean of 2.0 or more and 2.5 and above are considered significant on 3 and 4 point scales, respectively.

## 4. Results

Percentage distribution of responses on the availability and sources of 12 items of new technologies shows that computer is the most available, with 100% score on availability, and 65% and 35% on self and institutional provisions, respectively. Internet facilities, e-library, and e-mail are the three most available new technologies provided by the institutions with percentage scores of 97.5, 82.5 and 57.5, respectively on availability, and 67.5, 57.5 and 55, respectively on institutional provision. Camcorder is the least available with 35% availability and 35% institutional provision, while iPad/iPod is the least provided by the institutions on 7.5% score.

Mean ($X$) and standard deviation ($SD$) of the responses of teachers on the extent of their access to the new technologies measured on a 3 point scale reveal that computer is the most accessible with $X = 2.63$ and $SD = 0.54$. This is followed by printer ($X = 2.58$; $SD = 0.50$), internet facilities ($X = 2.55$; $SD = 0.55$) and photocopier ($X = 2.55$; $SD = 0.60$). Ipad/Ipod ($X = 1.70$; $SD = 0.62$), midget ($X = 1.70$; $SD = 0.62$) and camcorder ($X = 1.75$; $SD = 0.73$) are not accessible to Igbo language teachers with mean scores $< 2.00$.

Mean and standard deviation of responses on competence measured on a 4 point scale show that teachers are competent in 8 out of the 12 items listed in which mean $\geq 2.5$, but not competent in power point preparation ($X = 2.03$; $SD = 1.01$) and presentation ($X = 2.46$; $SD = 1.05$), the use of photocopier ($X = 2.39$; $SD = 1.24$) and digital camera ($X = 2.11$; $SD = 1.23$), which mean responses are $< 2.50$.

Percentage utilisation of the new technologies: five areas of utilisation surveyed reveal non-use of manual typewriter, blackboard technology, and lecturers' social network platform, each scoring 0%. On the other hand, surfing the net (95.0%), long hand notes (52.5%), writing on white/chalk board (97.5%), computer typing (57.5%) and hardcopy print out (57.5%) scored highest on each of the five areas of utilisation.

Mean and standard deviation of responses to challenges measured on a 3-point scale show that 2 of 14 items with mean < 2.00 pose no challenges of any extent. Others have mean ≥ 2.00 and so very significantly pose challenges to the teachers' use of new technologies with highest $X = 2.74$; $SD = 0.55$ and the least $X = 2.00$; $SD = 0.40$.

Mean comparisons of the extent of access to and expertise in the use of new technologies among the two institutions reveal t-values > 2.00 for 9 out of 12 items on access, and t-values > 2.00 for 5 out of 12 items on expertise in favour of the younger and state university. These indicate that teachers in the younger institution have more access to and expertise in the use of the relevant items than teachers in the older institution.

Mean comparisons of responses from the two institutions on the perception of the need for and challenges to the use of new technologies show that the older university teachers perceive new technologies as 'very needed' while the younger university teachers perceive them as 'needed' with t-value of the mean comparison of their needs perception set at 2.50. Moreover, 8 of 14 items measured on challenges produced t-values > 2.00 when mean responses from the two institutions were compared. This implies some significant differences in the perception of challenges to the use of new technologies among teachers in the institutions.

## 5. Summary of findings

The study suggests that new technologies are available and accessible to teachers in the two institutions. These teachers have skills in the use of these facilities. However, they make limited use of them for teaching the Igbo language because some symbols and diacritics used to write the Igbo languages are not available by default on the standard keyboard, neither are there software programmes (system and application) that support easy use of Igbo on the computer and internet. The implication of this is that in spite of the availability of, accessibility to and competence in the new technologies established in this study most teachers still adopt more traditional language teaching practices, such as preparing long handwritten notes, writing on a white/chalk board, while their students type assignments by combining keystrokes on standard keyboard and submit hardcopy printouts. Furthermore, the result of comparisons of responses of teachers from the two institutions surveyed shows more competence, perceptions of the need for and challenges of the use of new technologies on the part of teachers of the younger university. This confirms that age is a relevant factor in the utilisation of new technologies. Among other things, the study recommends that Igbo teachers should use the new technologies as a platform to collaborate with one another and with teachers of more commonly taught languages to seek interventions that will facilitate the teaching and learning of Igbo using the new technologies.

## References

Anderson, J. (1997). Integrating ICT and Other Technologies in Teacher Education: Trends, Issues and Guiding Principles. *Infoshare: Sources and Resources Bulletin* (pp. 33-35). Retrieved from http://www.educationcaribbean.com/eDocs/Teacher%20Education/4integrating.pdf

Godwin-Jones, R. (2013). Emerging Technologies: The Technological Imperative in Teaching and Learning Less Commonly Taught Languages. *Language Learning & Technology, 17*(1), 7-19.

Hennessy, S., Harrison, D., & Wamakote, L. (2010). Teacher Factors Influencing Classroom Use of ICT in Sub-Saharan Africa. *Itupale Online Journal of African Studies, 2*, 39-54. Retrieved from http://www.cambridgetoafrica.org/resources/Hennessy%20etal_FINAL.pdf

Hennessy, S., & Onguko, B. (Eds). (forthcoming). *Developing Use of ICT to Enhance Teaching and Learning in East African Schools: a Review of the Literature*. Cambridge and Dar es Salaam: Faculty of Education, University of Cambridge and Aga Khan University Institute for Educational Development - Eastern Africa.

Shyamlee, S. D., & Phil, M. (2012). Use of Technology in English Language Teaching and Learning: An Analysis. *International Conference on Language, Medias and Culture IPEDR vol. 33* (pp. 150-156). Retrieved from http://www.ipedr.com/vol33/030-ICLMC2012-L10042.pdf

Tella, A., Tella, A., Toyobo, O. M., Adika, L. O., & Adeyinka, A. A. (2007). An Assessment of Secondary School Teachers Uses of ICTs: Implications for Further Development of ICT's Use in Nigerian Secondary Schools. *Turkish Online Journal of Educational Technology, 6*(3), 5-17.

Uchechukwu, C. (2005). The Representation of Igbo with the Appropriate Keyboard. In C. Ikekeonwu & I. Nwadike (Eds), *Igbo Language Development: The Metalanguage Perspective*. Enugu: CIDJAP printing Press.

Winke, P., Goertler, S., & Amuzie, G. L. (2010). Commonly-taught and Less-commonly-taught Language Learners: Are they equally prepared for CALL and online language learning? *Computer Assisted Language Learning, 23*(3), 199-219. doi: 10.1080/09588221.2010.486576

Xing, X. (2008). *An Investigation of the Use of CALL by College English Teachers: Perspectives in a Chinese Normal University*. M. ED Thesis. Queensland University of Technology.

Zhao, Y. (2003). Recent Developments in Technology and Language Learning: A Literature Review and Meta-analysis. *CALICO journal, 21*(1), 7-27. Retrieved from https://calico.org/html/article_279.pdf

# The European Project TILA

Kristi Jauregi[1], Sabela Melchor-Couto[2], and Elina Vilar Beltrán[3]

**Abstract.** Telecollaboration for Intercultural Language Acquisition (TILA), is an EU-funded project within the Lifelong Learning Programme that will run between January 2013 and June 2015. TILA's overall objectives are: (1) to innovate, enrich and make foreign language teaching programmes more attractive and effective by encouraging the implementation of telecollaboration activities in secondary schools across Europe; (2) to assist teachers and teacher training programmes in developing information and communications technology (ICT) literacy skills as well as organisational, pedagogical and intercultural competences to guarantee adequate integration of telecollaboration practices; and (3) to study the added value that telecollaboration may bring to language learning in terms of intercultural understanding and motivation amongst younger learners. Our aim in this (albeit short) paper is to introduce the project, its background and outline the specific teaching needs of our participants with regards to languages and technology.

**Keywords**: telecollaboration, TILA, teacher training, CMC.

## 1. Introduction

The European TILA project (http://www.tilaproject.eu/) seeks to implement telecollaborative activities in secondary schools' foreign language curricula in order to make language learning a more authentic, attractive and relevant experience. Six countries are represented in the TILA consortium: France, UK,

---

1. Utrecht University, Utrecht, The Netherlands; k.jauregi@uu.nl
    Fontys University of Applied Sciences, Ttilburg, The Netherlands
2. University of Roehampton, London, UK
3. Queen Mary, University of London, UK

**How to cite this article**: Jauregi, K., Melchor-Couto, S., & Vilar Beltrán, E. (2013). The European Project TILA. In L. Bradley & S. Thouësny (Eds.), *20 Years of EUROCALL: Learning from the Past, Looking to the Future. Proceedings of the 2013 EUROCALL Conference, Évora, Portugal* (pp. 123-128). Dublin/Voillans: © Research-publishing.net.

Germany, Spain, the Netherlands and Czech Republic[4]. Each country collaborates with a secondary school and a teacher training institution.

## 1.1. Focus on foreign language learning at secondary education

TILA seeks to take full advantage of the capacity that younger learners seem to have to acquire foreign languages (particularly as far as fluency and pronunciation are concerned) (Muñoz, 2008) and to contribute to the research field on Computer Mediated Communication (CMC), as most research has been carried out within tertiary education.

## 1.2. Focus on intercultural communicative competence (ICC)

The development of ICC of language learners is a core objective in the project. As we know, culture and language are inseparable and constitute "a single universe or domain of experience" (Kramsch, 1991, p. 217). Interacting with others in a target language involves more than just knowing the correct syntax and lexicon; it is also an issue of developing interactional competence (Hall, 2004) according to specific cultural values, as culture permeates social interaction (Lantolf, 2000; Lantolf & Thorne, 2006). Consequently, an important goal of foreign language teaching should be to make learners aware of similarities and contrasts between cultures and interaction styles, prepare students to understand them and, if possible, help them mediate between them (Byram, 1997). TILA's efforts will be geared towards the creation of materials and tools aiming at developing and assessing ICC.

## 1.3. Telecollaboration and teacher training

For educational changes to be successful, they have to be embraced by teaching practitioners. Although efforts are being made by scholars to put digital literacy (Dooly, 2008; Levy, 2009; O'Dowd, 2007) and intercultural and pedagogical competences high in the educational agenda, reality shows how difficult it is to introduce innovation in traditional educational settings. Few are the institutions that include telecollaboration practices in their teacher training modules, and still smaller is the number of schools experimenting with interactive communication tools. If innovative ICT-based content and pedagogies are to be introduced in

---

4. The partner from the Czech Republic will be in charge of disseminating TILA experiences and results in the Czech Republic.

secondary education, teachers will have to be trained in CMC practices, and learn by doing, by experimenting with telecollaboration tools, reflecting about their experiences, analysing possible added-values, being aware of problems and developing strategies to handle them. TILA's efforts will be devoted to the development of teacher training components to improve teaching pedagogies and learning outcomes in secondary education.

## 2. Teachers' needs

As part of the TILA training stage, an electronic survey was circulated to the project teachers in order to determine what their training needs were. The survey included a total of 40 questions and it was distributed electronically through SurveyMonkey. A total of 210 secondary school teachers took part: 94 from Spain, 39 from the Netherlands, 31 from Germany, 32 from France and 14 from the UK. The data gathered shows the following conclusions.

### 2.1. Technology in the classroom

Of the total number of respondents, France (69%), UK (57%) and the Netherlands (51%) have the highest percentage of language teachers who use technology on a daily basis or very frequently. Spain (36%) and Germany (42%) have the highest percentage of teachers who rarely or never use technology. However, both countries also show an equally high percentage of teachers who sometimes use technology (29% of the respondents for Germany and 35% for Spain). YouTube is the most widely used tool across all countries. It is worth mentioning that mobile phones are regularly used by 28% of the Dutch teachers and 16% of the German ones, and that Facebook seems to be used reasonably frequently in Spain (24%). Other tools such as wikis, blogs, chat applications, Twitter, Skype and virtual worlds are reportedly used, although only marginally.

### 2.2. Why are teachers not using technology more frequently?[5]

Most teachers stated that they like using technology in the classroom; only 19% of the French respondents, 17% of the Spanish, 16% of the German, 7% of the British and 5% of the Dutch teachers expressed a dislike towards doing so. Only a minority of them reported not to feel confident enough to do so. The main deterrents seem to be of a technical nature, as described below.

---

5. The data gathered for this question comes from answers to open-ended questions. Therefore, the information included here reflects only what teachers felt that was relevant to report for every question.

## 2.3. Availability and appropriateness of the facilities

In Germany and Spain, the main limitations reported by the respondents are that there are few computer suites per school and they have to be booked in advance, which means that they may not always be available. Incidentally, this issue is described as the main difficulty in all the project countries, although to a lesser extent.

Not having enough computers for all the students is also a problem reported by 48% of the German respondents and 46% of the Spanish. This seems to be less of an issue in France (19%) and the UK (14%). In the Netherlands, 36% of the respondents mentioned this problem.

A bad Internet connection also seems to be a powerful deterrent for using technology more frequently in the classroom for Spanish teachers (34%), only mentioned by 19% of the German teachers, and 13% of the French and Dutch teachers.

## 2.4. Technical assistance

There seems to be a split between countries where the school's technical support is reportedly available and those where it is not. On the one hand, the UK, the Netherlands and Spain seem to have a majority of respondents who reported to have some kind of technical assistance. Germany, on the other hand, seems to have a mixed picture with 52% of the respondents reporting to have technical assistance and 48% who reported the opposite. Finally, in France a majority of teachers reported not to have technical assistance (59%).

It is important to note that the technical assistance available to teachers across most of the countries analysed here is arguably limited, as most respondents state that technicians are hard to find when they are needed. This situation is particularly acute in Spain and Germany, where 30% and 32% of the respondents for each country respectively reported that the role of the technicians is in fact undertaken by fellow teachers who may have some expertise in ICT or who teach IT. This obviously involves a workload issue, in addition to the inability to attend to technical problems that occur during class times, as those colleagues will be teaching themselves. This has not been reported as a problem in the Netherlands or the UK and only to an extent in France (13%). In any case, limited availability of technical staff is one of the main issues flagged in all countries (35% in Germany, 21% in the UK, 19% in France, 15% in Spain and 13% in the Netherlands) be it due to a work overload in Spain and France or to an insufficient number of technicians per school in the other countries.

## 3. Conclusions

The focus of telecollaboration, and TILA for that matter, is on students' collaborative construction of knowledge with the aid of technology. More importantly perhaps, it teaches students 21st century skills in the form of languages, intercultural competence and digital know-how, as well as content.

As it has been discussed here, an initial needs analysis revealed that attitudes towards technology amongst the secondary school teachers surveyed are positive and that some tools, although scarcely in some cases, are already in use.

The UK and the Netherlands seem to be at the forefront of technology use in the classroom, but also seem to be better equipped for it, both in terms of the facilities and technical support available to them. The main challenge seems to be that the resources available are not sufficient, both in terms of the number of computers per student and computer rooms per school. In addition to this, Internet connections are generally perceived to be unreliable, which is an added difficulty for the successful development of telecollaborative activities. Finally, the lack of readily available technical assistance seems to be a problem across the board, particularly so in Spain and Germany where the role of the IT specialist is often allocated to a fellow teacher. These conclusions suggest that additional investment is needed in this respect for telecollaboration to be a reality across Europe. A shift towards mobile devices might be an affordable solution to the logistics of accessing sought-after computer rooms, although it would also involve an investment in sound wireless networks. A more in depth analysis is underway and will also provide information about the respondents' context. The above-mentioned figures might not only be country specific but influenced by other factors.

Although still in the early days, we hope that TILA will inspire others to give conventional teaching a new, more authentic dimension. We are now in the process of training language teachers so that they can incorporate telecollaboration activities in their daily practices.

## References

Byram, M. (1997). *Teaching and assessing intercultural communicative competence*. Clevedon: Multilingual Matters.

Dooly, M. (Ed.). 2008. *Telecollaborative language learning: A guidebook to moderating intercultural collaboration online*. Bern: Peter Lang.

Hall, J. K. (2004). A prosaic of interaction: The development of interactional competence in another language. In E. Hinkel (Ed.), *Culture in Second Language Teaching and Learning* (pp. 137-151). Cambridge: Cambridge University Press.

Kramsch, C. (1991). Culture in language learning: A view from the States. In K. de Bot, R. B. Ginsberg, & C. Kramsch (Eds.), *Foreign language research in cross-cultural perspective* (pp. 217-240). Amsterdam: John Benjamins.

Lantolf, J. P. (Ed.). (2000). *Sociocultural Theory and Second Language Learning*. Oxford: Oxford University Press.

Lantolf, J. P., & Thorne, S.L. (Eds). (2006). *Sociocultural Theory and Second Language Learning*. Oxford: Oxford University Press.

Levy, M. (2009). Technologies in use for second language learning. *The Modern Language Journal, 93*(s1), 769-782. doi: 10.1111/j.1540-4781.2009.00972.x

Muñoz, C (2008). Symmetries and Asymmetries of Age Effects in Naturalistic and Instructed L2 learning. *Applied Linguistics, 29*(4), 578-596. doi: 10.1093/applin/amm056

O'Dowd, R. (Ed.). (2007). *Online Intercultural Exchange: an introduction for foreign language teachers*. Clevedon: Multilingual Matters.

# Using Smart Phones in Language Learning – A Pilot Study to Turn CALL into MALL

### András Kétyi[1]

**Abstract**. The popularity of smart phones has increased enormously in the last few years. Because of the increasing penetration of these devices and the above-average willingness of our students using new tools and devices in language courses, we decided to design a voluntary pilot project for mobile language learning for students who learn German as a second language ($N = 70$). In our project we decided to use busuu.com, because of its easy registration process, the clear design, the very active and helpful busuu community and primarily, because of the provided tasks and materials, which are available via PC and via mobile devices too. The voluntary pilot project started in March and ended in May 2013. Every week, the students had to finish a lesson of their own choice and they could give feedback and share their experience during the project in the learning management system of the school. In May, we asked the participants how they used their devices in language learning, their experiences with language learning with busuu, what they felt were ideal learning environments for mobile learning and the types of activities they felt that their mobile devices were suited for.

**Keywords**: smart phone, mobile learning, MALL, CALL.

## 1. Introduction

The popularity of smart phones has increased enormously in the last few years. In addition, MALL research has multiplied as well (Palalas, 2011; Steel, 2012; White & Mills, 2011), although according to a MALL literature review most of the reviewed studies are experimental, small-scale and conducted within a short period of time (Viberg & Grönlund, 2012).

---

1. Budapest Business School, Diósy Lajos u. Budapest, Hungary; ketyi.andras@kkk.bgf.hu

**How to cite this article**: Kétyi, A. (2013). Using Smart Phones in Language Learning – A Pilot Study to Turn CALL into MALL. In L. Bradley & S. Thouësny (Eds.), *20 Years of EUROCALL: Learning from the Past, Looking to the Future. Proceedings of the 2013 EUROCALL Conference, Évora, Portugal* (pp. 129-134). Dublin/Voillans: © Research-publishing.net.

According to a survey from 2011 ($N = 81$), one in every three students learning German as a second language at our institution owned a smart phone. In our last survey from 2013 ($N = 70$) we found that almost half of our students learning German as a second language now have a smart phone.

Building on the increasing penetration of these devices and the above-average of willingness of our students to using new tools and devices in the language courses, we designed a pilot project about mobile language learning for students who learn German as a second language ($N = 70$). Participants were enrolled for the project on a voluntary basis.

## 2. Method

### 2.1. The participants, the tool used and the pace of the project

The participants of the project were students of our college ($N = 59$, $M = 21.03$ years) who learned German as a second language. For the purposes of the project a mobile language learning tool had to be used. Because of its easy registration process, the clear and functional design, and the very active and helpful community, *busuu* was chosen for the present project. A special advantage of *busuu* was that it provided tasks and materials which are available via PC and mobile devices. The *busuu* mobile application can be run on both Android and iOS devices. The voluntary pilot project started in March and ended in May. During the project the participants had to finish a lesson of their own choice weekly and they could also give feedback or share their experience in the learning management system of the school.

### 2.2. The qualitative data of the project

In May we asked the participants about their opinions and experiences with *busuu*. We used three questionnaires: an ICT, a smartphone and a MALL questionnaire. They are available on our research blog (http://ict-research-blogspot.com).

## 3. Discussion

### 3.1. The main findings of the ICT questionnaire

As the results indicate, our students are technically well equipped. Every student has an internet connection at home and the majority (60%) have a quick internet connection (ADSL, cable modem, mobile internet).

97% of the students use a laptop instead of a desktop computer. In contrast, our institution almost exclusively owns desktop computers instead of laptops. 97% of our students own a mobile device and 82% of these devices are smart phones. Furthermore, almost every fifth student (19%) has a tablet.

Computers at home are mainly for fun, communication and homework. The vast majority of students (92%) use the computer at home for finding fun information and watching videos on the internet. 81% of them participate in social networks (e.g. Facebook) and send emails; 61% of them use chat. 69% of students do their homework on the computer.

Desktop computers available at school are used only by a fraction of the students on a daily basis. The highest every-day-value stands for "download, upload or browse material from the school's website" (15%) followed by "browse the internet for schoolwork" and "use e-mail at school" (10% alike). These ratios indicate that teachers (except for language teachers) at our institution use computers in the classrooms very rarely.

According to the survey, students use computers more than 60 minutes a week in mathematics, marketing and accountancy lessons (2% in each) and lessons that were not listed in the questionnaire (24%). The only exception are the language lessons where the ratio comes to 86%.

PowerPoint and Excel dominate the list of applications. Tasks that students can do by themselves are the following: create a presentation (100%), use a spreadsheet to plot a graph (85%), edit digital photos (68%), create a multi-media presentation (47%) and create a database (34%).

For the majority of the students it is very important to work with a computer (73%) and playing or working with a computer is really fun for them (76%). Nevertheless, the majority of students have a pragmatic approach to technology; they are not using computers because they are very interested in them (61%), but because they see their advantages.

### 3.2. The main findings of the smartphone questionnaire

73% of students own a smart phone, most of them have one from Apple, Samsung or Sony. Most students can control the frequency of smart phone usage, while only 12 % use it more than 4 hours per day. There are no restrictions at our institution regarding the use of mobile phones, so 37% of the students use their phone during lessons. Sending messages (15%), browsing the internet (14%) and listening to music (12%) are the three most frequently used services by our students.

On average the students have 18 installed applications on their devices. Only half of the students download an application every week. If they do so, they typically check either the appstore (35%) or follow the recommendations of their fellows (33%).

### 3.3. The main findings of the MALL questionnaire

Before the project started, only two students had used a language learning system like *busuu*. Apart from one feedback, all other reactions on the first impression were positive: "Funny, happy surface", "Just like a game or Facebook". The students participating in the project liked *busuu* very much, 79% rated it good or very good. Although the majority (64%) thinks that acquiring a foreign language only with *busuu* is not possible, they nonetheless see it as a helpful tool in language learning.

92% of students would not pay after a 7-day-trial-period for the premium membership. Interestingly there were only two students who paid for a service on the internet.

Almost all of the students mentioned vocabulary as the real strength of *busuu*. Because of lack of the Hungarian language the typical language setting of students was German-English (all of our students speak English) and in their comments many students added learning a lot of English words and idioms. Some of the students said that *busuu* was helpful not just for learning new stuff, but also for reviewing and practice.

According to the students' feedback, the strengths dominated clearly over the weaknesses. The mentioned strengths were that (1) language learning was playful and easy, and the information provided was not overwhelming, (2) audio helped acquire the pronunciation, and (3) the vocabulary supported many common situations and a vast variety of topics. Students also liked the interactive online communication with other users, the immediate feedback, and the idea that their writing tasks were corrected very quickly by other *busuu* users.

Most students did not add any weakness, but if they did so, they found the fee for premium membership too high. Additionally, some of them missed their native language (Hungarian) equivalents from the bilingual glossaries and had imagined more challenging tasks. Some of the students found *busuu* boring after a while.

Students also articulated their opinion about effective language learning methods. Despite the fact that the mobile language learning application *busuu* was very well received by most of the participants, they still need, according to the feedback, real (mostly oral) communication with real persons; so language learning is still something lively and non-artificial.

The majority of the students think that the most effective way to learn a foreign language is learning it abroad. For many students oral skills are essential (e.g. communicating with native speakers, learning through conversations, dialogues). Private lessons are welcome by many of them as well. Some of the students are aware of the importance of every-day-practice and motivation, and there are still many students who believe that the "conservative learning method" with books and exercises is the key to success ("Everyone should learn the basics first").

## 4. Conclusions

As the technical conditions for mobile language learning are given – smart phones are available for the vast majority of students (82%) and everyone has an internet connection and a laptop at home – , in the present project we looked for a mobile language learning solution, which combines computers and mobile devices. If we could integrate the mobile devices in our language teaching practice, our students could gain valuable additional learning time outside the school and that could improve their language learning efficiency.

The mobile language learning application chosen for the project, *busuu*, was positively received by our students. However, *busuu*, at least for the time being, had a serious limitation in large scale language teaching. The 7-day-trial-period is way too short for an effective use of the app in practice. And since teachers may not expect their students to pay an extra fee for a language learning tool, free alternatives or a, presently not available, educational package of the provider is sought after. A further alternative would be the collaboration of several educational institutions to get funding for common MALL projects.

## References

Palalas, A. (2011). Mobile-assisted language learning: Designing for your students. In S. Thouësny & L. Bradley (Eds.), *Second language teaching and learning with technology: views of emergent researchers* (pp. 71-94). Dublin: Research-publishing.net. Retrieved from http://research-publishing.net/publications/thouesny-bradley-2011/

Steel, C. (2012). Fitting learning into life: Language students' perspectives on benefits of using mobile apps. In M. Brown, M. Hartnett & T. Stewart (Eds.), *Future challenges, sustainable futures. Proceedings of ascilite Wellington 2012* (pp. 875-880).

Viberg, O., & Grönlund, Å. (2012). Mobile assisted language learning: A literature review. In *11th World Conference on Mobile and Contextual Learning, mLearn 2012*. Helsinki.

White, J., & Mills, D. J. (2011). Get Smart!: Smartphones in the Japanese classroom. *JALT Conference Proceedings - JALT2011* (pp. 328-337).

# Data-Driven Learning of Speech Acts Based on Corpora of DVD Subtitles

## S. Kathleen Kitao[1] and Kenji Kitao[2]

**Abstract**. Data-driven learning (DDL) is an inductive approach to language learning in which students study examples of authentic language and use them to find patterns of language use. This inductive approach to learning has the advantages of being learner-centered, encouraging hypothesis testing and learner autonomy, and helping develop learning skills. The approach has grown out of corpus linguistics, and it has been used to help students learn grammar and vocabulary usage. It is also possible to use it for teaching speech acts. In this paper, we contrast inductive and deductive learning and discuss an example of an exercise using data-driven learning to learn about the expressions and strategies used in apologies.

**Keywords**: speech act, apology, data-driven learning, inductive approach.

## 1. Introduction

An important aspect of language education is the development of communicative competence, including use of speech acts. In this paper, we will discuss inductive and deductive approaches to learning and look at data-driven learning, one inductive approach, and its application to teaching apologies.

### 1.1. Inductive and deductive approaches

One way to categorize approaches to language teaching is to divide them between deductive and inductive approaches. A teacher using a deductive approach explains grammar rules, meanings of words, etc., and then the students

---

1. Doshisha Women's College, Kyoto, Japan; kkitao217@yahoo.com

2. Doshisha University, Kyotanabe, Japan

**How to cite this article**: Kitao, S. K., & Kitao, K. (2013). Data-Driven Learning of Speech Acts Based on Corpora of DVD Subtitles. In L. Bradley & S. Thouësny (Eds.), *20 Years of EUROCALL: Learning from the Past, Looking to the Future. Proceedings of the 2013 EUROCALL Conference, Évora, Portugal* (pp. 135-140). Dublin/Voillans: © Research-publishing.net.

do activities to apply what they have learned. This is a teacher-centered approach and a traditional way of teaching.

In contrast, in an inductive approach, the teacher gives students examples of the grammar point or uses of the vocabulary words and the students make observations and make generalizations from those observations. This involves hypothesis formation and testing of the hypotheses, and it is a student-centered approach.

Inductive approaches have both advantages and disadvantages. On the one hand, they allow more student participation and involvement. Students understand better and remember more, and using inductive approaches helps students develop autonomy. On the other hand, they do take longer, especially if the concepts are complex (Tian, 2005).

### 1.2. Data-driven learning

Data-driven learning is an inductive approach that makes use of corpora to find examples of lexical usage or grammatical points so that students can make generalizations about them. It is defined by Johns and King (1991) as "the use in the classroom of computer generated concordances to get students to explore the regularities of patterning in the target language, and the development of activities and exercises based on concordance output" (p. iii). Students use examples from a corpus to find patterns and develop rules.

While DDL was originally developed as a way to study grammar and vocabulary, it has also been used to teach speech acts and sociopragmatic guidelines.

## 2. An example of data-driven learning

In this section, we will explain an example of the use of DDL to teach apologies.

### 2.1. Apologies

Because they are searchable in a corpus, apologies are an appropriate speech act to use for data-driven learning. Most apologies can be found using lemmatised searches of five performative words: sorry, pardon, excuse, forgive, and apologize. In one study, using a corpus of downloaded subtitles from DVDs, lemmatised searches for the five keywords found 98% of the apologies in the corpus (Kitao, 2012).

## 2.2. Developing materials

A corpus of DVD subtitles can by compiled by downloading the subtitles from DVDs using a program called SubRip (http://www.videohelp.com/tools/Subrip). This program creates .srt files, which, if the srt extension is changed to txt, can be searched with concordancing software. The files include minutes and seconds indicating how far from the beginning each subtitle occurred, which can be useful in finding scenes.

SubRip files are often posted online. A search for the title of a movie or television program and "srt" will find links to these files. Also, a large collection of .srt files can be found at http://www.tvsubtitles.net/. You can compile the .srt files for individual series' episodes or movies into a text file. In addition, scripts can be found at such websites as Drew's Scripts-O-Rama Index at http://www.script-o-rama.com/table.shtml.

The choice of material is important. Huang (2004) found that movies of the genre romance/comedy and dramas portrayed ups and downs in relationships that required apologies that reflect real life. Television comedies and dramas would have similar characteristics. In contrast, Huang (2004) found that science fiction and action movies concentrated more on action and had few apologies. Rose (2001) suggested that material used to teach speech acts be less than 15 years old and depict contemporary characters in real-life situations.

Depending on the type of class and goals, the teacher can have students compile their own corpora and search for themselves, search for themselves in corpora provided by the teacher, or provide examples from a corpus with explanations of the background, names of speakers, etc. If the focus of the class is corpus linguistics, one of the former two methods would be preferable; if the focus of the class is on speech acts or linguistic pragmatics, the latter is preferable. If students search for themselves, they will need to look at the scenes on DVDs in order to understand what the context of the apology was, for instance, which character spoke which line. A concordancer can be used to find the apologies (and certain other speech acts). A concordancer, developed by Laurence Anthony can be downloaded at http://www.antlab.sci.waseda.ac.jp/software.html.

When one of the authors developed a data-driven learning activity to teach apologies in a linguistic pragmatics course, she used a corpus of DVD subtitles that had been developed from the first three seasons (2009, 2010 and 2011) of the US situation comedy *Modern Family* (Levitan & Lloyd, 2009). She had compiled a list of apologies from the corpus for a study of apologies (Kitao & Kitao, 2013) and she chose twenty examples of apologies. In choosing the apologies, she considered the variety of expressions and strategies and also the ease of explaining the context briefly in a way that students could easily understand. She also included examples that could be used to make specific points, such as one that used "I'm sorry" to express sympathy rather than an apology, one that used the apology in an ironic way, and one that did not have an Illocutionary Force Indicating Device (IFID) such as "I'm sorry" (Searle & Vanderveken, 1985, p. 2).

Students were given information about the characters in the series and the following instructions, along with the list of twenty apology interactions:

> The following are examples of apologies from the US family situation comedy *Modern Family*. Read the conversations and answer the following questions.
>
> 1. What is the expression used for the actual apology? (For example, "I apologize") Make a list of the common/useful expressions.
>
> 2. What other strategies are used in each conversation, that is, what else does the speaker try to do? (For example, if the speaker says, "I didn't mean to do it," they are saying that they hadn't intended to commit the offense.) Make a list of the strategies.

### 2.3. Classroom procedures

Students work together in groups to identify common expressions and strategies that were used in the examples and then the teacher goes through the list with the students, identifying which expressions and strategies are used in each example. Obviously, students describe the strategies in their own terms rather than using technical terms. Depending on the purpose of the class, the teacher can follow up by introducing students to a typology of apology strategies, with a lecture on theoretical aspects of apologies, with a discussion of the problems related to compiling a corpus, etc.

### 2.4. Examples

Below are examples of the apologies and an explanation of the strategies involved.

1. Whitney, a woman 11-year-old Manny met online, has come to meet him, believing he is an adult. She is talking to Manny's mother Gloria after learning he is only 11.

> Whitney: This is so humiliating. I am sorry.
>
> Gloria: It's okay.
>
> Whitney: He just seemed so mature online. How could I be so stupid?
>
> Manny: You're not stupid. "Stupid" is not following your heart and taking a chance on love.

Whitney expresses the emotion she is feeling ("This is so humiliating"), uses an IFID ("I am sorry"), explains why she made a mistake ("He seems so mature online"), and criticizes herself for making the mistake ("How could I be so stupid?").

2. Phil talks with an acquaintance about a problem his wife Claire has.

> Phil: But if she lets me help her, I can make her problem go away.
>
> Woman: Oh! That is such a male thing to say.
>
> Phil: Well, forgive me for being a man.

In this example, Phil is using an IFID ("Forgive me for…") and explains what he is apologizing for ("…for being a man"). In this case, students should recognize that the apology is being used ironically, since Phil has no control over the fact that he is a man.

## 3. Discussion and conclusion

When using this activity in a small linguistic pragmatics class, one author found that students could identify most of the strategies in the apologies. In an informal survey of the students, they indicated that they liked the approach. One student wrote,

> "I think this is an effective way. By doing the exercise before listening to explaining, we can consider deeply, and it is important, I think. If we knew points before exercising, we only think the way that the teacher told [sic]".

A limit on the use of DDL for speech acts is that many speech acts are not easily searchable. However, it might be possible to use speech acts such as asking permission and expressing gratitude. More research is necessary on the use of DDL to teach speech acts as well as an exploration of which speech acts would work well with this approach.

**Acknowledgements.** This work was supported by JSPS KAKENHI Grant Number 25580142.

# References

Huang, H. (2004). Apologies in film: Implications for language teaching. *Paper presented at the 13th International Symposium on English Teaching, November 12-14, Chien Tan Overseas Youth Activity Center, Taipei.* Retrieved from http://personnel.sju.edu.tw/改善師資研究成果/92年度/黃馨週--編號89.doc

Johns, T., & King, P. (Eds.). (1991). *Classroom concordancing. English Language Research Journal, 4.* University of Birmingham: Centre for English Language Studies.

Kitao, S. K. (2012). Using a spoken corpus compiled from subtitles to study apologies. *Asphodel, 47,* 50-77.

Kitao, S. K., & Kitao, K. (2013). Apologies, apology strategies, and apology forms for non-apologies in a spoken corpus. *Journal of Culture and Information Science, 8*(2), 1-13.

Levitan, S., & Lloyd, C. (2009). *Modern Family* [Television Series]. Hollywood: American Broadcasting Company.

Rose, K. R. (2001). Compliments and compliment responses in film: Implications for pragmatics research and language teaching. *International Review of Applied Linguistics, 39*(4), 309-326. doi: 10.1515/iral.2001.007

Searle, J. R., & Vanderveken, D. (1985). *Foundations of illocutionary logic.* Cambridge: Cambridge University Press.

Tian, S. (2005). Data-driven learning: Do learning tasks and proficiency make a difference? *Proceedings of the 9th Conference of the Pan-Pacific Association of Applied Linguistics.* Retrieved from http://www.paaljapan.org/resources/proceedings/PAAL9/pdf/TianShiaup.pdf

# Expert Views on How Language Education May Develop in the Next 20 Years and What CALL Could Contribute

## Ton Koenraad[1]

**Abstract**. The celebration of EUROCALL's twentieth anniversary also provides a proper occasion to reflect on the future of language teaching and the role of CALL in these developments. In this paper we present the views of five authorities on language teaching and learning from different EU countries. Most of them are also CALL experts and well respected EUROCALL members, including the late Graham Davies. Our presentation is based on a summary of the Skype interviews in which they contributed to a symposium entitled 'And now for another century of modern language teaching…' organised by the Dutch national Association of Language Teachers on the occasion of its first centennial in 2011. To provide a more global (or at least European) perspective the interviewees were asked to cover the same topics that were central to the live panel discussion by six Dutch participants representing a variety of perspectives: secondary and university teachers, students, curriculum experts and teacher educators. By way of preparation all involved had been given a number of challenging statements related to some aspects of the discussion theme: the characteristics of the future learning environment, teacher, learner, pedagogy and technology. In this audio-supported document we will focus on interesting points of view particularly related to pedagogy and technology expressed in the interviews. A video report summary of the live discussion (in Dutch) is available on the limited edition CD with recordings of the centennial festivities.

**Keywords**: CALL trends, future of MFL education, expert views, discussion, panel, educational trends watching.

---

1. TELLConsult, Vleuten, The Netherlands; ton.koenraad@gmail.com

**How to cite this article**: Koenraad, A. L. M. (2013). Expert Views on How Language Education May Develop in the Next 20 Years and What CALL Could Contribute. In L. Bradley & S. Thouësny (Eds.), *20 Years of EUROCALL: Learning from the Past, Looking to the Future. Proceedings of the 2013 EUROCALL Conference, Évora, Portugal* (pp. 141-148). Dublin/Voillans: © Research-publishing.net.

Ton Koenraad

## 1. Introduction

The Dutch national Association of Language Teachers (Levende Talen)[2] celebrated its first centennial on May 27, 2011. Part of the festivities was a symposium with the title: '…and now for another century of modern language teaching'.

The focus point of this symposium was a panel discussion. Six Dutch participants (teachers, pupils, curriculum experts and teacher educators) shared their views on the future of mainstream language learning/teaching. As food for thought they were given the following introduction and reflections to the theme.

In a 100 years' time… will there still be thirty students in three rows in a classroom with a language teacher working their way through text- and workbooks during two or three weekly, fifty-minute periods? Or will the concept of classroom and form disappear and will school be more like a social meeting place? After all, learning can take place anywhere: in social networks, virtual learning environments, with the help of intelligent agents or a private teacher at a distance. On the other hand, we should take into account that changes in education have proven to be slow and that all our 2011 prophecies may well stand little to no chance to come true in the traditional classroom.

> 1. **The future learning environment.** What changes can be predicted about the 'learning environment'? What implications are there for schools and school buildings?
>
> 2. **The future teacher.** Will subject teachers (f/m) and their task load of some 26 lessons per week disappear in the next one hundred years? And if so, who or what will replace them? Will they become merely coaches assisted by robots to transfer knowledge?
>
> 3. **The future student.** Pupils have changed in the course of time. Nowadays they are less willing to just consume educational content. They prefer to find information themselves but distinguish between personal and school-related learning.
>
> 4. **Future methodologies.** What are the current views on how languages are taught? Will didactics in mainstream language courses still be driven

---

[2]. Living Languages.

by textbooks produced by educational publishers? Or will web-based and interactive materials replace the traditional means?

5. **Future technology**. Technological developments are bound to continue the next one hundred years. How will this affect language learning and teaching? What technical developments will support future teachers and students in the second language acquisition process?

To provide a more global (or at least European) perspective five international experts were invited to be Skype interviewed individually and discuss the same topics that were central to the live panel debate.

The following colleagues accepted the request: Jozef Colpaert (Belgium), Nicolas Guichon (France), Andreas Müller-Hartmann (Germany), Andreas Lund (Norway) and Graham Davies (UK), who regrettably died a year later.

Below we summarize the key points of their opinions about the symposium topics. The present document has links to the original audio sequences for a number of statements. The extended version of this paper[3] includes links to all the audio references and the complete summaries of all the interviews. Although the standard language was English, Colpaert and Guichon have been invited to use their mother tongues so as to also add a multi-lingual dimension to this venture.

## 2. The views of the international experts on the symposium topics

### 2.1. Learning in the future learning environment

Andreas Müller-Hartmann does not expect the learning environment to change dramatically in the short term as for societies, schools are the spaces where the training of the future potential workforce takes place. Because of this interest, states consequently want to have much influence and control over these institutions [Müller-Hartmann, 1].

Nicolas Guichon finds it difficult, possibly even dangerous to make predictions, but observes that technologies develop faster than the changes that take place in schools [Guichon, 1]. From his research on the integration of ICT in language

---

3. The extended, online version of this paper is available here: http://www.koenraad.info/content/international-perspective-future-language-education

teaching it appears that teachers understand the importance of ICT but it still takes them too much time to learn to use applications.

Graham Davies observes that the learning environment in the United Kingdom (UK) is developing rapidly [Davies, 1]. In particular the Web and the interactive whiteboard have contributed to these changes.

Andreas Lund concludes that the computer function to support (oral) communication is becoming more important in language education. He elaborates on *telecollaboration* [Lund, 1] and sketches the future development of this concept towards speech communities, in which the role of the teacher is increasingly of an organizing and coaching nature.

Jozef Colpaert starts off by saying that the order of the symposium propositions, with the learning environment as a starting point, is well chosen [Colpaert, 1]. Experience has shown that first the entire learning environment must be well defined before choices as to technological instrumentation can be made.

## 2.2. The future teacher

Davies [15] expects that teachers will increasingly be developing their own materials thanks to the availability of software tools and the related competencies developed in teacher education. Furthermore he expects participation in Personal Learning Networks (PLN) as a form of continuing professional development to contribute to the development of skills needed to manage the "open classroom" [Davies, 16].

Although Lund expects the book as such will survive, he [Lund, 6] doubts if textbooks, also in their hybrid form with media and Internet content supported components, are here to stay. This is in contrast to Müller-Hartmann [10], who on the other hand, despite the very vast supply of information the web offers, thinks that teachers will not become redundant. Youngsters can find lots of content but the teacher is still needed to support the process of meaning making. Related new teacher competences that Lund mentions include the ability to design learning environments, curriculum trajectories and communication activities based on an understanding of the effects of the choice of technologies to the learning and communication process.

Colpaert [2] considers it of great importance that teachers take pride in their work and are able to feel comfortable in their learning environment. He invites them to actively participate in improvement of the quality of the learning environment in which they operate [Colpaert, 5.1].

Also Müller-Hartmann attaches great value to the teacher's comfort zone. He therefore calls for more attention in initial training and more time in professional development [Müller-Hartmann, 12] for familiarisation with, both personally and professionally, (technological) innovations such as the adoption of more learner- and task-oriented approaches and technology-enhanced telecollaboration [Müller-Hartmann, 14].

### 2.3. The future student

Davies [6] regrets that students in the UK after they have turned 14 are no longer obliged to expand their language skills. At the same time he endorses the suggestion that there is an extra demand on one's motivation to learn other languages if English is your first language [Davies, 7].

Müller-Hartmann, Lund and Guichon see an increase in informal learning because students use social media and so called web 2.0 applications. Studies by Guichon reveal that Facebook is very popular among grammar school students and their use also leads to (more) cooperation between pupils outside the school context [Guichon, 5].

### 2.4. Future language learning pedagogy

With regard to the possible influence of methodological innovations Guichon expects further growth of bilingual education in content and language integrated learning (CLIL) [ Guichon, 7]. Although Davies [13] also views CLIL as a valid approach, he does not expect a wide implementation in the UK. Lund [9] and Müller-Hartmann [4] consider it a most relevant development mainly because of the emphasis on the content that it characterizes. Both Müller-Hartmann [8] and Lund [8] observe a growing influence of the task-oriented approach also in classroom practice and on the materials currently produced by the publishers.

According to Guichon and Lund, language teachers should not attempt to integrate informal learning that could take place with the help of web 2.0 applications in education [Guichon, 6]. On the other hand, because of the relevance of the related communication processes and development of new genres for the formal curriculum, the awareness levels within the professional community of these developments should be raised [Lund, 4].

Colpaert [7] does not expect significant short-term changes in language teaching methodologies. Like Lund, he hopes that insights from other disciplines will be better integrated in modern foreign languages (MFL) pedagogy [Colpaert, 8, 9].

## 2.5. Technology of the future

Both Guichon [9] and Davies [12] expect that mobile technologies will provide flexibility and interesting applications for language teaching. Like Lund [3] they think that communicative use of language will get a much more central place in the curriculum thanks to Web 2.0 applications – also because they can support social networking and telecollaboration. Müller-Hartmann shares this view but notes that for the realization of these developments at any scale a generation of adequately trained teachers is required.

Other relevant technologies mentioned are touch screens [Davies, 11] and translation tools, for example to support the development of intercultural understanding [Guichon, 10]. Colpaert [10], finally, sees a more limited impact of technological developments on language education as choices in this domain, also in the near future, represent "only" one aspect of the whole of the learning environment.

## 3. Conclusion

When we focus on the common aspects in the views of these five experts, a trend appears to emerge with a number of characterstics. Key elements of future modern language teaching and learning that are mentioned are the (oral) use of the target language for communicaton based on authentic content. The related schoolbased processes are teacher orchestrated and facilitated by information and communication technologies. The speed at which innovation will take place is expected to be largely dependent on the availability of teachers with the necessary competences and willingness to function in the related learning environment.

**Acknowledgements**. We would like to thank the interviewees for their time and contribution to both the Levende Talen 2011 Centennial and the EUROCALL 2013 conference.

## References

**Prof. Dr Jozef Colpaert** teaches Instructional Design and Computer Assisted Language Learning at the University of Antwerp. He is vice-chairman of the Institute for

Education and Information Sciences (IOIW) and director R&D of LINGUAPOLIS, the Language Institute of the University of Antwerp. Homepage: http://www.ua.ac.be/main.aspx?c=jozef.colpaert

**Graham Davies** (2012) was employed as a Lecturer in German at Ealing College (later integrated into Thames Valley University) from 1971 to 1990, and then as Director of the Multimedia Language Centre from 1990 to 1993. He had been involved in CALL since 1976. He was conferred with the title of Professor of Computer Assisted Language Learning in 1989 and the founder president of EUROCALL from 1993 to 2000. Homepage: http://grahamdavies.wikispaces.com/

**Dr Nicolas Guichon** is professor at Lyon 2 University in Language education. He is a member of ICAR research team (CNRS) and was the director of the Masters programme language education and CALL until 2012. Homepage: http://nicolas.guichon.pagesperso-orange.fr/

**Dr Andreas Lund** is Associate Professor at the Department of Teacher Education and School Research and Vice Dean at the Faculty of Education, University of Oslo, Norway. Homepage: http://www.uv.uio.no/ils/english/people/aca/andlund/index.html

**Prof. Dr Andreas Müller-Hartmann** is head of the English Department of the University of Education (Pädagogischen Hochschule) Heidelberg. Homepage: http://www.ph-heidelberg.de/englisch/personen/lehrende/prof-dr-mueller-hartmann.html

## Audio references

Colpaert [1]: https://soundcloud.com/tellconsult/1-symposiumtopics?in=tellconsult/sets/josef-colpaert
Colpaert [2]: https://soundcloud.com/tellconsult/2-teacher-learning-environment?in=tellconsult/sets/josef-colpaert
Colpaert [5.1]: https://soundcloud.com/tellconsult/5-1-educational-engineering?in=tellconsult/sets/josef-colpaert
Colpaert [7]: https://soundcloud.com/tellconsult/7-methodological-developments?in=tellconsult/sets/josef-colpaert
Colpaert [8]: https://soundcloud.com/tellconsult/8-sla-research-input-4?in=tellconsult/sets/josef-colpaert
Colpaert [9]: https://soundcloud.com/tellconsult/9-other-research-fields-1?in=tellconsult/sets/josef-colpaert
Colpaert [10]: https://soundcloud.com/tellconsult/10-no-didactic-revolution?in=tellconsult/sets/josef-colpaert

Davies [1]: https://soundcloud.com/tellconsult/1-learningenvironment-1?in=tellconsult/sets/graham-davies
Davies [6]: https://soundcloud.com/tellconsult/6-no-languages-after-14-1?in=tellconsult/sets/graham-davies
Davies [7]: https://soundcloud.com/tellconsult/7-english-l1-disadvantage-1?in=tellconsult/sets/graham-davies
Davies [11]: https://soundcloud.com/tellconsult/11-interactive-mobile-1?in=tellconsult/sets/graham-davies
Davies [12]: https://soundcloud.com/tellconsult/12-mall-1?in=tellconsult/sets/graham-davies
Davies [13]: https://soundcloud.com/tellconsult/13-clil-1?in=tellconsult/sets/graham-davies
Davies [15]: https://soundcloud.com/tellconsult/15-role-of-textbooks-1?in=tellconsult/sets/graham-davies
Davies [16]: https://soundcloud.com/tellconsult/16-telecollaboration-1?in=tellconsult/sets/graham-davies

Guichon [1]: https://soundcloud.com/tellconsult/1-lt-topics-impact-on?in=tellconsult/sets/nicolas-guichon
Guichon [5]: https://soundcloud.com/tellconsult/5-research-facebook-use?in=tellconsult/sets/nicolas-guichon

Guichon [6]: https://soundcloud.com/tellconsult/6-communication-strategies?in=tellconsult/sets/nicolas-guichon
Guichon [7]: https://soundcloud.com/tellconsult/7-impact-future-methodologies?in=tellconsult/sets/nicolas-guichon
Guichon [9]: https://soundcloud.com/tellconsult/9-mobile-learning?in=tellconsult/sets/nicolas-guichon
Guichon [10]: https://soundcloud.com/tellconsult/10-translation-tools?in=tellconsult/sets/nicolas-guichon

Lund [1]: https://soundcloud.com/tellconsult/1telecollaboration?in=tellconsult/sets/andreas-lund
Lund [3]: https://soundcloud.com/tellconsult/3-language-use?in=tellconsult/sets/andreas-lund
Lund [4]: https://soundcloud.com/tellconsult/4-informal-learning-1?in=tellconsult/sets/andreas-lund
Lund [6]: https://soundcloud.com/tellconsult/6-future-of-textbook-1?in=tellconsult/sets/andreas-lund
Lund [7]: https://soundcloud.com/tellconsult/7-teacher-roles-and-1?in=tellconsult/sets/andreas-lund
Lund [8]: https://soundcloud.com/tellconsult/8-methodology-1?in=tellconsult/sets/andreas-lund
Lund [9]: https://soundcloud.com/tellconsult/9-clil-1?in=tellconsult/sets/andreas-lund

Müller-Hartmann [1]: https://soundcloud.com/tellconsult/1-school-learningenvironment?in=tellconsult/sets/andreas-m-ller-hartmann
Müller-Hartmann [4]: https://soundcloud.com/tellconsult/4-clil-in-germany?in=tellconsult/sets/andreas-m-ller-hartmann
Müller-Hartmann [8]: https://soundcloud.com/tellconsult/8-changes-in-methodology?in=tellconsult/sets/andreas-m-ller-hartmann
Müller-Hartmann [10]: https://soundcloud.com/tellconsult/10-evolution-of-teaching?in=tellconsult/sets/andreas-m-ller-hartmann
Müller-Hartmann [12]: https://soundcloud.com/tellconsult/12-teachers-comfort-and-new-1?in=tellconsult/sets/andreas-m-ller-hartmann
Müller-Hartmann [14]: https://soundcloud.com/tellconsult/14-teleunsafeteachered?in=tellconsult/sets/andreas-m-ller-hartmann

# iTILT and SmartVET: 2 EU Projects to Promote Effective Interactive Whiteboard Use in Language and Vocational Education

Ton Koenraad[1], Shona Whyte[2], and Euline Cutrim Schmid[3]

**Abstract**. Although the interactive whiteboard (IWB) is becoming increasingly prevalent in classrooms throughout the more affluent parts of the world and research has shown how this tool can increase the effectiveness of teaching and even transform pedagogy (Kennewell & Beauchamp, 2007), research literature overviews (Higgins, Beauchamp, & Miller, 2007; Koenraad, 2008) also identify obstacles to the realisation of added value and to the uptake of this technology by teachers in some educational contexts and in language education in particular (Cutrim Schmid & Whyte, 2012; Thomas & Cutrim Schmid, 2010). One such obstacle is the lack of pedagogical quality and sustained support in teacher development. A desire to meet this need has motivated a number of European projects. This paper focuses on two such projects, iTILT and SmartVET, funded via the Lifelong Learning Programme, which address teacher education and professional development with the IWB. Both based their approach on findings from IWB specific and general professional development research and on needs analysis, using related research instruments.

**Keywords**: interactive whiteboard, IWB, classroom technologies, EU project, professional development, SmartVET, iTILT.

---

1. TELLConsult, Vleuten, The Netherlands; ton.koenraad@gmail.com
2. Université Nice Sophia Antipolis, Nice, France
3. University of Education Schwäbisch Gmünd, Schwäbisch Gmünd, Germany

**How to cite this article**: Koenraad, A. L. M., Whyte, S., & Cutrim Schmid, E. (2013). iTILT and SmartVET: 2 EU Projects to Promote Effective Interactive Whiteboard Use in Language and Vocational Education. In L. Bradley & S. Thouësny (Eds.), *20 Years of EUROCALL: Learning from the Past, Looking to the Future. Proceedings of the 2013 EUROCALL Conference, Évora, Portugal* (pp. 149-157). Dublin/Voillans: © Research-publishing.net.

Ton Koenraad, Shona Whyte, and Euline Cutrim Schmid

## 1. Introduction

Interactive whiteboards are subject to general principles of effective use of information and communication technology (ICT). If teachers have digital learning materials that are of practical use and if they have been trained in using the technology and are aware of its pedagogical possibilities an IWB can be beneficial for teaching and learning (Kennisnet, 2012). Both the iTILT and the SmartVET projects aim to address these issues by providing teachers with several instruments/tools that help them to exploit the potential of the IWB. Below, we briefly describe the individual projects and their results and summarise some research findings.

## 2. The iTILT project (2011-2013)

The overall aim of the European project, iTILT (Interactive Technologies in Language Teaching) is to promote effective interactive whiteboard use in communicative language teaching. Following the design of a training module and examples of good practice materials, language teachers from six European countries were trained in accordance with the principles of the communicative approach, and video-based illustrations of teachers using the IWB in classroom practice were collected.

The publicly accessible version of the project website www.itilt.eu was officially launched in January 2013, three months before the end of the project. It hosts the key deliverables of the project that can be consulted and/or downloaded for free. These include IWB video resources, a training manual, electronic teaching materials, video tutorials, a library, a community of teachers, research and publications, and Comenius courses.

### 2.1. IWB video resources

The video resources offer examples of classroom practice showing teachers using IWBs in classes of English, French, Spanish, Dutch, Welsh and Turkish as a second/foreign language in a variety of educational contexts (primary, secondary, university and vocational education). These IWB practice reports consist of (a) video clips of classroom interactions with IWBs, (b) comments from learners, teachers and trainers reflecting on good IWB-practice and (c) related resources such as lesson plans, IWB materials, etc. They are designed to function as learning objects which encourage reflection on IWB use in modern language education.

## 2.2. A training manual

The iTILT training manual[4] was developed for pre- and in-service training with the main goal of supporting teachers in exploiting the potential of the IWB and helping them to teach in accordance with communicative and task-based approaches to foreign language teaching. The manual contains technical as well as pedagogical information on IWB use, with many examples of activities based on the four skills and chapters on teaching grammar and vocabulary. The examples are based on a set of criteria for task design for IWB materials listed in the manual.

## 2.3. Electronic teaching materials

The electronic teaching materials[5] for language teachers are based on a communicative and task-based pedagogical framework. They provide classroom-ready teaching resources, but also include explanatory information for teachers describing each activity, its aims, how it was designed and how the IWB provides potential added value.

Available in 6 language versions and for different types of IWB software, they include explanations of the aim, activity, design and potential of each task. Furthermore, each resource provides descriptions of the target context and learning objectives.

## 2.4. Video tutorials

In order to help users make optimal use of the iTILT website, nine video tutorials[6] were developed, for example on how to conduct advanced searches or use the site for teacher training.

## 2.5. The library

A library[7] offers over 200 annotated links to additional resources in the field of IWB and Language Education including related research, relevant collections of IWB (training) materials and related communities.

---

4. http://www.itilt.eu/itilt-training-handbook
5. http://www.itilt.eu/teaching-materials
6. http://www.itilt.eu/tutorials
7. http://www.itilt.eu/Library

## 2.6. A community of teachers

The development of a community of teachers, experts and educators interested in exchanging ideas and best practice related to interactive technologies and language teaching has also been encouraged. In addition to the possibilities offered on site (www.itilt.eu/forum/) to exchange ideas, opinions and IWB files, other social media have been exploited for dissemination and community building purposes (iTILT-Facebook, iTILT-Twitter, iTILT-LinkedIn, iTILT-Scoop.it); see Whyte (2012) for further discussion of social media.

## 2.7. Research and publications

Several conference and research papers have been published, including the following topics:

- The challenges and opportunities associated with developing an open educational resource (OER) such as the iTILT website (Whyte, Cutrim Schmid, van Hazebrouck Thompson, & Oberhofer, 2013).

- Analysis of iTILT data partners' baseline data in relation to Beauchamp's (2004) transitional framework (Hillier, Beauchamp, & Whyte, 2013).

- Researching iTILT data partners' actual IWB use for particular language learning objectives and teaching methods and related both primary teachers' and learners' perceptions on effectiveness (Whyte, Beauchamp, & Hillier, 2012).

## 2.8. Comenius courses

During the project's lifetime the iTILT website and expertise gained have been exploited in 23 courses taught by the partners, reaching nearly 1,000 students. Partners will continue exploiting iTILT results in future courses, including EU Comenius courses[8].

## 3. The SmartVET project (2011-2013)

The EU project 'Supporting Continuous Professional Development of VET teachers in the use of Interactive Whiteboards' (SmartVET) is a Leonardo

---

8. http://www.itilt.eu/courses

transfer of innovation project funded under the Lifelong Learning Programme of the EU. The project's (2011-2013) main focus is on supporting the continuous professional development of vocational teachers in the use of interactive technology for teaching and learning. Based on findings in the literature and reported experiences it was decided to adopt a train-the-trainer approach in this project. To initiate and guide this process a number of IWB 'Champions' were identified. These early adopters across the VET sector have been trained through their participation in the project to organise professional development events for their peers. The ambition is to also develop a Community of Practice which will enable VET teachers across Europe to exchange their ideas and experience, to share new and innovative lessons and to have access to a wide variety of professional development materials. More information on the SmartVET project and its results is available on the website www.smartvetproject.eu. A brief description of the various project results is provided below.

### 3.1. Needs analysis report

To provide research-based input for the design of materials for and delivery of the professional development programme a needs analysis was carried out as a first project activity. Key questions were: to what extent and in what ways are IWBs being used in the Irish vocational education sector?, and what should be the content and delivery mode of a training programme to provide teachers/tutors in the Irish vocational education sector with the necessary competences?

Data from 200 respondents on the topics A. Personal Profile, B. Using the Interactive Whiteboard and C. General use of ICT, was collected with the help of an online questionnaire. A majority of the SmartVET respondents reported not to use the IWB although they were available in most schools. The main reasons for non-use appeared to be (a) lack of regular access to IWBs, (b) insufficient (subject specific) training and (c) no need: Internet + data projector are seen as adequate support for current teaching.

Analysis of all data (Figure 1) led to the conclusion that the rationale for the SmartVET project could be said to be borne out by the fact that the majority of the respondents indicate that they (a) do not use the IWB, (b) are interested in using it in their teaching and (c) would welcome training in the use of IWBs. The needs analysis also resulted in defining a number of recommendations for the design of a training programme and related materials, such as the development of a set of generic modules covering the basic IWB functionalities and those that support general cognitive activities such as ordering, categorising, comparing, etc., that are applicable in all subject areas (Koenraad, 2012, p. 35). For more information, the full report may be consulted on the project website www.smartvetproject.eu.

Figure 1. Needs analysis report

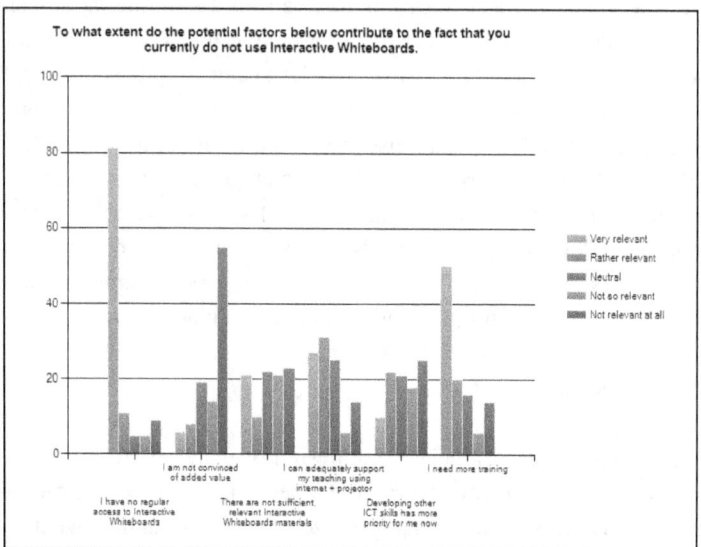

### 3.2. Training programme

The training programme (and related learning resources) are based on the needs analysis of VET teachers in county Wicklow VEC, as well as the knowledge and expertise of the project partnership, in particular on experience gathered with the EU Project Smarteach[9]. The training programme is not only about the technical features of the IWB and their use, but also on the experimentation of IWBs as a teaching tool for everyday activities, in order to promote the progression from technology to pedagogical and methodological innovation using an action research approach.

### 3.3. Learning manual

A learning manual has been developed to assist IWB Champions and teachers participating in the programme and to guide them step by step on how to implement IWB teaching resources in the classroom environment. The main focus of this

---

9. http://www.adam-europe.eu/adam/project/view.htm?prj=4213#.UeFI3UG9nh8

manual is to introduce teachers to Interactive Whiteboards, their technical aspects, main features as well as different approaches to training.

### 3.4. Professional development materials

The continuing professional development (CPD) materials respond to the objective of training the technological skills, especially those that have been identified and explored in the needs analysis survey. They include short tutorials that show how to use the IWB features on Smartboard and Promethean IWBs in practice.

### 3.5. Online community of practice

The SmartVET Community of Practice is part of the eTuition Community of Practice site, an online network for teaching and supporting teaching staff in VET in Ireland and UK. The virtual community[10] enables EU teachers to exchange their ideas and experience, to share new and innovative lessons and give them access to a wide variety of professional development materials.

### 3.6. Model on interactive whiteboards training implementation (Irish context)

The Model on Interactive Whiteboards training implementation (Irish Context) will present the whole process of IWB training development, an overview of identifying and implementing the best practice in terms of IWB training and their use in the classroom.

This document will present the development and adoption of IWB training in an Irish context and will act as a model for training and will be of interest to VET organisations that are planning to implement Interactive Whiteboards.

## 4. Conclusion

This paper focuses on the following results of both iTILT and SmartVET projects, i.e. the outcomes of and recommendations based on needs analysis, the design and content of the training models and materials, the available final and interim web-based resources, and reflections on the project-related processes and research results. It also discusses the process of developing quality OERs and how they can best be exploited in language teacher education (Whyte et al., 2013). For instance,

---

10. http://etuitionnetwork.ning.com/group/smart-vet

the iTILT project focuses on foreign language teaching in four educational sectors in six languages and seven European countries and has produced an open educational resource (OER) at http://itilt.eu including over 250 video examples of classroom activities with teacher and learner commentary, as well as a training manual and sample teaching/training materials, plus a resource library. SmartVET, on the other hand, addresses issues related to the IWB competence levels of (Irish) teachers in the vocational education and training (VET) sector. More specifically, the project is developing materials to support a train-the-trainers approach based on the results of local needs analysis research and good practice as identified in international IWB training contexts and initiatives.

## References

Beauchamp, G. (2004). Teacher use of the interactive whiteboard in primary schools: towards an effective transition framework. *Technology, Pedagogy and Education, 13*(3), 327-348. doi: 10.1080/14759390400200186

Cutrim Schmid, E., & Whyte, S. (2012). Interactive Whiteboards in School Settings: Teacher Responses to Socio-constructivist Hegemonies. *Language Learning & Technology, 16*(2), 65-86. Retrieved from http://llt.msu.edu/issues/june2012/cutrimschmidwhyte.pdf

Higgins, S., Beauchamp, G., & Miller, D. (2007). Reviewing the literature on interactive whiteboards. *Learning, Media and Technology, 32*(3), 213-35. doi: 10.1080/17439880701511040

Hillier, E., Beauchamp, G., & Whyte, S. (2013). A study of self-efficacy in the use of interactive whiteboards across educational settings: a European perspective from the iTILT project. *Educational Future, 5*(2), 3-23. Retrieved from http://www.educationstudies.org.uk/materials/emily_hillier_besa.pdf

Kennewell, S., & Beauchamp, G. (2007). The features of interactive whiteboards and their influence on learning. *Learning, Media and Technology, 32*(3), 227-241. doi: 10.1080/17439880701511073

Kennisnet. (2012). The four in balance model. In *Four in balance monitor 2012: IXT in Dutch primary, secondary and vocational education* (pp. 21-25). Retrieved from http://www.kennisnet.nl/fileadmin/contentelementen/kennisnet/1_deze_map_gebruiken_voor_bestanden/Over_ons/About/pdf/Four-In-Balance-Monitor-2012.pdf

Koenraad, A. L. M. (2008). *Interactive whiteboards in educational practice: the research literature reviewed*. Retrieved from http://www.researchgate.net/publication/237065574_Interactive_Whiteboards_in_educational_practice_the_research_literature_reviewed

Koenraad, A. L. M. (2012). *Needs analysis research report*. EU Project SmartVET. Retrieved from http://www.academia.edu/4641641/Needs_Analysis_Research_Report_for_SmartVET_project_promoting_effective_IWB_use_in_Vocational_Education_

Thomas, M., & Cutrim Schmid, E. (Eds.). (2010). *Interactive whiteboards for education: Theory, research and practice*. Hershey, PA: Information Science Reference.

Whyte, S. (2012). The iTILT project: interactive Technologies in Language Teaching. *Web2LLP Video showcase*. Retrieved from http://www.web2llp.eu/videos/video-showcase-itilt

Whyte, S., Beauchamp, G., & Hillier, E. (2012). Perceptions of the IWB for second language teaching and learning: the iTILT project. In L. Bradley & S. Thouësny (Eds.), *CALL: Using, Learning, Knowing, EUROCALL Conference, Gothenburg, Sweden, 22-25 August 2012, Proceedings* (pp. 320-326). Dublin: Research-publishing.net. Retrieved from http://research-publishing.net/publications/2012-eurocall-proceedings/

Whyte, S., Cutrim Schmid, E., van Hazebrouck Thompson, S., & Oberhofer, M. (2013). Open educational resources for CALL teacher education: the iTILT interactive whiteboard project. *Computer Assisted Language Learning*. doi: 10.1080/09588221.2013.818558

# Learning French Through Ethnolinguistic Activities and Individual Support

### Celia Lafond[1] and Nadia Spang Bovey[2]

**Abstract**. For the last six years, the university has been offering a Tutorial Programme for learning French, combining intensive courses and highly individualised learning activities. The programme is based on an ethnolinguistic approach and it is continuously monitored. It aims at rapid progress through contact with the local population, real-life experience in the urban environment and confrontation to cultural differences. The 6-week programme, highly regarded by the attendees who enjoy learning French *in situ*, also grants students 6 ECTS, if all requirements are met. It is facilitated by a supporting team of tutors and an online learning environment allowing for distance pedagogical interaction. The target audience includes actual or to-be university students and immigrants in professional integration (20-40y.).

**Keywords**: individual tutoring, individualised learning scenario, tutoring tools.

## 1. Theoretical background

The programme is designed according to the underlying assumptions of ethnolinguistics. Progress is stimulated by a double active observation process in which both learner and tutor are involved. Language is not considered as knowledge to be mastered, but as a communication means whose use is facilitated by the intercultural competence of the learner and the ability to observe and compare (Limentani, 2010). Context and cultural interaction are taken into account to narrow the gap between learned language and used language. With the guidance of a tutor, pictures and audio samples of real situations provide the language

---

1. Université de Lausanne, Cours de vacances, Lausanne, Switzerland; celia.lafond@unil.ch

2. Université de Lausanne, Faculté des Lettres, Lausanne, Switzerland; nadia.spangbovey@unil.ch

**How to cite this article**: Lafond, C., & Spang Bovey, N. (2013). Learning French Through Ethnolinguistic Activities and Individual Support. In L. Bradley & S. Thouësny (Eds.), *20 Years of EUROCALL: Learning from the Past, Looking to the Future. Proceedings of the 2013 EUROCALL Conference, Évora, Portugal* (pp. 158-163). Dublin/Voillans: © Research-publishing.net.

student with spatiotemporal mnemonic devices that are efficient in reproducing words, sentences and idiomatic expressions in French. While being reinforced by learning-to-learn discussions, deep learning processes are thus set into motion even in such a short period (Clerc & Rispail, 2008; Montredon, 2005; Zarate, 1991).

The approach is also inspired by the research and assumptions that led to the development of the European Language Portfolio, namely the work related to its language biography section (see webography below). The actual learning scenario of the programme relies on notions such as learner's autonomy, formal and informal learning situations, and action-oriented learning processes.

## 2. The learning scenario in practice

In practical terms, students follow an iterative sequence of activities. Each week, they collect ethnolinguistic material, observations and pictures, record and transcribe conversations, then transcribe and comment on them. The resulting Diary of Stay is made of three types of contributions, with instructions adapted according to the student level:

- A photograph to be taken in a real situation that shows the use of a written statement, the description of the situation and a personal interpretation.

- An audio recording of a real-life conversation, with its transcription (more advanced students will be expected to conduct a linguistic observation of the situation - oral marks, gesture, tone, hesitations, repetitions, etc.).

- A written work in personal tone, using a real or fictional identity.

To help autonomous learners select useful activities, a set of propositions is available in the online learning environment (Table 1). After a few guided experiments, students become able to design their own activities. The proposed activities are organised by level of difficulty. They really are propositions, as opposed to instructions. Their main aim is to facilitate the appropriation of the approach by the student, and learners are encouraged to design their own activities as soon as they feel confident. An additional benefit is that the student realises that he becomes able to use the approach by himself after the course has ended.

In parallel, a second set of activities lead the learner to identify and work on lexical or grammatical aspects in the Learning Journal.

Table 1. A proposed activity

| Bookshop (A2-C1) |
|---|
| **I. Ethnographic collection** |
| At the place<br>1) Take photos of the situation<br>2) Take a photo of a detail which contains some text. |
| At your place<br>3) Describe briefly the situation<br>4) Write a commentary<br>Your description and your commentary must contain at least 200 signs |
| **II. Ethnolinguistic recording** |
| At your place<br>1) Before starting your recording, if necessary, prepare your questions for the redaction<br>You will be offering a book to someone. Think to whom you would like to give this gift. You can choose a real or a fictional person. If so, imagine her life, her interests. For example, a woman in her 40's, who works in a bank, who likes to read in a park on a sunny day, etc.). |
| At the place<br>2) Start your recording by telling where you are, the date and the time.<br>Ask the seller which book in French he would suggest for this person. Ask if it's possible to get a gift voucher, if an exchange would be possible, etc.<br>The dialogue should at least include 4 questions. Do not hesitate to take initiatives during the interaction! |
| At your place<br>3) Listen to the recording and transcribe the dialogue. It does not matter if you do not understand everything, but try to write as much as you can, even phonetically. Your tutor will help you complete the transcription during the meeting.<br>4) From the transcription, observe how the people express themselves in French:<br><br>For example :<br>- Does the person hesitate?<br>- Does the person repeat himself? Why ?<br>- Does the person have a funny pronunciation? Some words in particular?<br>- etc. |
| During the meeting with the tutor<br>5) With your tutor, complete the transcription if necessary and speak about your observations on the transcription. |
| **III. Short essay** |
| At your place<br>Letter : from a lover to the person of his/her heart<br>You are in love and you write her/him a love letter.<br>Your letter should contain about 1000 signs. |
| **IV. Meeting with the tutor** |
| 1) Print your work and show it to your tutor. |
| 2) With the tutor, get to understand the meaning of the words. Compare both the bookshop and the romantic customers from your country with the ones in Lausanne. Would they behave the same way? |
| 3) After the meeting with your tutor, you will have to edit your work a second time and put it in your Electronic Notebook. Then you can start your Learning Journal. |

Based on the Diary of Stay, the lexical work integrates three aspects: the context in which the vocabulary was used, the subjective perception of the student, and the linguistic and cultural insights of the tutor (Montredon, 2005). As far as grammar is concerned, the learner is led to identify frequent mistakes and their explanations. Imprecisions and inter-languaging are allowed, as long as the explanations allow the student to deepen his or her understanding and avoid the error the next time a similar situation is encountered.

More advanced students work alongside on writing an academic essay (Mini-mémoire). After attending four talks in academic settings, the learner will choose one of them as a base to his/her written production. Guidance is provided at each stage of the writing process.

Each piece of work is corrected in detail and rewritten twice, both at a distance and during the weekly one-hour tutorial session, until being considered suitable for insertion into the student's Notebook. During the tutorial session (2 x 60 minutes), the teacher provides support and encouragement, linguistic and cultural explanations, and discusses remaining errors as well as context, idioms, typical oral forms, and any relevant topics.

The sequences of activities culminate in the production of an exportable student's Notebook, whose structure replicates the Diary of Stay, the Learning Journal and the Mini-mémoire, including pictures and audio recordings. When returning home, along with their credentials, the students will thus be able to showcase their progress and keep tangible tracks of their learning experience.

The student engaged in the programme is expected to devote about 85 hours of work over a 6-week period, which add up to the 42 hours of traditional classroom attendance in the morning. This sums up to a weekly average of 42 hours of intense study. Additional leisure activities in French are also provided. A tutor will devote between 21 and 25 hours to each student over the duration of the programme.

## 3. Supportive learning technology

Such a complex learning scenario proved being difficult to run without supportive technology. Though providing a varied set of tools, the existing infrastructure could not cope with both the requirements of the correction process and of the production of the Notebook. Therefore, in addition to the replication of courses templates including activities and instructions adapted to language levels A1, A2 and B1-C1, two add-ons were developed for the Tutorial Programme:

an extension to the Moodle standard editor allowing the tutors to specify nine types of language errors in the text itself and providing them with a history of the corrections.

Figure 1. Online tool for text annotation

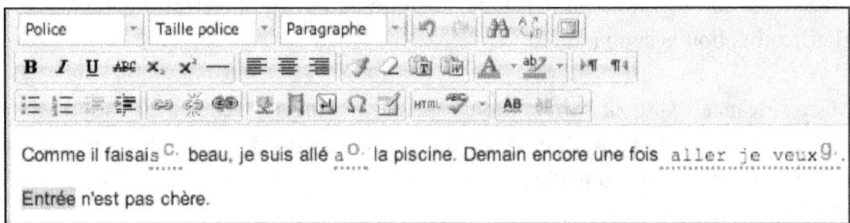

An external interface for the Notebook, with a database for texts and artefacts storage, that allows modifications by both students and the tutor while maintaining the given structure when generating the final PDF file (a document of about 20 pages including images and audio references).

Figure 2. Student's notebook interface

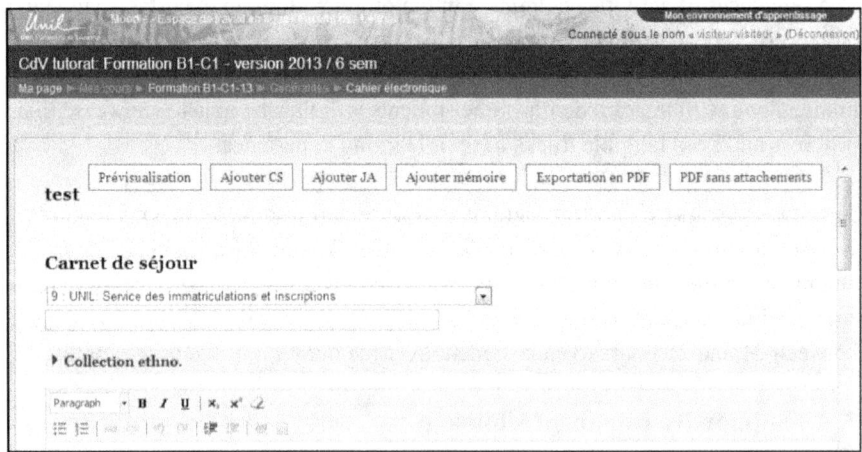

## 4. Conclusion

As described above, the tutorial programme requires that the students get deeply involved in the learning experience. It is aimed at those learners who intend to take full advantage of their stay in a French-speaking region and are ready to engage themselves in interpersonal activities that can be disconcerting. But when undertaken without resistance, the progress made in only six weeks is remarkable.

However, the overall positive appreciation of the programme should be nuanced by the following difficulties. First, both the ethnolinguistic approach and learner autonomy necessary to successfully complete the course can cause blocking resistance, since most students and sometimes tutors are not prepared for the actional learning approach. Then, the practicalities of the programme can be discouraging for those students who are not familiar with computers and learning technologies. Last, as the tutoring tools were developed in the context of a small-scale experimental project, they lack the usability which would be required for comfortable use. In the time being, these limitations would hinder a large scale deployment of the programme, should it be necessary.

## References

Clerc S., & Rispail, M. (2008). Former aux langues et aux cultures des autres, une gageure ? *Ela: Études de linguistique appliquée, 2008/3*(151), 277-292.
Limentani, R. (2010). La doublure d'une écriture des autres. In B. Olezewska, M. Barthélémy, & S. Laugier (Eds.), *Les données de l'enquête* (pp. 149-166). Paris: PUF.
Montredon, J. (2005). *De bouche à oreille, dictionnaire des étudiants étrangers de Besançon*. Besançon: Cêtre.
Zarate, G. (1991). The observation diary : an ethnographic approach to teacher education. In D. Buttjes & M. Byram (Eds), *Mediating languages and Cultures : Towards an Intercultural Theory of Foreign Langague Education* (pp. 248-260). Clevedon: Multilingual Matters.

## Webography

Anthropologie et observation participante : http://fr.wikipedia.org/wiki/Observation_participante
Autobiographie de rencontres interculturelles : http://www.coe.int/t/dg4/autobiography/default_FR.asp?
Biographie langagière : http://www.coe.int/t/dg4/education/elp/elp-reg/elp_biography_FR.asp
Expérimentation du Portfolio européen des langues (PEL) dans le secteur de l'enseignement supérieur: un projet transnational ELC/CEL : http://userpage.fu-berlin.de/elc/bulletin/6/fr/forster.html
Portfolio européen des langues pour l'éducation supérieure (PEL) : http://userpage.fu-berlin.de/elc/portfolio/fr-info.html

# Interactive Whiteboards in Japanese Education

Gordon Liversidge[1]

**Abstract**. The use of interactive whiteboards (IWBs) is widespread in the United Kingdom, Australia, and to some extent in the United States and Canada. However, this potentially learning enhancing technology has been adopted very little in Japan at any level of education, apart from some international schools. Furthermore, one of the world's two leading IWB manufacturers has recently closed their Japan office. This paper examines cultural issues and reports of fieldwork mainly from within Japan, but also from Australia, and Thailand. The overall conclusion is that the main factor is the very different philosophy of education.

**Keywords**: interactive whiteboards, compatibility, iPad, reflective practice.

## 1. Introduction

Shimizu (2006) revealed his concern about interactive whiteboards: "Our country aims to be one of the world's leading IT nations, but has made little progress in embracing it in education" (p. ii). Almost ten years later the number of IWBs in use in educational institutions is still less than one per school or university. This is well below the number of boards necessary to get the take-off or to the tipping point necessary to achieve the learning rewards for the cost and effort invested in installation and training. This poor usage has prompted one of the two world's main manufacturers, SmartBoard, to recently close their Tokyo office and withdraw from Japan.

The IWBs and other interactive technologies are not necessarily a panacea. However, if used well with the correct kind of support, IWBs can be a very important part of the curriculum framework, as they are in the UK education system and some international schools. In 2006, spending a year at London University's

---

1. Otsuma Women's University, Tokyo, Japan; gordon@otsuma.ac.jp

**How to cite this article**: Liversidge, G. (2013). Interactive Whiteboards in Japanese Education. In L. Bradley & S. Thouësny (Eds.), *20 Years of EUROCALL: Learning from the Past, Looking to the Future. Proceedings of the 2013 EUROCALL Conference, Évora, Portugal* (pp. 164-168). Dublin/Voillans: © Research-publishing.net.

Institute of Education many, not familiar with Japan, were surprised to discover that technologies developed in Japan were often not used in education (Liversidge, 2007).

Although the leading IWBs are not Japanese, the following study sought to re-examine the reasons for the lack of use of IWBs. Thailand was included because of certain cultural and historical similarities to Japan, especially that it was the only East Asian country, other than Japan, which did not come under Western colonial domination in the 19th century.

## 2. Method

Visits were made to observe classes in international schools in Tokyo in 2010 and 2013, Canberra and Melbourne in Australia in 2011, and schools and universities in Bangkok and Chiang Mai, Thailand in spring 2013. Information technology (IT) and information and communication technology (ICT) directors, principals and teachers were also interviewed. Full-time faculty at fifteen universities in Tokyo were interviewed, and visits were made to media and IT centres. Consultations were held with both SmartBoard and Promethean at their Tokyo offices, and representatives were invited to universities to demonstrate their products, both to faculties and administrations.

## 3. Results

Some of the international schools in Tokyo and Bangkok were outstanding examples of how a technology should be blended into and become an integrated part of the curriculum. Usually teachers used the IWBs at the beginning of classes, especially to introduce new topics. Students were encouraged to gather close to the IWBs and participate with questions, discussion and actually writing on or touching the IWBs. The teachers could access materials from the school server or the Internet. Two schools followed the prescribed Japanese curriculum but had gathered a large data base of materials from which activities and lesson plans were developed and stored on the institutions' servers. This enabled the schools to teach these subjects in English.

In universities, the number of IWBs is exceedingly low. Most lecturers or teachers, even non-Japanese, have never seen or used one. In the case of larger universities, the fragmentation of faculties means that people do not know what is happening elsewhere. Media centres knew of IWBs but said that attempts to encourage faculty staff to use them had failed.

The SmartBoard and Promethean offices were helpful in providing information as to where their boards were being used. In the case of one well-known university in Tokyo with sixty thousand students, the only IWB was to be found in the rugby club's office, presumably because it allowed the manager, coach and players to save diagrams of formations and tactics. The internationally highly-ranked universities in Bangkok and Chiang Mai also had almost no IWBs.

## 4. Discussion

### 4.1. Technical

In Japanese schools, the number of students ranges from around thirty in primary education classes, to up to as many as fifty in high school classes. Moving desks, so students can all be closer or nearer to the front of the class, does not happen very often. So, even with the ever increasing quality of IWBs and their projection systems, at times it is difficult for all the students to see the screen.

Compatibility issues are no longer the problem they used to be. Betcher and Lee (2009) in discussing software stated that "While there is limited compatibility between brands, the value of this online community should be a major factor in any evaluation of an IWB product" (p. 34). However, software has now been developed that enables teachers to move materials between SmartBoard and Promethean and other brands. There are also interactive monitors 'TV whiteboards' which are non-proprietary in that they will run using any software Mac, PC, or Linux, not just IWB software. As such they may lessen the need for IWBs. iPads and other tablets have attractiveness in that they are easy to use, and students can now interact with computers and the projector using Wi-Fi, again weakening arguments for the use of IWBs. Some schools in Thailand and Australia now provide students with iPads, and have decided against installing IWBs.

New short-throw projectors provide full-touch interactivity when projected onto a normal wall or standard whiteboard. This again renders some of the special functions of IWBs as unnecessary. With technologies changing so rapidly, it appears that it will be more difficult to persuade administrations to install a large number of IWBs.

### 4.2. Financial

It can be argued that the slowness of spread of IWBs in Japan is simply because there was, and still is, not enough profit for Japanese companies and other vested interests. Japanese companies do make IWBs but only have a very small market share. The two world leaders are Canadian and British companies. They have the systems that allow teachers to post, share, access, and adapt materials.

A second reason why IWBs have not spread is that they were really the first electronic instructional technology designed primarily for use by teachers. Other electronic technologies such as film, radio, television or personal computers, were first designed for the general consumer or offices, and then adapted for use in education. So there was no existing primary market for products for which educational institutions become a secondary market.

### 4.3. Philosophy

When discussing the potential of IWBs, Liversidge (2010) states that "For teachers and lecturers, most important are ease of use of the technical aspects, reliable and learnable software, support from the producers, and access to good materials with an online community" (p. 30). Generally speaking, teachers and lecturers, especially at the university level are very reluctant to share materials, discuss how courses are proceeding and what worked or did not work. Furthermore, 'reflective' practice, the closest translation of which is 'hanseiteki na' in Japanese implies a negative criticism. The constructive analysis of reflective practice and sharing and discussion is not encouraged within the teaching environment. Institutions also do not see any reason to provide or allow time for it. Thus, one of the core strengths of IWBs of sharing and collaborating does not occur often within or across Japanese educational institutions.

In junior and senior high schools where IWBs are used, the methodology used is 'lecture and explain', often not even asking or allowing opportunities for questions. The purpose of the methods used is directed at passing the entrance examinations. Despite the criticism, there are many capable Japanese teachers. However, they are restricted by having to keep on the entrance exams which have multiple-choice or select an item type questions. This does not allow or encourage participation or presentation on topics where in the classroom IWBs would be an invaluable tool.

## 5. Conclusion

Using the interactive whiteboard as a computer screen in a class or lecture allows the teacher and also the student to be at the front of the class, while taking full advantage of all the multimedia available. At the university level in Japan, it seems unlikely that IWBs will be adopted on a large scale. The most sensible and productive approach would be to install some IWBs in smaller rooms for content courses and seminars.

## References

Betcher, C., & Lee, M. (2009). *The Interactive Whiteboard Revolution: Teaching with IWBs.* Camberwell, Australia: ACER Press.

Liversidge, G. (2007). *Made in Japan, but not Used: Paradoxes and Change in Japanese Education.* Lecture March 2007. London University: The Institute of Education.

Liversidge, G. (2010). E-Teaching and How Interactive Whiteboards Can Enhance the Learning Process. *Kiyo Bunkei, 42,* 25-45. Otsuma Women's University. Retrieved from http://ci.nii.ac.jp/naid/110007535719

Shimizu, M. (2006). *Denshi kokuban de jugyo ga kawaru* [How Interactive Whiteboards can Change Classes]. Tokyo: Koryosha Shoten.

# Exploring Culture-related Content in the COCA with Task-based Activities in the EFL Classroom

## António Lopes[1]

**Abstract**. The Corpus of Contemporary American English (COCA) at the Brigham Young University website has been used in the English as a Foreign language (EFL) classroom to help learners better understand how language works at different levels of analysis and also to develop their writing skills. However, it also allows learners to explore culture-related content by giving them access to invaluable information about the social, ideological, political and historical contexts. Moreover, it provides the means to examine the ways in which such aspects intersect with language and condition its use. The understanding of this cultural and discursive dimension of language is pivotal in the training of undergraduate students in the areas of humanities and social sciences. To determine how far the COCA can contribute to increase this awareness, a series of task-based activities involving writing was drawn up and carried out in an EFL class of undergraduate students. They were first introduced to this corpus analysis tool and encouraged to explore it further. Later on, in order to complete a writing task, they were prompted to resort to a series of strategies to collect information about relevant events, personalities and social or cultural phenomena, to analyse and interpret data, and to draw conclusions about the modes in which culture and language can interact. This paper provides (a) the rationale and a brief literature review on this topic, (b) a description of the task-based activities, the implementation process, the students' strategies and the evaluation procedures, and (c) a critical reflection on this study that may open the path for further developments in this area.

**Keywords**: corpus analysis tools, culture-related content, discourse, EFL, higher education.

---

1. University of the Algarve, Campus da Penha, Faro, Portugal; alopes@ualg.pt

CETAPS – Centre for English, Translation and Anglo-Portuguese Studies, Avenida de Berna, Lisboa, Portugal

**How to cite this article**: Lopes, A. (2013). Exploring Culture-related Content in the COCA with Task-based Activities in the EFL Classroom. In L. Bradley & S. Thouësny (Eds.), *20 Years of EUROCALL: Learning from the Past, Looking to the Future. Proceedings of the 2013 EUROCALL Conference, Évora, Portugal* (pp. 169-174). Dublin/Voillans: © Research-publishing.net.

## 1. Introduction

There is a whole range of online corpus analysis tools (Compleat Lexical Tutor, Sketch Engine, Wmatrix, etc.) which provide interfaces to corpus linguistic methodologies. The COCA[2] has been used in the EFL classroom to help learners better understand how language works at different levels of analysis (Bennett, 2010; Boulton, 2011; Callies, 2013; Orenha-Ottaiano, 2012). It has also been used to enhance their text production and develop their writing skills (Kim, 2009; Nurmukhamedov & Olinger, 2013) by helping them to fine-tune grammatical points and by putting them in contact with different genres and styles. However, it also offers the opportunity to explore culture-related content by shedding light on a huge variety of social, ideological, cultural and historical issues, and on the ways in which these issues intersect with language. Culture-related approaches based on corpus analysis can increase our awareness of the discursive practices within institutions, groups and society at large.

The cultural and discursive dimension of language is pivotal in foreign language learning (Andersen, Lund, & Risager, 2006; Byram & Grundy, 2003; Corbett, 2010; Elsness, 2013; Kramsch, 1998; Lange & Paige, 2003). In order to determine how far the COCA can contribute to heighten not only their linguistic and metalinguistic awareness in the writing process, but also their comprehension of the linguistic treatment accorded to cultural referents, a series of task-based activities involving writing was drawn up and carried out in an EFL class of undergraduate students attending a media and communication studies programme.

## 2. Objectives and pedagogical goals

The objectives of this study were:

- to determine whether the use of the COCA can improve learners' writing skills;

- to test the learners' ability to use its functionalities;

- to ascertain whether the learners could interpret data displayed by the COCA concerning cultural referents and integrate them in the composition of a text.

On the other hand, the pedagogical goals were:

---

2. Corpus of Contemporary American English was created by Mark Davies.

- to encourage learners to use relevant cultural information in their writing;
- to make them acquainted with tools that help them understand how language works;
- to improve their writing skills in the genres they are expected to produce as professionals.

## 3. Implementation

Mostly composed by students within the 18-21 age bracket, a group of 18 learners had been required to take a placement test at the beginning of the school year. It showed that the majority was at B2 level of the CEFR[3], a classification further corroborated by a series of written assignments prior to this study. Besides the linguistic limitations typical of this level, those assignments revealed inability to incorporate cultural references, overgeneralisations, poor organisation of ideas, lack of focus and inability to quote or paraphrase adequately.

Firstly, students were introduced to this corpus analysis tool and encouraged to explore it. Emphasis was laid on the explanation of the modes of display and the search string. They were given examples and homework was assigned to make them more familiar with the system and the procedures (drills that compelled them to go through each mode of search). Afterwards, they were taught a series of strategies to help them to extract information about cultural referents including individuals, social movements, political events, social and cultural phenomena, etc. They were also taught the basics of how to analyse the linguistic context of the tokens, and to draw conclusions about the modes in which culture and language can interact. Attention was paid to the way in which perceptions and judgments of the political events find expression, for example, through lexical choices, subjective descriptive modifiers, or the ways in which one single cultural referent may be worded differently in sources and genres.

The taxonomy of strategies and modes recommended was as follows:

- **Strategy A**: Finding out how an influential individual, social group, country or organisation was judged/evaluated in a particular type of publication/ spoken language resorting to collocates. Modes advised: KWIC[4] and LIST.

---

3. The Common European Framework of Reference for Languages: Learning, Teaching, Assessment.

4. Key Word in Context.

- **Strategy B**: Comparing two public figures. Mode of display advised: COMPARE.

- **Strategy C**: Following and collecting as much information as possible about individuals, events or movements. Different modes of display advised.

- **Strategy D**: Frequency data analysis to determine how influential/significant was an individual or cultural phenomenon through the years or in what type of publication. Mode of display advised: CHART.

The above strategies had to be applied in the completion of the following tasks:

- writing a news story (providing objective information);

- writing an editorial (expressing an opinion);

- preparing an interview (eliciting information);

- setting up a quiz (producing closed-ended questions).

Students were asked to make reference to the source of information taken from the COCA through footnotes. The purpose was twofold: on the one hand, it served to quantify how much of the content of the text produced had its origin in the COCA; on the other, it was intended to make students understand the ways in which texts can be embedded inside other texts without committing plagiarism. The completion of the task was mandatory for the students' final evaluation.

Texts were then evaluated according to the IELTS[5] writing assessment criteria (GT version): task response, coherence and cohesion, lexical resource, grammatical range, and accuracy.

In the end, students filled in a questionnaire comprising 19 questions to explain how they were able to cope with the tool, and, on the other hand, to express their views on the whole teaching and learning process. The questionnaire addressed the following topics: usefulness of the tool in the writing process, usefulness of the tool in the learning of English grammar, usefulness of the tool in providing relevant information about cultural referents, and usefulness of the activity in their learning.

---

5. International English Language Testing System.

## 4. Results and discussion

In the texts produced by the students, no significant progression was detected at the level of grammatical range and accuracy in relation to their previous production. Students failed to use the COCA to avoid frequent errors, either because of a limited perception of their own linguistic difficulties, lack of commitment or habit, or inability to take the best advantage of the tool. These texts typically fall within the IELTS band 6: students resorted to a mix of simple and complex sentence forms, errors in grammar and punctuation not impeding communication. Concerning their lexical resources, students also scored 6, having revealed an adequate range of vocabulary for the task, despite some inaccuracy in less common vocabulary. Regarding coherence and cohesion, students progressed from band 5 to band 6, in that they sought to avoid repetitions and arrange their ideas more coherently. The same happened at the level of task response. Instead of an inappropriate format, unclear development of ideas or lack of detail, the texts showed that, despite some inadequately developed ideas, students were able to address all parts of the task, to focus more clearly on the main ideas, and to present a relevant position throughout the text.

Students' answers to the questionnaire indicate an overall positive response to the learning potential of the tool. Concerning the use of the COCA as an aid in the writing process, two thirds of the respondents ranked it as the third most useful aspect of the interface. When asked if they would continue to use the COCA as a writing tool of reference, 50% stated it was probable, whereas 19% said that it was almost certain. In relation to the learning of English grammar through the COCA, students ranked it as the least important aspect out of six. Paradoxically, in the same question they ranked the learning of the uses of a word/phrase in context as the second most important aspect. With regard to usefulness of the tool in providing relevant information about cultural referents, 43% stated that it was relevant and 31% that it was very relevant. Finally, in an overall appreciation, 93% agreed that the COCA met their needs as learners of EFL.

## 5. Conclusions

For the first time, students explored a tool that gave them a clear view of the grammatical workings of real-life language. To use it efficiently, they were compelled to revisit grammatical concepts and adopt a more analytical perspective. Yet, despite preparatory work, students still offered substantial resistance to metalinguistic reflection and to the use of grammatical categories. They also revealed some difficulty in coping with some technical aspects of the tool.

They were shown the way in which language is used at an ideational level to prompt judgments, corroborate or challenge ways of thinking regarding specific cultural referents, since the tool allowed them to easily identify evaluative elements. As far as the tasks were concerned, both the deliverables and the questionnaire showed that the COCA was useful insofar as it provided ideas that were integrated in the compositions, in compliance with the conventions governing quotation and paraphrasing.

## References

Andersen, H. L., Lund, K., & Risager, K. (2006). *Culture in language learning*. Aarhus University Press.

Bennett, G. R. (2010). *Using corpora in the language learning classroom: Corpus linguistics for teachers*. Ann Arbor: University of Michigan.

Boulton, A. (2011). Language awareness and medium-term benefits of corpus consultation. In A. Gimeno Sanz (Ed.), *New Trends in Computer-Assisted Language Learning : Working Together* (pp. 39-46). Madrid: Macmillan ELT.

Byram, M., & Grundy, P. (Eds.). (2003). *Context and Culture in Language Teaching and Learning*. Clevedon: Multilingual Matters.

Callies, M. (2013). Advancing the research agenda of interlanguage pragmatics: The role of learner corpora. In J. Romero-Trillo (Ed.), *Yearbook of Corpus Linguistics and Pragmatics 2013: New Domains and Methodologies* (pp. 9-36). New York: Springer.

Corbett, J. (2010). *Intercultural Language Activities*. Cambridge: Cambridge University Press.

Elsness, J. (2013). Gender, culture and language: Evidence from language corpora about the development of cultural differences between English-speaking countries. In G. Andersen & K. Bech (Eds.), *English Corpus Linguistics: Variation in Time, Space and Genre. Selected papers from ICAME 32* (pp. 113-137). Amsterdam and New York: Rodopi.

Kim, Y. J. (2009). *Effectiveness of on-line corpus research in L2 writing: Investigation of proficiency in English writing through independent error correction*. Master thesis. University of North Texas. Retrieved from http://digital.library.unt.edu/ark:/67531/metadc12140/m1/1/

Kramsch, C. (1998). *Language and Culture*. Oxford: Oxford University Press.

Lange, D. L., & Paige, R. M. (Eds.). (2003). *Culture As the Core: Perspectives on Culture in Second Language Education*. Information Age Publishing.

Nurmukhamedov, U., & Olinger, A. R. (2013). Computer-mediated collocation: Resources for exploring word choice in English academic writing. *Writing & Pedagogy, 5*(1), 121-150.

Orenha-Ottaiano, A. (2012). English collocations extracted from a corpus of university learners and its contribution to a language teaching pedagogy. *Acta Scientiarum Language and Culture, 34*(2), 241-251. Retrieved from http://www.periodicos.uem.br/ojs/index.php/ActaSciLangCult/article/view/17130/pdf

# Creating and Nurturing a Comunity of Practice for Language Teachers in Higher Education

## Teresa MacKinnon[1]

**Abstract**. This case study investigates the implementation of a virtual learning environment designed for language teachers for an institution-wide language programme in a UK higher education institution. This development has taken place over a 3 year period and included a pilot virtual learning environment for 300, followed by a full implementation to more than 3,000 users. It was informed at all stages by users, usage analysis and research into best practice for language teaching and learning. The users have complete ownership of the spaces and the tools they need to facilitate interaction and communication, allowing greater freedom to experiment with learning design. Social media are used to help tutors find their personal learning network. An empirical design methodology and the Community of Practice approach to implementation embeds continuing professional development (CPD) within a supportive and open community. This case study will provide a quantitative analysis of the activity in the portal over time. It will also draw on qualitative data using Steiner Kvale's (1996) "traveler metaphor" approach in order to reach conclusions about factors important to the use of technology in CPD. It points to the need for tutors to find relative advantage in the technologies they are given as their engagement is closely linked to that of their learners (Levy, 1997). It also highlights the opportunities presented to foster interest in and discussion of the theoretical aspects of subject specific learning design.

**Keywords**: community of practice, CPD, digital literacies, language teaching, HE, VLE, innovation.

---

1. University of Warwick Language Centre, Coventry, UK; t.mackinnon@warwick.ac.uk

**How to cite this article**: MacKinnon, T. (2013). Creating and Nurturing a Community of Practice for Language Teachers in Higher Education. In L. Bradley & S. Thouësny (Eds.), *20 Years of EUROCALL: Learning from the Past, Looking to the Future. Proceedings of the 2013 EUROCALL Conference, Évora, Portugal* (pp. 175-182). Dublin/Voillans: © Research-publishing.net.

## 1. Introduction

The Language Centre at the University of Warwick is a long established support service delivering language learning opportunities to Warwick's student and staff population as well as to members of the public. Annually it supports about 3,500 students with approximately 50 teaching and support staff. Faced with the rapidly growing pressures in a competitive market, the Centre puts a strategic priority upon maintaining a delivery that is effective and meets consumer expectations for support beyond the classroom. We also aim to deliver research based innovation in language teaching. In recent years it has become clear that we need to prioritise the accessibility of our resources over the internet. Developments in our teaching have also included greater reliance on web based resources and some interest in digital affordances for innovation, e.g. voice over the internet and use of video. These concerns presented some important challenges:

- there was no institutional provision for a virtual learning environment such as Moodle or Blackboard;

- the available tools were not sustainable given our limited technical and training resources and did not meet the requirements for international language use, fundamental to our work;

- nor did they foster the development of transferable digital skills to support career development of our staff.

The case study reported here attempted to address the challenges detailed above in order to provide a basis for the digital skills development of our staff. It was decided that we would invest in a hosted moodle and integrate sustainable technologies, some of which were already in use, in order to offer flexible online areas to support tutor development of blended delivery.

An initial pilot study with a limited number of tutors and courses proved popular and so, with support from an Institutional Teaching and Learning review and Fellowship[2] funding through our Institute for Advanced Teaching and Learning, a full deployment of Languages@Warwick[3] began in 2010.

---

2. http://www2.warwick.ac.uk/fac/cross_fac/iatl/funding/fundedprojects/fellowships/mackinnon2/

3. http://m2.warwicklanguage.org.uk/

## 2. Method

The approach used draws upon Wenger's (2000) Community of Practice model, which identifies three elements that define a Community of Practice:

- the domain – all members are committed to the same domain, in this case teaching languages to non specialist students;

- the community – members interact with each other and learn together;

- the practice – the members engage in sustained interaction which results in a shared repertoire.

Additionally, it was recognised that tutor confidence is an important factor in the effective use of technologies for teaching (Levy, 1997) and so the approach adopted prioritised ownership, autonomy and sharing. At the outset, all tutors were enrolled as students in a course area called "Using moodle for language teaching" (101), in order to explore the pedagogical aspects of course design and easily locate useful resources including a staff user guide[4], video tutorials[5] and a quick tool guide[6]. Staff also had access to shared sandbox areas for testing.

A mixed methods approach was used to evaluate the project and establish its effectiveness in fostering tutor confidence and engagement in blended delivery. Every year quantitative usage data[7] has been collected in order to inform developments and we knew that engagement in Languages@Warwick by both students and staff was growing (Table 1).

Table 1. Growth in user base

| Growth of Languages@Warwick | December 2011 | July 2013 |
|---|---|---|
| number of users | 2127 | 3491 |
| number of courses | 105 | 182 |

For this evaluation, quantitative data used included usage patterns of the 101 course over the three years and student satisfaction scores from 2013. Student

---

4. http://www.scribd.com/doc/125351686/Languagesv5
5. https://www.youtube.com/user/warwicklanguage
6. http://www.slideshare.net/teresamac/moodle2-toolguideforteachers-v11tm
7. http://www.slideshare.net/teresamac/languages-warwick

feedback responses were used as an indicator of how course design principles were being applied.

Qualitative data was elicited from a small purposive sample of tutors in order to collect their reflections on the Community of Practice approach we had adopted. The sample was selected on the basis that they had been using technology for language teaching in our context prior to the launch of Languages@Warwick. The data was collected via an anonymous Google form sent by email to each participant. The short questionnaire[8] asked for reflection upon their use of technology before and after the deployment of Languages@Warwick. The data was then analysed as a "Bildungsreise" (Kvale, 1996) in order to reveal further research questions for closer investigation.

## 3. Data analysis

The 101 course usage showed spikes of activity at certain times of each year (Figure 1). During the first year (Oct 2010-May 2011) the course ran as a time-released course and started with lots of interest, mainly views rather than active participation. However, during that year only a small cohort of staff were using a Languages@Warwick course for their students. During the ensuing years the course content was managed as a set of topics and the forum was used as a way of transmitting information to site users.

Figure 1. 101 course usage

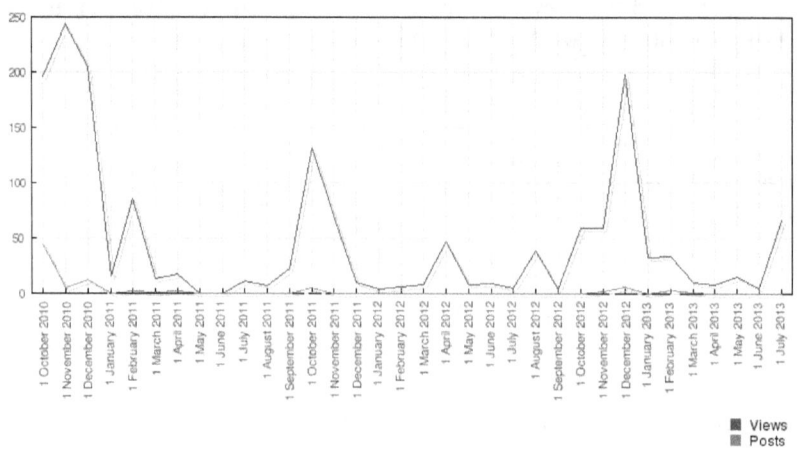

---

8. https://docs.google.com/forms/d/1fYFeWsxaqzSY5IT28eL7DhWhNAbwZ_U3vSgM9NUiZYw/viewform

Examined in more detail it is clear that the increased views are linked to the timings of our face-to-face sharing sessions where staff showed what they had been doing in their online courses. Other smaller spikes also follow forum messages. These patterns are to be expected. They show our staff behaving as many students do, reactively attending to the messages they are sent by the tutor and using the course resources to follow up on relevant items of interest which have been brought to their attention in a "classroom" setting. However, the lack of posting indicates that the Community of Practice is not residing within this course. Looking more broadly at staff interactions outside the course, it was interesting to see that most of the questions arising out of the 101 course came through e-mail and face-to-face questions as staff were less comfortable posting "publically" on the course forum. It was clear that there was also a lack of understanding of moodle messaging settings. Staff often replied to forum posts thinking they were personal emails. These trends were visible during the past 2 years and interventions were put in place to increase staff awareness of messaging settings and encourage the formation of personal learning networks (PLN) relative to activities of interest such as voice tools and more recently video usage. The aim was to disrupt the expectation that learning could only happen as a result of the course tutor's actions and encourage ownership of skills development. This realisation is significant if tutors are to transfer control to learners and increase autonomy (Tumposky, 1982, p. 5; Vandergrift, 2008, p. 90). The role of the 101 course is as a central point of contact and the emerging Communities of Practice (e.g. teachers using voice tools) are satellites around it.

Using the student satisfaction data it was clear that tutors were able to manage their courses by 2012-13 in a way which was judged broadly satisfactory by students. On average 84.9% of students on courses rated the use of Languages@Warwick as satisfactory or better. Courses with a wider variety of activities including use of the interactive features available such as voice boards and quizzes showed greater levels of student satisfaction as illustrated in Table 2.

Table 2. Student satisfaction levels

| Activities | Course A 91% scored 3 or above | Course B 27% scored 3 or above |
|---|---|---|
| assignments | 17 | 10 |
| fora | 2 | 1 |
| quizzes | 3 | 0 |
| resources | 118 | 20 |
| voice boards | 5 | 0 |
| voice podcasts | 4 | 0 |

The results are not unexpected but are worthy of bringing to the attention of the emerging Community of Practice.

The qualitative survey[9] contributed insights from a small cohort of tutors interested in technology enhanced learning. All respondents said that since they have been using the site their technical skills have improved. Their range of strategies for finding help was broad; all had accessed tutorial videos and asked colleagues for help, but there was evidence of using a wide range of support networks both internal and external and experimentation in sandbox areas. There was unanimous agreement that the following factors impacted positively on their technology usage: ease of use, positive feedback from students, re-usability of resources and a perception of professional development. For this group of tutors these factors contributed to the relative advantage they had found in using Languages@Warwick.

The qualitative responses indicate an awareness of an emerging Community of Practice from one participant:

> "I showed colleagues how to upload documents to Forum and to each week, how to create activities, e.g. assignment… I remember better in showing them how to do those tasks".

Another, reflecting on the face-to-face sessions:

> "Colleagues demonstrated how to make quizzes and how to upload videos. I remembered them because I could use them straight away in my design of online courses, and they are very practical and quite easy to implement. The sharing has been useful and did prompt me to try a new technology in my teaching".

This feedback shows tutors taking ownership of their skills development and nurturing their colleagues' skills, whilst at the same time fostering the conditions for discussions about learning design. They are the technology champions whose skills feed the development of the wider Community of Practice, they also share their learning beyond our local context with their language associations.

## 4. Conclusions

It is widely acknowledged in the literature of CALL that tutors struggle with the transfer and application of technology use to their teaching situation (Hegelheimer et al., 2004; Peters, 2006). The tutor champions in our context provide scaffolding

---

9. A summary of responses can be seen at https://docs.google.com/forms/d/1fYFeWsxaqzSY5IT28eL7DhWhNAbwZ_U3vSgM9NUiZYw/viewanalytics#start=publishanalytics

in support of Lave and Wenger's (1991) notion of the "cognitive apprenticeship" offering practical examples of how the tools can fit the teaching tasks. The 101 course (Figure 2) signposts the theory and professional resources.

Figure 2. 101 course screenshot

The approach allows for situated learning whereby collaboration between novice and expert users of technology for learning co-operate in relevant, task based contexts, facilitating the transfer process. Shared participation in problem solving and negotiation of meaning allow for discussion of learning design. However, this is not a rapid development solution. Growth takes place in an organic way and the Community has to be "tended" to in order to ensure that timely interventions are available to support the expansion of the Community. The 101 course is built on the assumption that our tutors identify with a shared domain of practice, that of "language tutors who use technology". The extent to which this is true will vary and could be investigated more closely but our champions will play a key role in convincing others that belonging to this domain is to their advantage. It would appear that we should continue to investigate our progress and provide focused interventions in order to nurture an enterprise which is bringing positive impact to our teaching and learning.

**Acknowledgements**. I would like to thank all participants in the Languages@ Warwick project for their contributions to my learning and my wider PLN for their support.

## References

Hegelheimer, V., Reppert, K., Broberg, M., Daisy, B., Grgurovic, M., Middlebrooks, K., & Liu, S. (2004). Preparing the new generation of CALL practitioners and researchers: What nine months in an MA program can (or cannot) do. *ReCALL, 16*(2), 432-447. doi: 10.1017/S0958344004001223

Kvale, S. (1996). *InterViews: An introduction to qualitative research interviewing*. Thousand Oaks, California: Sage Publications.

Lave, J., & Wenger, E. (1991). *Situated learning: Legitimate peripheral participation*. Cambridge: Cambridge University Press.

Levy, M. (1997). *Computer-assisted language learning*. Oxford: Oxford University Press.

Peters, M. (2006). Developing computer competencies for pre-service language teachers: Is one course enough? In P. Hubbard & M. Levy (Eds.), *Teacher education in CALL* (pp. 153-166). Philadelphia, PA: John Benjamins Publishing Company.

Tumposky, N. (1982). The learner on his own. In M. Geddes & G. Sturtridge (Eds), *Individualisation* (pp. 4-7). London: Modern English Publications.

Vandergrift, L. (2008). Learning strategies for listening comprehension. In S. Hurd & T. Lewis (Eds.), *Language Learning in Independent Settings*. Bristol: Multilingual Matters.

Wenger, E. (2000). Communities of Practice and social learning systems. *Organization, 7*(2), 225-246. doi: 10.1177/135050840072002

## Appendices

Further data produced as part of this investigation can be accessed here: http://www.scribd.com/doc/172819468/Appendices-for-Eurocall-2013-Paper

# Podcasts for Learning English Pronunciation in Igboland: Students' Experiences and Expectations

Evelyn E. Mbah[1], Boniface M. Mbah[2], Modesta I. Iloene[3], and George O. Iloene[4]

**Abstract.** This paper studies students' experiences and expectations on the use of podcasts in learning English pronunciation in Igboland. The Igboland is made up of five states in Southeastern Nigeria where Igbo is spoken as a mother tongue. The states are Abia, Anambra, Ebonyi, Enugu, and Imo. The study is a survey research where two universities were studied. A proportional sampling technique was used with the aid of a structured questionnaire that was used to elicit information. The data gathered were analysed using mean, standard deviation, t-test, and ANOVA with the aid of Statistical tool for the Social sciences. The study concluded that the students agreed to the fact that podcasts improved their English pronunciation. The hypotheses tested generally showed that there was no significant difference in the internet background, level of students or gender in the use of podcasts. Thus, technology was indispensable in learning a second language.

**Keywords**: podcasts, English pronunciation, Igboland, technology.

## 1. Introduction

English is learned as a second language in Igboland (and all over Nigeria). Learning English in Nigeria is confronted with some challenges. One of them, according to Oluikpe (1978), is that English is not taught to solve the language problems

---

1. Department of Linguistics, Igbo and Other Nigerian languages, University of Nigeria, Nsukka; ezymbah@yahoo.co.uk
2. Department of Linguistics, Igbo and Other Nigerian languages, University of Nigeria, Nsukka
3. Department of Linguistics, Igbo and Other Nigerian languages, University of Nigeria, Nsukka
4. Department of Linguistics, Ebonyi State University, Abakaliki

How to cite this article: Mbah, E. E., Mbah, B. M., Iloene, M. I., & Iloene, G. O. (2013). Podcasts for Learning English Pronunciation in Igboland: Students' Experiences and Expectations. In L. Bradley & S. Thouësny (Eds.), *20 Years of EUROCALL: Learning from the Past, Looking to the Future. Proceedings of the 2013 EUROCALL Conference, Évora, Portugal* (pp. 183-187). Dublin/Voillans: © Research-publishing.net.

relating to the linguistic peculiarities of Nigerian learners. Some of these include the fact that rather than writing textbooks for commercial purposes as it is the practise in the country, they should be written for different language groups to solve their particular linguistic issues. Language teaching in Nigeria like in other parts of the world involves teaching pronunciation, vocabulary, grammar and the culture of the target language. The place of pronunciation in L2 teaching is often relegated to the background when compared to the place of grammar, vocabulary and culture (Lord, 2008). Part of the reason for the relegation is that many teachers assume that with more input on the L2, students will learn pronunciation, or it will be acquired sometime later.

Native-like pronunciation is needed especially now that the world is becoming globalised and considering the position of the English language internationally. To be meaningful from an international perspective, effective communication is required. Thus, an L2 learner should strive to acquire native-like pronunciation to achieve intelligibility because it is a key factor for effective communication. Technology is essential in minimizing L1 segmental transfer to L2. Podcasting is one of the techniques used to enhance L2 pronunciation (Knight, 2010). The net-generation students are often very busy and involve themselves in multitasking (Tapscott, 2009) and many of them have devices for playing audio files (Rainie & Madden, 2005; Schmidt, 2008; Tapscott, 2009). These reasons combined make podcasts relevant to be one of the tools used in delivering L2 materials to the students.

## 2. Purpose of the study

The general objective of this research is to identify podcasts for learning English pronunciation by students in Igboland. Its specific objectives are to find out whether or not the students' background in internet or computer assisted language learning (CALL) affect the use of English as a second language (ESL) podcasts. For this, how the types of gadgets that students use for podcasts affect their interest in listening to podcasts is worth exploring together with background information on the students' first knowledge of podcasts. Further objectives are to explore the reasons students listen to podcasts as well as their expectations, and if listening to podcasts influence the students' performance in English phonetics related courses and their spoken English and English phonetics. Additional objectives include to test some hypotheses that seek to know the level of difference in the mean ratings of the four levels of undergraduate studies on the influences of students' background information on the knowledge of podcasts, on podcasts and performance in English phonetics, and on students' experiences in the use of podcasts. In addition, the objectives are to examine the level of difference in the mean ratings of gender on influences of students' background on internet or CALL, the types of gadget in the active use of podcasts, reasons for listening to podcasts, and students' expectations in using podcasts to learn English pronunciation.

## 3. Findings and discussion

The study suggests that the students' background on internet or computer assisted language learning affects their use of ESL podcasts and that there are significant differences in the mean ratings of male and female students on accessing courses and class assignments, listening to online podcasts, and posting comments to online groups and social networks. There are no significant differences in the mean ratings of the responses of male and female students in making PowerPoint slides, downloading online podcasts, creating/working on a webpage, journal and weblog, checking emails with different browsers, and sharing ideas using e-learning forum platforms.

The respondents agreed that an ipod/Mp3 player, desktop computer, laptop/ notebook computer, cell phone, Blackberry, Mp4 and the like, digital camera, and webcam are the types of gadgets that affect active use of podcasts. Concerning the students' background information on the knowledge of podcasts, there are no significant differences in the mean ratings of the responses of students at all levels of undergraduate education. The knowledge of podcasts was through a friend who had an interest in acquiring the native speaker's pronunciation. Learning of podcasts is considered necessary. There are no significant differences in the mean ratings of the responses of students at all levels of undergraduate studies on the point that the knowledge of podcasts was through the teacher.

The respondents agreed that vocabulary, pronunciation, composition, grammar, logical reasoning, socialisation, lectures, and entertainment are the students' reasons for listening to podcasts. There are no significant differences in the mean ratings of the responses on students' reasons for listening to podcasts at all levels of education on the above eight items. The respondents agreed that podcasts have positively affected scores in English phonetics courses, improved oral English performance more than vocabulary, grammar, and level of logical reasoning. There are no significant differences in the mean ratings of the responses of students. At all levels of education on podcasts they have positively affected scores in English phonetics courses. Podcasts have improved English pronunciation more than vocabulary, grammar, and level of logical reasoning, while the fact that podcasts have improved oral English performance shows a significant difference.

The respondents agreed that it is convenient to listen to podcasts at any place and any time. They possess the ability to download and save podcasts to computer/portable devices conveniently/easily, listening to podcasts on a computer, ipod or Mp3 player. Listening to any kind of podcasts is interesting and there are no significant differences in the mean ratings of the responses on students' experiences in using podcasts for learning English pronunciation at all levels of education. The respondents agreed that the presenter's voice should be clear, podcasts should be interactive, free/cheap internet access should be provided by the university administration, and teachers of English phonetics and other related courses should be abreast of new technologies in learning pronunciation. These are the students' expectations in using podcasts to learn English pronunciation. There are no significant differences in the mean ratings of the responses of students' expectations in using podcasts to learn English pronunciation at all levels of education.

The overall results of the study showed that there was a significant improvement on the students' performance in English phonetics. As such, we employ teachers of another language to encourage the use of authentic audio technology in native speakers' accent in delivering their learning materials. This kind of audio will equip the students more than solely relying on the teacher's production which may be affected by mother tongue interference.

## 4. Conclusion

This study sought to investigate students' experiences and expectations on the use of podcasts to learn English pronunciation in the Igbo speech community. Most students testified to the fact that although their first knowledge of podcasts was independent of their teacher, they see podcasts as an effective tool that has reasonably improved their oral as well as written performance in English phonetics related courses through the use of portable gadgets. Podcasts are therefore a pedagogic instrument that learners of English language in Igbo speech community embrace in learning English as a second language in all levels of undergraduate education irrespective of gender.

## References

Knight, R-A. (2010). Sounds for study: Speech and language therapy students' use and perception of exercise podcasts for phonetics. *International Journal of Teaching and Learning in Higher Education, 22*(3), 269-276.

Lord, G. (2008). Podcasting communities and second language pronunciation. *Foreign Language Annals, 41*(2), 364-379. doi: 10.1111/j.1944-9720.2008.tb03297.x

Oluikpe, B. O. (1978). *English in Igboland*. Onitsha: Africana Publishers Ltd.

Rainie, L., & Madden, M. (2005). Podcasting catches on. *Pew Internet & American Life Project*. Retrieved from http://www.pewinternet.org/~/media//Files/Reports/2005/PIP_podcasting2005.pdf.pdf

Schmidt, J. (2008). Podcasting as a learning tool: German language and culture every day. *Die Unterrichtspraxis/Teaching German, 41*(2), 186-194. doi: 10.1111/j.1756-1221.2008.00023.x

Tapscott, D. (2009). *Grown up digital: How the net generation is changing your world*. New York, NY: McGraw-Hill.

# Understanding Presence, Affordance and the Time/Space Dimensions for Language Learning in Virtual Worlds

## Susanna Nocchi[1] and Françoise Blin[2]

**Abstract**. Notwithstanding their potential for novel approaches to language teaching and learning, Virtual Worlds (VWs) present numerous technological and pedagogical challenges that require new paradigms if the language learning experience and outcomes are to be successful. In this presentation, we argue that the notions of presence and affordance, together with the time/space dimensions of interactions in virtual worlds (e.g. Bakhtin's (1981) chronotope, Foucault's (1984) heteropia, and Lemke's (2000) heterochrony), provide new insights into language learners' trajectories as they attempt to carry out tasks that are designed to make use of virtual worlds' characteristics and potentialities. We explore and analyse a critical incident that occurred during the realisation of a language learning task by university learners of Italian in Second Life©. Recordings of the session, teacher observations, learner reflections and interviews have provided large amounts of data highlighting a number of critical incidents that emerged during their execution. Analysing these critical incidents through the lenses of presence, affordance, and time/space inseparability allows us to highlight the non-linearity of temporal and spatial aspects of interactions in virtual worlds, and to reveal the emergence of affordances and learning chronotopes linked to such interactions. In turn, the analysis of these emerging learning chronotopes helps us refine the design and implementation of language learning tasks in virtual worlds.

**Keywords**: language learning, virtual worlds, affordances, learning chronotopes.

---

1. Dublin Institute of Technology, Dublin, Ireland; susanna.nocchi@dit.ie

2. Dublin City University, Dublin, Ireland

**How to cite this article**: Nocchi, S., & Blin, F. (2013). Understanding Presence, Affordance and the Time/Space Dimensions for Language Learning in Virtual Worlds. In L. Bradley & S. Thouësny (Eds.), *20 Years of EUROCALL: Learning from the Past, Looking to the Future. Proceedings of the 2013 EUROCALL Conference, Évora, Portugal* (pp. 188-193). Dublin/Voillans: © Research-publishing.net.

## 1. Introduction

In the last decade VWs have been used and studied by the educational community, with a particular focus on their potential for immersive learning, simulation and cross-cultural exchanges. Language learning has become a popular activity in VWs (see experiences, such as Avalon, Euroversity, Virtlantis), and the enthusiasm of the foreign language (FL) teaching community has led many to tap into the potentialities offered by VWs such as Second Life©.

Research in the pedagogy of FL teaching and learning in VWs is however still quite young and an analysis of some of the first language courses in these environments showed that early adopters tended to reproduce known and safe pedagogical choices; this brought the researchers' attention on how to best exploit the unique characteristics of this new technology (Blin, Nocchi, & Fowley, 2013; Girvan & Savage, 2010; Zheng, 2012; Zheng & Newgarden, 2011).

In this short paper, we show how the concepts of presence and affordance, as well as the spatial and temporal dimensions of VWs can be useful tools for making sense of these spaces as learning environments.

### 1.1. Presence and affordances

The cyber psychologist Riva defines presence in a mediated environment as "the intuitive perception of successfully transforming intentions into action" (Riva, Waterworth, Waterworth, & Mantovani, 2011, p. 2) and social presence as "the capacity to act on one's intentions and to understand the intentions of the others" (Riva, 2004, p. 51). According to Riva (2004), a high degree of presence can give an indication of how successful one has been in using the medium; through full usability of the medium one can act how one wants and become more fully aware of the medium's possibilities for action, i.e. its affordances (Kaptelinin & Nardi, 2012). Our understanding of affordances draws on an activity theoretical perspective, which highlights the strong link between affordance, context, activity, the user's previous history and experience and the mediational aspect of the technological tool/artefact and its cultural and historical significance for the user and the educational activity (Morgan, 2007).

### 1.2. Spatial and temporal dimensions – heterotopia and the chronotope

VWs do not only provide a new learning environment with exciting affordances; a VW is a separate space, but it is also part of the user's physical world. Foucault's

(1967) concept of heterotopia as a space that is in relation to other sites but, at the same time, contains in a single place different spaces and locations that can be incompatible with each other, seems apt to describe the cyber experience. Heterotopias "always presuppose a system of opening and closing that both isolates them and makes them penetrable at one at the same time" (Foucault, 1967, p. 7). VWs, as well, are located in the world and outside it and assemble a variety of real and imagined spaces and realities.

Time is also an interesting dimension of the cyber reality. When we are immersed in a VW's historical period, season and time, we are also still living and acting in our own real time, whose reality intersects with the VW reality. Bakhtin's (1981) concept of chronotope, a "connectedness of temporal and spatial relationships […] in literature" (Bakhtin, 1981, p. 84), can be usefully utilised to observe how time is conceptualised in a learning space and in computer-assisted collaboration (Ligorio & Ritella, 2010).

## 2. Method

SLitaliano was an Italian language course that took place in Second Life© in 2011/2012. The course was designed for International Business and Languages students at the Dublin Institute of Technology, who wanted to work on their Italian language and intercultural competence, in view of spending their Erasmus year in an Italian university. SLitaliano consisted of 9 in-world sessions. Each session was preceded by pre-session tasks on the course wiki.

### 2.1. Si Mangia! (Let's eat!)

Session 4 of SLitaliano was called "Si mangia!" (Let's eat) and focused on Italian food, food habits and food culture. The session took place on Imparafacile Island, and most of it was spent in an Italian restaurant/pizzeria. The participating students, Bea, Ita and Dub, had met a group of Italian native speakers outside the restaurant and had already tackled a language task with their help.

At this point in the session, students and Italians are facing a table covered with food and kitchen tools and have been asked to devise a recipe using the objects and ingredients they see on the table. These scripted objects show lexical and morphological information about them if the users hover their mouse over them. As part of their wiki pre-session tasks, students had been asked to make sure their hover tips were active.

## 2.2. Data collection and analysis

The session was recorded and multimodal interactions were transcribed for subsequent analysis. Focus shifts were identified, which defined episodes that were then analysed. Such focus shifts were primarily triggered by technical issues or breakdowns, and lexical or intercultural queries. Some were expected, others emerged as students set out to complete the tasks assigned to them.

The episode discussed in this article was the result of an unexpected technical issue that affected the flow of the activity and caused a shift in the focus of the action.

## 3. Results

Before starting to devise a recipe, the students needed to properly identify the objects they were to use, by zooming in on them and/or hovering their mouse over them to get lexical and grammatical information if needed. Two students, Bea and Dub, had not activated their hover tips as instructed. As a result, they could not take advantage of the affordances provided by the hover tips and by the zooming option.

As they were unable to access information on the objects on the table, the group momentarily left the simulation to create an alternative solution that would enable students to complete the task. Ita was given the role of the 'seer' for the group and helped her colleagues find the names of the objects they could not recognise. Also, the Italians left their spectator role and actively helped the students in Local Chat, providing technical and lexical tips.

The group had to resort to alternative actions which caused the emergence of various affordance based actions. The actions connected to this episode were: languaging in local and voice chat, native speaker support in local and voice chat, technical support in voice chat, language reflection, and target language input in local chat.

Also, the 'hover tips' incident brought about extensive language production from the students, with a total of 51 exchanges in Voice Chat and 3 in Local Chat (Bea: 7 instances; Dub: 18 instances; Ita: 29 instances).

As illustrated in Figure 1 below, the technical issue caused a shift in the focus of attention of the group while giving rise to the emergence of a new chronotope and of different affordances.

Figure 1. Hover tips episode triggering a focus shift
as well as a temporal and spatial one

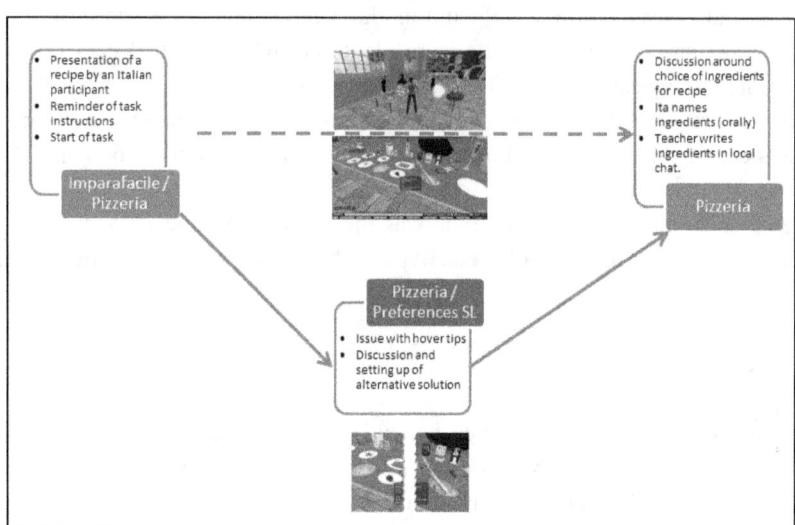

## 4. Discussion and conclusions

The hover tips incident illustrates the breakdowns and repairs that are likely to occur in a virtual world. Such episodes enable us to better understand the relationship between affordance, presence, and the spatio-temporal aspects that are characteristic of "in-world" interactions. The learning environment briefly described above provided educational, technological, and linguistic affordances to students. While some of these affordances were enacted, others were not. As Bea and Dub were not in a position to realise the technological affordances offered by Second Life©, they could not enact the linguistic affordances offered by the scripted ingredients. Yet, unexpected affordances soon emerged, following the teachers' and students' temporary withdrawal from the simulation, also known as *virtual corpsing* (Marsh, 2003). However, virtual corpsing may potentially contribute to a loss of presence and to the emergence of chronotopes that not only interrupt the flow of the simulation but may also weaken the group cohesion and collaborative learning processes and outcomes.

**Acknowledgements.** We would like to thank Imparafacile Runo and all the people gravitating around Imparafacile Island for their priceless help in terms of work, time and enthusiasm. Also, we would like to acknowledge DIT for funding Ms Nocchi's attendance to the EuroCALL 2013 conference.

# References

Bakhtin, M. M. (1981). Forms of time and of the chronotope in the novel: Notes toward a historical poetics. In M. Holquist (Ed.), *The Dialogic Imagination: Four Essays* (pp. 84-258). Austin: University of Texas Press.

Blin, F., Nocchi, S., & Fowley, C. (2013). Mondes virtuels et apprentissage des langues : Vers un cadre théorique emergent. *Recherches et applications, 54*, 94-107.

Foucault, M. (1967). *Of other spaces: Utopias and heterotopias*. Retrieved from http://web.mit.edu/allanmc/www/foucault1.pdf

Foucault, M. (1984). Dits et écrits, des espaces autres (conférence au Cercle d'études architecturales, 14 mars 1967). *Architecture, Mouvement, Continuité, 5*, 46-49.

Girvan, C., & Savage, T. ( 2010). Identifying an appropriate pedagogy for virtual worlds: A Communal Constructivism case study. *Computers & Education, 55*(1), 342-349. doi: 10.1016/j.compedu.2010.01.020

Kaptelinin, V., & Nardi, B. (2012). Affordances in HCI: Toward a mediated action perspective. *Proceedings of CHI 2012, New York* (pp. 967-976). doi: 10.1145/2207676.2208541

Lemke, J. L. (2000). Across the scales of time: Artifacts, activities, and meanings in ecosocial systems. *Mind, Culture, and Activity, 7*(4), 273–290. doi: 10.1207/S15327884MCA0704_03

Ligorio, M. B., & Ritella, G. (2010). The collaborative construction of chronotopes during computer-supported collaborative professional tasks. *International Journal of Computer-Supported Collaborative Learning, 5*(4), 433-452. doi: 10.1007/s11412-010-9094-4

Marsh, T. (2003). Staying there: an activity-based approach to narrative design and evaluation as an antidote to virtual corpsing. In G. Riva, F. Davide, & W. A. IJsselsteijn (Eds.), *Being There: Concepts, effects and measurement of user presence in synthetic environments* (pp. 85-96). Amsterdam: Ios Press.

Morgan, M. (2007). Evaluating ICT in education using the concept of mediation. In S. Wheeler & N. Whitton (Eds.), *ALT-C 2007: Beyond control Learning technology for the social network generation, Research Proceedings, Nottingham* (pp. 13-24). Retrieved from http://www.alt.ac.uk/altc2007/altc2007_documents/altc2007_research_proceedings.pdf

Riva, G. (2004). *Psicologia dei nuovi media*. Bologna: Il Mulino.

Riva, G., Waterworth, J. A., Waterworth, E. L., & Mantovani, F. (2011). From intention to action: the role of presence. *New Ideas in Psychology, 29*(1), 24-37. doi: 10.1016/j.newideapsych.2009.11.002

Zheng, D. (2012). Caring in the dynamics of design and languaging: exploring second language learning in 3D virtual spaces. *Language Sciences, 34*(5), 543-558. doi: 10.1016/j.langsci.2012.03.010

Zheng, D., & Newgarden, K. (2011). Rethinking language learning: Virtual World as a catalyst for change. *International Journal of Learning and Media, 3*(2), 13-36. doi: 10.1162/ijlm_a_00067

# The Impact of Employing Mobile Technologies and PCs for Learning Coursera Online Lectures and TOEIC Practice Kit

## Hiroyuki Obari[1]

**Abstract**. Mobile (m)-learning is motivating to learners to improve foreign language skills, as it offers them a rich, informal, contextual, and ubiquitous learning environment. In this paper I report on the results of two empirical studies that focused on two projects, both of which incorporated e-learning and m-learning, to determine if a blended-learning environment could improve the Test of English for International Communication (TOEIC) (Educational Testing Service, 2011) and presentation skills of native Japanese undergraduate students. The goal of the first study was to examine the effectiveness of blended and mobile learning activities on the students' English language proficiency and oral communication skills. The second study focused on the use of an on-line TOEIC training kit. The results revealed that the students' communication skills improved as a result of the on-line activities. Questionnaires administered at the end of each study indicated the students were satisfied with the online Coursera lectures and motivated by the blended-learning environment incorporating m-learning.

**Keywords**: Coursera, TOEIC, e-learning, m-learning, mobile technologies, iPhone, iPad, online learning.

## 1. Introduction

"Five years from now on the web for free you'll be able to find the best lectures in the world." The above quote, uttered by Bill Gates at the first Techonomy conference in August 2010, was his prediction of the future state of "open"

---

1. Aoyama Gakuin University, Tokyo, Japan; obari119@gmail.com

**How to cite this article**: Obari, H. (2013). The Impact of Employing Mobile Technologies and PCs for Learning Coursera Online Lectures and TOEIC Practice Kit. In L. Bradley & S. Thouësny (Eds.), *20 Years of EUROCALL: Learning from the Past, Looking to the Future. Proceedings of the 2013 EUROCALL Conference, Évora, Portugal* (pp. 194-199). Dublin/Voillans: © Research-publishing.net.

lectures, social media, and smartphones, which helped to usher the world into "the next era" of the web. Gates' bold prediction is what we are now experiencing around the world.

Coursera is an educational technology company that offers free online courses in a wide variety of areas, including the humanities, medicine, biology, business, computer science, and others. E-mobile learning technologies such as the iPhone, iPad, podcasting, and video-casting to name but a few, are rapidly gaining popularity as an effective way to improve foreign language skills around the world. Coursera is one of the most useful e-learning resources available and it is very conducive to mobile learning, whereby learning takes place at any time and at any place due to the swift development of mobile technologies. According to Vinu, Sherimon, and Krishnan (2011), mobile technologies have succeeded in transforming learning methodologies. One such methodology that has received great attention in recent years is blended learning (BL). BL combines traditional face-to-face classroom methods with computer-mediated activities, resulting in a more integrated approach for both instructors and learners.

The goal of the present paper is to examine the effectiveness of BL activities using mobile devices for the purpose of improving the English language proficiency of native Japanese undergraduates, including their writing, oral communication and presentation skills. This paper reports on two empirical studies that focused on two projects, both incorporating e-learning and m-learning, to determine if a blended-learning environment can improve the TOEIC and presentation skills of native Japanese undergraduate students at a private university in Tokyo, Japan.

## 2. Method

The research questions targeted in this paper were as follows:

- Can online Coursera courses help to improve the TOEIC scores of native Japanese students?

- Can online Coursera courses help to improve students' oral communication and writing skills?

- Are BL activities using mobile devices useful in improving students' overall English skills?

## 2.1. The first study

The first study was conducted over a period of four months during a single academic semester (October 2012 to January 2013). A total of 50 undergraduates, all native speakers of Japanese studying at a private university in Tokyo, were the participants of the study. The students were administered the TOEIC test as a pretest in October 2012 and again as a posttest in January 2013, the purpose of which was to ascertain the effectiveness of the BL program. The blended-learning activities included: (1) students watching online Coursera lectures with the use of a PC and mobile devices; (2) students presenting oral summaries of the lectures to their classmates both face-to-face and in front of the class; and (3) students spending extensive time watching several online lectures during their commuting hours and writing a 400-word summary of each lecture during each week. At the end of the course, a questionnaire was administered to the students after their exposure to the above activities. The goal of the first study was to examine the effectiveness of the blended and mobile learning activities on the students' English language proficiency and oral communication skills.

## 2.2. The second study (TOEIC training kit)

The second study focused on examining the use of an on-line TOEIC training kit to help determine the effectiveness of the e-learning and m-learning activities. The study started in October 2012 and ended in January 2013, and targeted approximately 60 Japanese undergraduate students. Students were required to spend roughly 50 hours in total to complete the online TOEIC course using a PC and mobile phones for the purpose of improving their reading and listening comprehension skills. By the end of the semester in January 2013, the students had completed nearly 80% of the online course contents. The students were administered the TOEIC test as a pretest in October 2012 and once again as a posttest in January 2013. A questionnaire was also administered to the students after their exposure to the above activities at the end of the course.

## 3. Results

For assessment purposes, we present a sampling of the data results below, including the results from TOEIC, which revealed that the students' overall English proficiency had improved after their exposure to the BL activities. Also included are some of the results of the survey which were administered to the students for the purpose of attaining feedback on how they felt about the BL activities.

## 3.1. TOEIC

The TOEIC results of the first study revealed that the students' mean scores had significantly increased from 585 ($SD = 25.3$) in the pretest to 645 ($SD = 24.6$) in the posttest. Likewise, in the second study, the mean TOEIC scores improved from 452 ($SD = 112$) to 566 ($SD = 122$) over a three-month period. In both cases, the pretest and posttest TOEIC scores were analysed using a t-test, which indicated that the difference between both scores were statistically significant at a 1% level. This improvement would seem to indicate that our utilisation of a language learning environment that integrated m-learning and e-learning had significantly helped the students to improve their English skills and had a positive effect on their overall English language proficiency.

## 3.2. Questionnaire

In the first study, a survey was administered to participants after their exposure to the blended-learning program incorporating the Coursera lectures. In response to the survey question "did you find the Coursera lectures useful in improving your English proficiency", 61% of students felt that the online lectures were very useful. In response to the question "to what extent did you use mobile technologies to learn online Coursera lecture", 30% of students responded having used their mobile devices to study the on-line English lectures. Overall, the questionnaire results indicated that the students were satisfied with the online Coursera lectures and TOEIC training kit and were motivated by the blended-learning environment incorporating m-learning.

## 3.3. Assessment of English writing and oral summaries (first case study)

At the start of the semester, the students had made numerous grammatical and structural mistakes in their summary writings. However, by the end of semester the students' writings, for the most part, had fewer grammatical errors, were better organised, and were longer in length. In addition, by comparing their first and final oral summaries, many students demonstrated significant improvement in their oral skills, particularly in terms of segmental and prosodic features, including pitch, intonation, and vowel duration.

## 4. Discussion and conclusion

An assessment of pre- and post-training TOEIC scores in the first study revealed that the Coursera lecture activities had a positive effect on the students' overall

English skills. In addition, the students' listening and oral communication skills improved as a result of the online English lecture activities with English subtitles. A questionnaire administered after their exposure to the BL activities indicated the students were satisfied with the online Coursera lectures and motivated by the BL environment incorporating m-learning.

The goal of the second study was to improve the students' reading and listening comprehension skills. The results showed the students completed nearly 80% of the course contents with their mean TOEIC scores improving from 452 ($SD$ = 112) to 566 ($SD$ = 122) over a three-month period. The students appeared to be very satisfied with the online Teaching and Learning Technology (TLT) TOEIC Kit Software because e-Learning TLT TOEIC Kit Software is a form of Web-Based Training (WBT) education materials developed to allow full expression of the convenience that comes with e-learning within academic settings. Its merit lies in the fact that individual learners are not only able to repeat their studies anywhere, at any time, but teachers are also able to uniformly manage the progress and results of their students' work.

As shown by the results of the two studies, the on-line and BL activities can be employed for language learning assignments in regular classes apart from the necessity of using CALL and computer rooms. Since they enable students to learn regardless of time or place when used with tablet computers or smartphones, it holds the potential for significant improvement over traditional study modalities. Overall, these results seem to indicate that blended learning using mobile technologies can be effectively integrated into the language learning curriculum and can play a positive role in improving students' language proficiency. Additionally, the instructor's observations of the BL activities revealed that the students were excited by using a variety of IT tools, which helped them to more effectively engage in the Coursera lecture activities by accessing a variety of learning materials from their mobile devices.

The results overall confirmed that students considered the activities to be helpful in developing their English language skills. One plausible reason for the effectiveness of the language learning program may be due to the flexibility and personalised nature of m-learning, since it enables students to control the pace and place of their L2 learning both in and out of the classroom. The portability and convenience of m-learning empowers students to actively explore and regulate their own language learning. It also enhances collaborative and creative exchanges between students while working on classroom or during autonomous learning activities, which can result in making their language learning experience more positive and enjoyable.

**Acknowledgments**. This work was supported by Grant-in Aid for Scientific Research (C) KAKENHI (23520698). I would like to express my hearty thanks to Stephen Lambacher on reviewing this paper.

## References

Educational Testing Service. (2011). *TOEIC Test: Data & Analysis 2011, ETS.* IIBC: The Institute for International Business Communication. Retrieved from http://www.toeic.or.jp/toeic_en/pdf/data/TOEIC_DAA2011.pdf

Vinu, P. V., Sherimon, P. C., & Krishnan, R. (2011). Towards pervasive mobile learning – the vision of 21st century. *Procedia - Social and Behavioural Sciences, 15*, 3067-3073. doi: 10.1016/j.sbspro.2011.04.247

# Developing a Virtual Learning Community for LSP Applications

## Panagiotis Panagiotidis[1]

**Abstract**. Foreign language teachers are nowadays required to respond to the changes provoked by the advent of web 2.0 and the developments it has introduced in the learning behaviour of users, and to adopt a new teaching approach, integrating users' online social activities in their educational practice. In this new educational approach, users must be able to choose the appropriate content for their needs, interact and collaborate with others and learn in an informal online environment, similar to the environment they use in their everyday life. Towards this direction, the development of Personal Learning Environments (PLEs) seems to promise new possibilities in the field of language teaching and learning, especially concerning LSP applications. In this paper we first present the current research on PLEs, their philosophy, the pedagogical context they are based on as well as the different ways of their formation. Furthermore, we propose a PLE developed specifically for language learning using the Netvibes platform. More specifically, we present the components and the possibilities of this PLE, as well as the way the environment was used in the foreign language classroom. Finally, we draw conclusions deriving from this application and the perspectives that this type of environment creates for language learning.

**Keywords**: personal learning environments, PLE, Ajax Start pages, ICT, technology enhanced language learning, learning communities.

## 1. Introduction

The increasing popularity of web 2.0 applications and their deeper integration into users' everyday lives leads to significant changes in the way users perceive education and affects the strategies they choose to reach their learning objective(s).

---

1. Aristotle University of Thessaloniki, Panepistimioupoli, Greece; pana@frl.auth.gr

**How to cite this article**: Panagiotidis, P. (2013). Developing a Virtual Learning Community for LSP Applications. In L. Bradley & S. Thouësny (Eds.), *20 Years of EUROCALL: Learning from the Past, Looking to the Future. Proceedings of the 2013 EUROCALL Conference, Évora, Portugal* (pp. 200-205). Dublin/Voillans: © Research-publishing.net.

In this context, the current educational approach of Tertiary Education Institutions as well as the e-learning systems on which it is based start to seem outdated, as they are incompatible with the users' new learning behaviour.

The traditional knowledge management through institutional e-learning systems, and especially the strict structure and predefined content of virtual learning environments (VLEs), discourages users, who are required to follow a mandatory and teacher-predesigned learning scenario, being passive and limited to the functions authorised by the VLE role (Clark, Beer, & Jones, 2010; Sclater, 2008). On the contrary, in new environments created by web 2.0 services, students can choose, manage and reconstruct content according to their needs, enrich it with additional resources, share it with or redistribute it to others interested in the same subject, interact with peers and/or the teacher and form their own learning path. Operating in such an online environment does not restrict them as the institutional VLEs (Brown & Adler, 2008). It is in fact a new educational model, fully compatible with learners' lifestyle, in which the one-way delivery of knowledge is replaced by personal exploration, interaction with others and social production of knowledge, through the use of social networks and web 2.0 tools such as blogs, wikis, podcasts and the pursuit of knowledge in informal and distant outskirts of the web (long tail learning).

It is obvious that this kind of online learning behaviour is neither encouraged nor supported directly by existing e-learning systems, at least to the extent that users may wish. On the one hand, this fact leads e-learning applications designers to the modernisation and development of the existing systems towards a more social approach. On the other hand, the search for new tools is more compatible with the informal and free management of knowledge.

## 2. Method

The basic concept to achieve the above aims is the development of applications that will approach or simulate the way people act, communicate and learn in their everyday lives and will allow them to form learning spaces suitable for communication, knowledge sharing, interaction, and informal and collaborative learning. Most researchers in the field believe that Personal Learning Environments may be the next step, and complement, or even replace VLEs in e-learning applications (Godwin-Jones, 2009; Martindale & Dowdy, 2010; Sclater, 2008).

The term PLE is open to many different approaches, as it does not represent a specific type of software, but rather a concept that focuses on new user learning practices. However, PLEs present some common characteristics: they are open, fully customisable systems that are controlled and managed by individuals and function independently of educational institutions. PLEs adopt a user-centered approach and promote informal and lifelong learning, assigning users the basic role of knowledge building, via the formation of communities and the creation, remixing and sharing of resources. In this framework, a PLE must give users access to a number of applications and services, to a network of peer learners, and, mainly, to the control of the learning process (Martindale & Dowdy, 2010).

From a technical point of view, researchers agree that PLEs are personal systems, environments or collections of tools and external web 2.0 services (SAAS) which users select and organise in such a way as to build their Personal Knowledge Networks and serve their learning needs (Chatti, Agustiawan, Jarke, & Specht, 2010; Ingerman & Yang, 2010; Peter, Leroy, & Leprêtre, 2010). In its most complex and demanding form, a PLE may be specially developed software which integrates all the user's necessary features, at the same time providing an interface with institutional computational infrastructures (databases, libraries, administration, etc.).

Consequently, the design of custom PLE systems may be a very demanding task, as it requires high programming skills and financing. This is why ordinary users should focus on the use of web-available tools in order to develop a PLE that will be suitable for their needs. This type of software application is described by the terms "start pages", "Ajax/web desktops" or "aggregators", and is a relatively new approach to the design of PLEs. This category includes applications freely available on the net in their majority and specifically designed to allow users to form their personal learning spaces according to their needs. Start pages are based on the core web 2.0 technologies – AJAX, XML, mashups, RSS and Widgets (McLoughlin & Lee, 2007; Rollett, Lux, Strohmaier, Dösinger, & Tochtermann, 2007) – and do not demand high programming skills, beyond the familiarisation with the web 2.0 concepts, technologies and services, from the final users.

## 3. Discussion

The use of an Ajax start page allows users the detailed configuration of their personal learning space. This option involves not only the tools to be used, but the information/knowledge resources on the subject of interest. In the case of foreign language learning, a key challenge for the foreign language teacher is to design a learning environment that brings learners close to the natural environment and the native speakers of the target language.

To this aim, a variety of tools, components and characteristics in the form of widgets and mashups have been used in the PLE presented here, in order to help the students get in touch with authentic language resources: communications (videoconferencing, POP3 and webmail accounts), social networking (user accounts in social networks and social bookmarking), content creation (users blogs), media (video, images, slides, sounds), repositories, multimedia players (Podcasts, Web radio, WebTV) and media search tools (Web, Video and Image search). A set of language specific tools is also included (collaborative writing tools, translation, vocabulary and dictionary widgets, spell checker, text-to-speech synthesiser, voice recorder and playback), as well as a variety of French resources like bookmarks/web pages (recommended websites, French resources and activities, language learning exercises), RSS feeds (French newspapers/ magazines feeds and blog feeds) and Quizzing tools (online exercises tools). Finally, connections to the Institutional VLE and to the Institutional website are also provided.

To increase ergonomics and ease of use, the PLE is organised in tabs, in which the widgets have been arranged according to their functionality and the task they address. In the main tab the user has access to all his/her personal services (such as email accounts, social network accounts, personal blogs and tagging services) as well as to personal bookmark collections. Communication widgets (such as Skype) as well as some common widgets (such as to-do lists, calendars and calculators) and search tools are also available. From this tab, the user can also have access to courses, as well, and work normally in the Institutional VLE (in this case, Moodle). All other tabs are dedicated to language resources, organised by type: multimedia players and resources (videos, podcasts, educational resources, etc), RSS information flow (French newspapers and magazines, TV and radio emissions) activities/exercises (plus collaborative tools), and games/quizzes.

In a PLE, the learners can create connections and collaborate with peers and the teacher, forming a virtual learning community in this way. In this community, users act and learn in a digital substitute of the natural environment they normally learn outside institutional environment. The principal philosophy of virtual learning communities is based on informal learning and on social constructivism or "connectivism" (Siemens, 2005). The informal way of learning people use in their everyday life through study groups, discussions or collaboration with peers, can be simulated in a PLE. In an online community, the PLE acts as a mediating mechanism between geographically distributed learners helping them to communicate, search, acquire and/or create knowledge in the context and as a result of social interaction

(Van Harmelen, 2008). In an online community, learning takes place through knowledge and experience sharing, information exchange, interaction with peers in an informal and unbounded way. Activities, conversations and online exercises may be started by the teacher (who is also a member of this community) or any other member, i.e. a learner. The traditional one-way transmission of knowledge constitutes only a small proportion of online communities' learning activities, whereas interaction among peers leads to knowledge sharing and creation (Aceto, Dondi, & Marzotto, 2010).

## 4. Conclusions

The PLE described in this paper can be properly configured to the specific user's needs. Furthermore, the content can be specifically selected to suit the needs of any specific language subject. This high level of customisability makes it clear that PLEs present significant advantages for language education. Using PLEs users can form virtual learning communities and approach the language and its native speakers much easier and in a richer context than in any other traditional e-learning platform.

Especially in the case of PLEs for LSP applications, it is possible to reuse the entire set of tools and create a new application for a different subject, simply by changing the resources from which the PLE is fed content.

Regarding the subject of foreign languages, the creation of personalised and adaptable learning environments that extend the traditional approach of a course seems to promise a more holistic response to students' needs. Functioning in the PLE, students could combine learning with their daily practice and communicate and collaborate with others, thus increasing the possibilities of multiple sources, informal communication and practice and eventually acquiring the foreign language.

## References

Aceto, S., Dondi, C., & Marzotto, P. (2010). *Pedagogical innovation in new learning communities: an in-depth study of twelve online learning communities.* Luxembourg: Publications Office of the European Union. Retrieved from http://ftp.jrc.es/EURdoc/JRC59474.pdf

Brown, J. S., & Adler, R. P. (2008). Minds on fire. Open education, the long tail, and learning 2.0. *EDUCAUSE Review, 17,* 18-32. Retrieved from http://net.educause.edu/ir/library/pdf/ERM0811.pdf

Chatti, M. A., Agustiawan, M. R., Jarke, M., & Specht, M. (2010). Toward a personal learning environment framework. *International Journal of Virtual and Personal Learning Environments, 1*(4), 66-85. doi: 10.4018/jvple.2010100105

Clark, K., Beer, C., & Jones, D. (2010). Academic involvement with the LMS: an exploratory study. In C. H. Steel, M. J. Keppell, P. Gerbic, & S. Housego (Eds.), *Curriculum, Technology & Transformation for an Unknown Future* (pp. 487-496). Proceedings ascilite Sydney. Retrieved from http://ascilite.org.au/conferences/sydney10/procs/Kenclark-full.pdf

Godwin-Jones, R. (2009). Emerging technologies personal learning environments. *Language Learning & Technology, 13*(2), 3-9. Retrieved from http://llt.msu.edu/vol13num2/emerging.pdf

Ingerman, B. L., & Yang, C. (2010). Top-ten issues 2010. *EDUCAUSE Review, 45*(3), 46-60. Retrieved from http://net.educause.edu/ir/library/pdf/ERM1032.pdf

Martindale, T., & Dowdy, M. (2010). Personal learning environments. In G. Veletsianos (Ed.), *Emerging Technologies in Distance Education* (pp. 177-193). Athabasca University Press.

McLoughlin, C., & Lee, M. J. W. (2007). Social software and participatory learning: pedagogical choices with technology affordances in the web 2.0 era. *Proceedings Ascilite Singapore* (pp. 664-675). Retrieved from http://www.scribd.com/doc/33506949/Social-Software-and-Participatory-Learning-Pedagogical-choices-with-Technology-affordances-in-the-Web-2-0

Peter, Y., Leroy, S., Leprêtre, E. (2010). First steps in the integration of institutional and personal learning environments. *Proceedings Workshop Future Learning Landscape, Barcelona, Spain, EC-TEL, 2010* (pp. 1-5). Retrieved from http://www2.lifl.fr/~petery/PeterLeroyLepretre-2010.pdf

Rollett, H., Lux, M., Strohmaier, M., Dösinger, G., & Tochtermann, K. (2007). The web 2.0 way of learning with technologies. *International Journal of Learning Technology, 3*(1), 87-107. doi: 10.1504/IJLT.2007.012368

Sclater, N. (2008). Web 2.0, personal learning environments, and the future of learning management systems. *EDUCAUSE Center for Applied Research, 13*, 1-13. Retrieved from http://pages.uoregon.edu/not/LMS/future%20of%20LMSs.pdf

Siemens, G. (2005, April 5). Connectivism: a learning theory for the digital age. *eLearn Space*. Retrieved from http://www.elearnspace.org/Articles/connectivism.htm

Van Harmelen, M. (2008). Design trajectories: four experiments in PLE implementation. *Interactive Learning Environments, 16*(1), 35-46. doi: 10.1080/10494820701772686

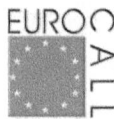 

# Toward Mobile Assisted Language Learning Apps for Professionals that Integrate Learning into the Daily Routine

Antonio Pareja-Lora[1], Jorge Arús-Hita[2], Timothy Read[3], Pilar Rodríguez-Arancón[4], Cristina Calle-Martínez[5], Lourdes Pomposo[6], Elena Martín-Monje[7], and Elena Bárcena[8]

**Abstract.** In this short paper, we present some initial work on Mobile Assisted Language Learning (MALL) undertaken by the ATLAS research group. ATLAS embraced this multidisciplinary field cutting across Mobile Learning and Computer Assisted Language Learning (CALL) as a natural step in their quest to find learning formulas for professional English that adapt to the changing profiles and needs of our modern society. A needs-analysis undertaken by group members highlights the way in which professionals need to have language learning activities available on their mobile devices. The SO-CALL-ME project has been established to enable such MALL apps, designed and developed within the ATLAS group, to be studied with real users to explore the way in which they can improve their oral language skills. Here one such app, ANT – Audio News Trainer, is presented as an example of the development being undertaken.

**Keywords**: MALL, second and foreign language, languages for special purposes.

1. Universidad Complutense de Madrid, Madrid, Spain; apareja@sip.ucm.es
2. Universidad Complutense de Madrid, Madrid, Spain
3. Universidad Española de Educación a Distancia, Madrid, Spain
4. Universidad Española de Educación a Distancia, Madrid, Spain
5. Universidad Complutense de Madrid, Madrid, Spain
6. Universidad Española de Educación a Distancia, Madrid, Spain
7. Universidad Española de Educación a Distancia, Madrid, Spain
8. Universidad Española de Educación a Distancia, Madrid, Spain; mbarcena@flog.uned.es

**How to cite this article**: Pareja-Lora, A. et al. (2013). Toward Mobile Assisted Language Learning Apps for Professionals that Integrate Learning into the Daily Routine. In L. Bradley & S. Thouësny (Eds.), *20 Years of EUROCALL: Learning from the Past, Looking to the Future. Proceedings of the 2013 EUROCALL Conference, Évora, Portugal* (pp. 206-210). Dublin/Voillans: © Research-publishing.net.

## 1. Introduction

We live in a society that is constantly on the move, where individuals have difficulties committing themselves to conventional face-to-face taught courses. These courses require physical presence and undivided attention, and even saving dedicated time and effort in front of a computing device, which is usually not completely integrated and/or compatible with many other activities. These difficulties are particularly evident in the case of second language learning (SLL) since it aims at real communication in an ever-changing variety of scenarios, situations and subject-matters. Besides, SLL involves not only the learning of various types of knowledge (i.e. phonetic, lexical, grammatical, pragmatic, and sociocultural), but also the development of a range of skills, which may be viewed in terms of semantic notions and functions. Thus, SLL is an extended and complex process, calling nowadays for novel adaptive solutions that integrate the various forms and contexts in which professionals need to engage in at work, when they travel, etc. Accordingly, the social mobility factor appears not as an obstacle to save for lifelong learning, but as a valuable opportunity in this whole process. In the next pages, we present the actions undertaken in the context of the SO-CALL-ME (Social Ontology-based Cognitively Augmented Language Learning Mobile Environment) project in order to (1) identify the needs of users, (2) explore the SLL-related apps existing in the market, and (3) develop our own apps.

## 2. Method

With the increasing need for immediate and customised solutions to satisfy social demands, learning is more dependent on technology than ever before. Concepts like lifelong learning and ubiquitous technology open up a number of possibilities for learning languages, particularly English. This is one of the eternal aspirations of the non-native population worldwide and a crucial capability in their professional and social lives nowadays. One of the fields that is receiving the attention of researchers is MALL, an approach to language learning that is assisted or enhanced through the use of handheld mobile devices. The original underlying idea of the 80's was that students would be able to both access their materials and communicate with their teachers and peers anytime and anywhere. This involved a notable increase of flexibility in comparison to desktop and laptop computers. However, since then, MALL research has moved from simulating more or less standard computer-based learning practice to designing specific mobile applications. The advantage is clear: whereas the former approach relies on small and light equipment and in formal educational institutions, the latter adapts to and benefits from the new forms and contexts of usage of mobile devices away from the classroom.

## 2.1. User needs and products available

Pomposo, Martín-Monje, and Bárcena (forthcoming) have undertaken a needs-analysis of the use of mobile devices for learning business English. In their study, firstly, they found out that middle managers and executives from national and multinational firms are regular mobile users who require English skills for key business activities that entail oral communicative situations such as meetings and product/service presentations. Secondly, they describe the precise communicative language competence needs of busy adult language learners to work effectively in such situations, such as conversational skills, register and intercultural competence.

This study served as the basis for the subsequent research on MALL undertaken by the ATLAS research group. A first step was the evaluation of some of the existing products in the SLL-related app market. To that end, a number of rubric-based evaluations of such apps were made (Arús-Hita, Rodríguez-Arancón, & Calle-Martínez, in press; Calle-Martínez, Rodríguez-Arancón, & Arús-Hita, in press; Martín-Monje, Arús-Hita, Calle-Martínez, & Rodríguez-Arancón, in press; Rodríguez-Arancón, Arús-Hita, & Calle-Martínez, in press). These evaluations show that some apps that are attractive to MALL users *a priori* do not necessarily have a sound linguistic content that is adequate for steady language learning. This represented a challenge that our group decided to face by engaging in the development of SLL apps that are attractive and pedagogically sound at the same time. We next describe one such application.

## 2.2. ANT: the first 'English on the Move' app for training oral comprehension for A2-B2 listeners

When faced with the development of an app for a mobile device, one of the first decisions to be made was which device was the intended target, and therefore, which operating system the app would run on. In general, this choice will limit how the app can be designed and developed. However, there are evermore options for developing cross-platform apps, which can then be run on multiple types of devices and operating systems. Hence, when the ATLAS research group started to focus on developing a series of related apps, called 'English on the Move', such a cross-platform solution was adopted.

The first app to be developed was the Audio News Trainer (or ANT). This app (1) dynamically collects a list of links to news podcasts available online every two days, (2) classifies and stores the podcast links in terms of three levels of difficulty, and (3) presents the classification to the student, colour-coded, following the standard traffic light system. Once a student has selected and listened to a particular recording, it presents a short questionnaire with three basic questions, regarding (1) the volume level used, (2) the presence of background noise, and (3) the understanding level of the podcast content (nothing / the key concepts / great level of detail). These data, about the factors that affect audio comprehension, are logged on the ATLAS server and the student is returned to the list to listen to other recordings. As more students use ANT their data is stored giving an overall indication of which audio broadcasts were found to be easier or harder, thereby enabling the researchers to identify the elements present in the recordings that caused the problems. This app in its current version does not represent a complete learning resource but is the first step toward a social collaborative app where the students move on to discuss and collectively analyse what they have listened to, thereby reaching understanding at a group level.

## 3. Discussion

Before engaging in the actual development of ANT, which is meant for use on portable devices, such as smartphones and tablets, a number of issues concerning usability had to be tackled. In the era of desktop computers connected to the Internet, the metaphor 'point and click' was a *de facto* standard for interaction in online browser-based second language learning websites and their related activities. Since the appearance and acceptance of smartphones and tablets as a common way to access online information via local apps, this metaphor has given way to a set of finger-based gestures (such as pinching to reduce the size of something or swiping to move from one page to another). As well as the way in which the user actually interacts with the device, there is also the question of which types of materials can actually be presented on such a device and how the user can effectively interact with them. The fact that a standard page of text can be displayed on a tiny smartphone does not imply that it will be sufficiently legible. Similarly, even though audio can be reproduced quite clearly from such a device, as the user context changes, background noise might make listening difficult. Furthermore, as well as intrinsic limitations of the device and app being used, and the nature of the materials being presented, there are also personal factors that each user will present that can limit interaction.

Once usability issues were taken care of and the app was created, we could move on to the analysis of the data logged on the ATLAS server. This analysis reveals that the students do generally find the difficulty of the podcasts to follow the three levels highlighted by the researchers. As was expected, background noise was also a factor for oral comprehension. As was noted above, even though the app was developed using a technology that would make it multiplatform, the majority of difficulties that the students have had were due to usability problems. For example, the app ran perfectly on iOS devices but had problems on Android when actually playing the podcast. On some devices the play button had to be pressed several times to get the recording running and on others it would just not work.

## 4. Conclusions

This paper has described the steps leading to the creation of the ANT mobile app. We started with the identification of users' needs. This was followed by a scrutiny of educational apps in the market, with a focus on SLL apps. After this, and preceded by a number of considerations concerning the usability of apps on mobile devices, ANT was developed and tested. Finally, the users' data logged on the ATLAS server was analysed, with the results described in Section 3. Before the app can be used by a larger number of students or development of the next social component can take place, the technical problems specified in Section 3 need to be resolved. That will be our next task.

**Acknowledgements**. We would like to thank the Spanish Ministry of Science and Innovation for funding the SO-CALL-ME research project (Research grant number: FFI2011-29829).

## References

Arús-Hita, J., Rodríguez-Arancón, P., & Calle-Martínez, C. (in press). A pedagogic assessment of mobile learning applications. In *Proceedings of ICDE 2013, Mobilizing Distance Education, UNED, Madrid.*

Calle-Martínez, C., Rodríguez-Arancón, P., & Arús-Hita, J. (in press). A scrutiny of the educational value of EFL mobile learning applications. In *Proceedings of World Conference on Learning, Teaching and Educational Leadership 2013, Barcelona, Spain.*

Martín-Monje, E., Arús-Hita, J., Calle-Martínez, C., & Rodríguez-Arancón, P. (in press). REALL: Rubric for the evaluation of apps in language learning. In *Proceedings of Jornadas ML: 13, Logroño, Spain.*

Pomposo, L., Martín-Monje, E., & Bárcena, E. (forthcoming). *A needs-analysis of the use of mobile devices for professional English language learning.*

Rodríguez-Arancón, P., Arús-Hita, J., & Calle-Martínez, C. (in press). The use of current Mobile learning applications in EFL. In *Proceedings of IETC 2013, Kuala Lumpur, Malaysia.*

# Developing Swedish Spelling Exercises on the ICALL Platform Lärka

### Dijana Pijetlovic[1] and Elena Volodina[2]

**Abstract.** In this project we developed web services on the ICALL platform Lärka for automatic generation of Swedish spelling exercises using Text-To-Speech (TTS) technology which allows L2 learners to train their spelling and listening individually at home. The spelling exercises contain five different linguistic levels, whereby the language learner has the choice between word, inflected word, phrase, sentence and performance based levels. The embedded avatar pronounces a random item of the desired level, which the user has to spell. Furthermore, the users have the possibility to train their own words for different linguistic levels. A result tracker containing a total and correct answer score keeps track of the language learner's performance. In order to analyse typical spelling errors and provide better feedback, misspellings are collected in a database. The usability of the spelling exercises, concerning the different linguistic levels and the quality of speech, has been evaluated through a questionnaire with 10 participants.

**Keywords**: Swedish spelling game, ICALL, text-to-speech, spelling errors, L2.

## 1. Introduction

The motivation behind this project is to support the ICALL platform Lärka (Volodina & Borin, 2012) in broadening the spectrum of exercises by implementing spelling exercises and integrating text-to-speech technology (Pijetlovic, 2013). The web-based platform Lärka is used for computer-assisted language learning that generates a number of exercises based on corpora available through Korp (Borin,

---

1. University of Gothenburg, Göteborg, Sweden; p3_dijana@yahoo.de
2. Språkbanken, University of Gothenburg, Göteborg, Sweden

**How to cite this article**: Pijetlovic, D., & Volodina, E. (2013). Developing Swedish Spelling Exercises on the ICALL Platform Lärka. In L. Bradley & S. Thouësny (Eds.), *20 Years of EUROCALL: Learning from the Past, Looking to the Future. Proceedings of the 2013 EUROCALL Conference, Évora, Portugal* (pp. 211-217). Dublin/Voillans: © Research-publishing.net.

Forsberg, & Roxendal, 2012), using also lexical resources through Karp (Borin, Forsberg, Olsson, & Uppström, 2012).

Spelling constitutes a part of vocabulary knowledge, therefore it is indispensable when it comes to language learning. Spelling errors can be broadly distinguished between performance-based errors, e.g. accidental typing errors and knowledge-based errors, i.e. a user not knowing how to spell a word or confusing words. A more detailed distinction could be, for instance, non-word errors, real-word errors, orthographical errors, or phonological errors. Furthermore, different aspects of word knowledge such as word form, its spelling, pronunciation, word inflection and derivation, meaning of words, grammatical functions and collocations are trained in the implemented exercises (Volodina, 2010).

The project consists of four main tasks: (1) Implementing web services for adaptive spelling exercise generation using TTS for Swedish, where target words, inflected words, phrases or sentences are pronounced and the user has to type what he/she hears. The user can either choose different linguistic levels or let the generator decide according to the user's performance. (2) Implementing the user interface for the spelling exercise to be used on the ICALL platform Lärka. (3) Creating a database for storing all possible misspellings associated with each individual word for providing better feedback, the latter by performing user tests and analysing logged errors. (4) Evaluating the usability of the exercise type for Swedish language learners by means of a questionnaire.

The project addresses two main research questions: (1) Is text-to-speech technology for Swedish mature enough for the use in L2? (2) Does the spelling game meet the requirements set by the Common European Framework of Reference (CEFR, 2001) for listening and orthography?

## 2. Material and method

The Swedish spelling game is integrated as a separate module in Lärka while the layout of the spelling exercises is inherited from Lärka's already existing exercises in order to have a coherent layout within the application. First, several available text-to-speech systems have been evaluated regarding their performance quality. Sitepal (www.sitepal.com) has been selected due to the mature text-to-speech technology, user-friendliness and availability of avatars. Second, four linguistic levels have been considered for exercise generation motivated by pedagogical considerations: word level, inflected word level, phrase and sentence levels, described shortly below.

The *word level* provides the user with random words in base form selected from the frequency based vocabulary list Kelly-list (Volodina & Johansson Kokkinakis, 2012), which is simple in implementation. At the *inflected word level* the user has the possibility to train inflected words retrieved from Karp's morphology lexicon Saldom (Borin & Forsberg, 2009). The *phrase level* allows the user to train words in phrase context. In order to find the best method for retrieving suitable phrases, different approaches have been tested. A selection of Korp's corpora is reused for setting the target vocabulary item into a suitable phrase-long context. On the *sentence level* the user trains spelling and listening on the basis of sentences. The challenge at this level is to both spell and at the same time remember the pronounced sentence. Sentences are retrieved by calling a web service for ranking sentences selected from Korp corpora according to their readability (Pilán, 2013). The *performance-based level* has been implemented in order to allow language learners to train all above-mentioned linguistic levels according to their performance in an adaptive fashion.

Figure 1. Lärka's architecture for automatic generation of spelling exercises

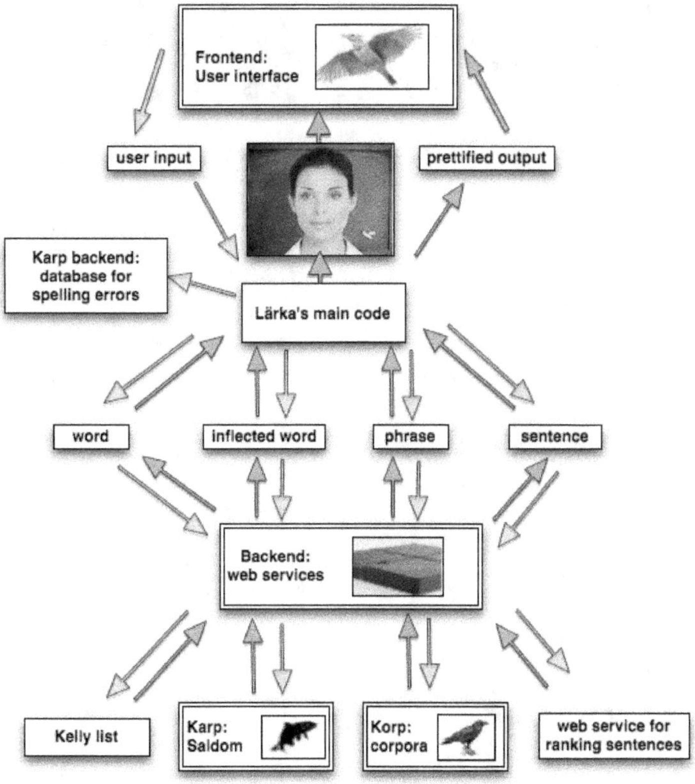

After all necessary resources have been analysed, a number of tests on appropriateness of extracted items have been performed; the web services have been linked to the user interface and an evaluation with 10 participants has been undertaken. The spelling errors have been saved to the spelling errors database (SPEED) during the evaluation stage and analysed in order to provide language learners with useful feedback in the future (Figure 1).

## 3. Spelling exercise functionality

Two exercise modes are available for the spelling exercises: 'self-study' and 'test mode'. The 'self-study' mode allows language learners to improve their answers, as the correct answer is not revealed. In the 'test' mode the language learner has only one chance to answer each item as the correct answer is revealed immediately after the submission.

Figure 2. User interface for word level

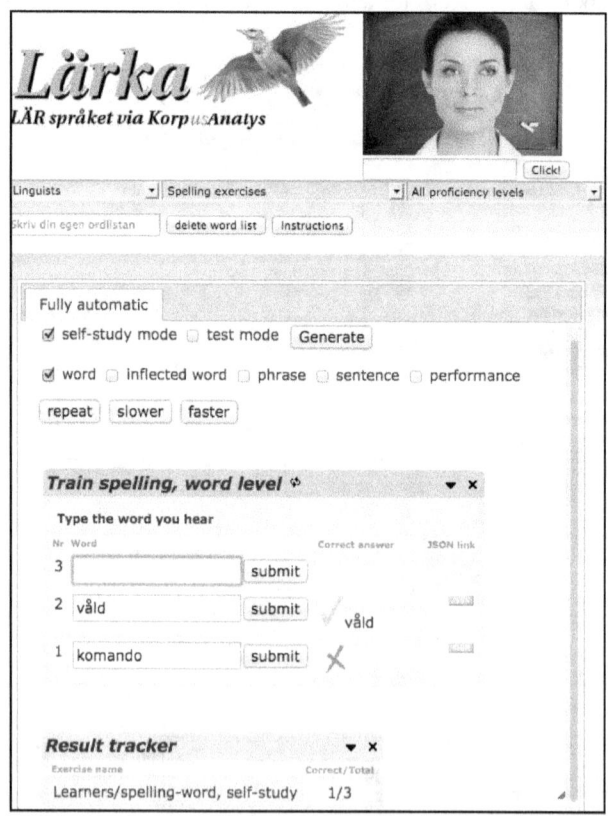

The language learner has the possibility to train words in different contexts by selecting the relevant linguistic level (word, inflected word, phrase, sentence and performance-based). Once the language learner selects a linguistic level, the avatar pronounces the item to be spelled. The user has also the option to rehear an item in a normal, slower or faster rate by clicking the corresponding buttons.

All the user selections are automatically added to the URL in order to save the user's effort of going through the menus on the main webpage (Figure 2).

## 4. Evaluation

The evaluation of the spelling exercises was carried out with 10 participants of which eight belong to the category language learners, one to linguists and one to native speakers. In order to provide the evaluation participants with detailed information, an evaluation page was created, containing the project description, the spelling game instructions, the evaluation questionnaire in English and Swedish as well as a link to Lärka (http://spraakbanken.gu.se/eng/larka/tts). Each of the participants spelled 10 items for the word and inflected word levels, 5 for phrases and 5 for sentences, all results being saved to the spelling error database.

For the analysis of the evaluation results, the evaluation participants were divided into 4 subgroups according to their proficiency levels (A – Basic User, B – Independent User, C – Proficient User, Native speaker). In order to evaluate the spelling exercise, a questionnaire containing a scale from 1 to 5 was applied (1 = very good and 5 = very poor). Additionally, the evaluators had the possibility to add extra comments for every question as well as free comments at the end of the questionnaire.

The purpose of the evaluation was, besides collecting spelling errors, to evaluate the user interface for its user friendliness as well as to assess the text-to-speech usability in a language learning environment, but primarily to assess the usefulness of the exercise regarding the different linguistic levels.

According to the evaluation results (Figure 3), the avatar (5) appears to be the least effective element for the spelling exercises. The unsatisfying results for the avatar are firstly based on the missing facial expressions and secondly on its location within the spelling game. The user interface (2) and the quality of pronunciation (7) were the most satisfying criteria in this evaluation. Comparing the word (including inflected word) (9), the phrase (10) and the sentence level (11), the diagram clearly shows that the word level was the most appropriate level for training spelling followed by the phrase level. However, phrases have to be more adapted to the respective proficiency level in order to achieve the best possible learning success. The sentence level was assessed as the least appropriate level, as the length and the speed rate were perceived as unsuitable for training spelling and listening. Furthermore, an appropriate error feedback was missing, for example, an indication of misspelled words or characters within a sentence, which is planned for later implementation based on error log analysis.

Figure 3. Diagram with evaluation results for all proficiency levels

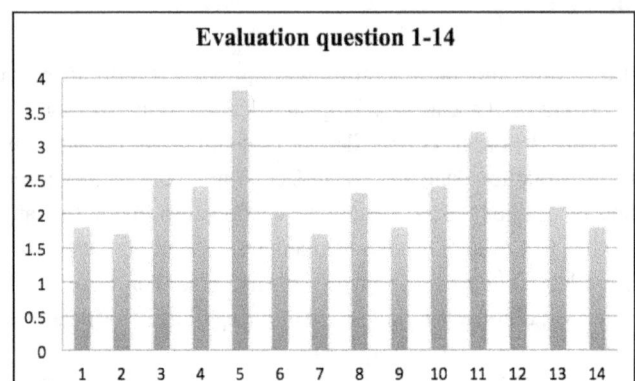

## 5. Conclusions

The goal of this project has been, firstly, the implementation of Swedish spelling exercises on an already existing ICALL platform in order to provide language learners with a tool for training spelling and listening on the basis of different linguistic levels. Secondly, the evaluation of the newly implemented module regarding its effectiveness and usefulness. The main focus of the evaluation was to find out whether the TTS technology is mature enough for the use in L2 context and to verify whether the spelling exercises meet the expectations of CEFR.

Overall, the evaluation results show that the implemented spelling game, which fulfills the expectation of CEFR, is an effective tool for training spelling and listening at home. Moreover, the TTS technology for Swedish has proven to be mature enough for use in L2 context. However, since the spelling game was evaluated specifically from the language learner's point of view, an evaluation from the teacher's position has to be carried out in the future, since the pedagogical perspective is essential for implementing exercises for L2 learners.

**Acknowledgements.** We would like to thank all the participants in the spelling game evaluation. Furthermore, we wish to thank Jonatan Uppström and Leif-Jöran Olsson for setting up the spelling error database, SPEED.

# References

Borin, L., & Forsberg, M. (2009). All in the family: A comparison of SALDO and WordNet. In *Proceedings of the Nodalida 2009 Workshop on WordNets and other Lexical Semantic Resources – between Lexical Semantics, Lexicography, Terminology and Formal Ontologies.* Odense.

Borin, L., Forsberg, M., & Roxendal, J. (2012). Korp – the corpus infrastructure of Språkbanken. *Proceedings of LREC 2012* (pp. 474-478). Istanbul: ELRA. Retrieved from http://www.lrec-conf.org/proceedings/lrec2012/pdf/248_Paper.pdf

Borin, L., Forsberg, M., Olsson, L. J., & Uppström, J. (2012). The open lexical infrastructure of Språkbanken. *Proceedings of LREC 2012* (pp. 3598–3602). Istanbul: ELRA. Retrieved from http://www.lrec-conf.org/proceedings/lrec2012/pdf/249_Paper.pdf

CEFR. (2001). *Common European Framework of Reference for Languages.* Council of Europe: Cambridge University Press. Retrieved from http://www.coe.int/t/dg4/linguistic/Source/Framework_EN.pdf

Pijetlovic, D. (2013). *Swedish spelling game: Developing Swedish spelling exercises on the ICALL platform Lärka using Text-to-Speech technology.* Master Thesis. University of Gothenburg.

Pilán, I. (2013). *NLP-based Approaches to Sentence Readability for Second Language Learning Purposes.* Master Thesis. University of Gothenburg.

Volodina, E. (2010). *Corpora in Language Classroom: Reusing Stockholm Umeå Corpus in a vocabulary exercise generator.* Saarbrücken: Lambert Academic Publishing.

Volodina, E., & Borin, L. (2012). Developing an open-source web-based exercise generator for Swedish. In L. Bradley & S. Thouësny (Eds.), *CALL: Using, Learning, Knowing, EUROCALL Conference, Gothenburg, Sweden, 22-25 August 2012, Proceedings* (pp. 307-313). Dublin: Research-publishing.net. Retrieved from http://research-publishing.net/publications/2012-eurocall-proceedings/

Volodina, E., & Johansson Kokkinakis, S. (2012). Introducing Swedish Kelly-list, a new lexical e-resource for Swedish. *LREC 2012, Turkey.* Retrieved from http://www.lrec-conf.org/proceedings/lrec2012/pdf/264_Paper.pdf

# Automatic Selection of Suitable Sentences for Language Learning Exercises

## Ildikó Pilán[1], Elena Volodina[2], and Richard Johansson[3]

**Abstract**. In our study we investigated second and foreign language (L2) sentence readability, an area little explored so far in the case of several languages, including Swedish. The outcome of our research consists of two methods for sentence selection from native language corpora based on Natural Language Processing (NLP) and machine learning (ML) techniques. The two approaches have been made available online within Lärka, an Intelligent CALL (ICALL) platform offering activities for language learners and students of linguistics. Such an automatic selection of suitable sentences can be valuable for L2 teachers during the creation of new teaching materials, for L2 students who look for additional self-study exercises as well as for lexicographers in search of example sentences to illustrate the meaning of a vocabulary item. Members from all these potential user groups evaluated our methods and found the majority of the sentences selected suitable for L2 learning purposes.

**Keywords**: sentence readability, Swedish, NLP, ICALL, CEFR, GDEX, retrieval, machine learning, supervised classification, corpus-based evidence.

## 1. Introduction

Native language (L1) texts are a valuable source of authentic sentences suitable for the purposes of L2 learning, either as exercise items or as examples illustrating the meaning of a word. Before being able to use such sentences in CALL systems, however, we have to ensure that these examples are *readable*, i.e. understandable

---

1. Språkbanken, University of Gothenburg, Göteborg, Sweden; ildiko.pilan@gmail.com

2. Språkbanken, University of Gothenburg, Göteborg, Sweden

3. Språkbanken, University of Gothenburg, Göteborg, Sweden

**How to cite this article**: Pilán, I., Volodina, E., & Johansson, R. (2013). Automatic Selection of Suitable Sentences for Language Learning Exercises. In L. Bradley & S. Thouësny (Eds.), *20 Years of EUROCALL: Learning from the Past, Looking to the Future. Proceedings of the 2013 EUROCALL Conference, Évora, Portugal* (pp. 218-225). Dublin/Voillans: © Research-publishing.net.

by learners both lexically and structurally. Identifying these sentences manually would require a considerable amount of time. Instead, we propose two automatized selection methods which perform this task for Swedish. Both approaches have been integrated into the online ICALL platform *Lärka* (Volodina, Borin, Loftsson, Arnbjörnsdóttir, & Leifsson, 2012) as part of a sentence readability module called *HitEx* (Hitta Exempel [Find Examples] or Hit Examples). The selection is based on a number of linguistic factors which were found influential for L2 readability, as well as principles of Good Dictionary Examples (GDEX) (Husák, 2008; Kilgarriff, Husák, McAdam, Rundell, & Rychlý, 2008). The sentences selected by the current version of the system have been evaluated by L2 Swedish teachers, learners and linguists, who provided us with positive feedback.

## 2. Materials and method

The materials used throughout the study included Swedish native language corpora of various genres (novels, newspapers and blog texts) which are accessible through an online tool called *Korp* (Borin, Forsberg, & Roxendal, 2012). Korp offers annotations at different linguistic levels for each sentence including parts of speech (POS), morphosyntactic and syntactic (dependency) relations, which have all been exploited in our selection methods. Furthermore, we employed the scale described in the *Common European Framework of Reference for Languages* (CEFR) when distinguishing L2 difficulty levels. Besides native language corpora, we also utilized the *CEFR corpus* (Volodina, Pijetlovic, Pilán, & Johansson Kokkinakis, 2013), a collection of L2 Swedish materials currently under development, and the *Kelly-list* (Volodina & Johansson Kokkinakis, 2012), a frequency-based word list with CEFR levels for each item. The platform Lärka, besides the HitEx module in which our selection methods have been incorporated, also includes an exercise generator module (Volodina et al., 2013).

The material described above served as basis for our two selection methods: a rule-based and a combined approach using rules as well as ML techniques. As a starting point, we used an algorithm described in Volodina, Johansson, and Johansson Kokkinakis (2012) based on four selection criteria. This initial set of rules was extended with additions from the GDEX literature (Kilgarriff et al. 2008; Husák, 2008), as well as sentence selection research in the L2 context (Segler, 2007) and readability studies for L1 Swedish (Heimann Mühlenbock, 2013; Sjöholm, 2012). The ML method used in the combined approach consisted of *supervised classification*, a process in which our model learned to predict whether a sentence is understandable at B1 (intermediate) proficiency level or not, based on training examples from the CEFR corpus and native language corpora. The classification algorithm employed was a Support Vector Machine (SVM) classifier which aimed at finding a line separating the two classes in the training data (within and above B1 level) based on the linguistic characteristics (*features*) of each sentence. A visual representation of this idea is presented in Figure 1 below.

Figure 1. Support vector machine classification

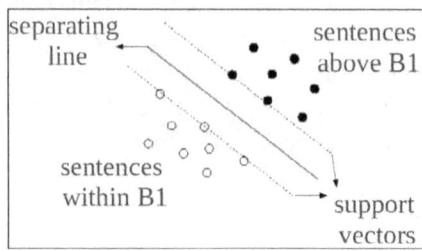

Once trained, the SVM tried to place previously unseen sentences from L1 corpora into the right class. The accuracy of the classifier expresses what percentage of these classifications were correct.

## 3. HitEx: the L2 sentence readability module

Through the graphical user interface of the HitEx module in Lärka a number of search criteria for the selection of sentences can be set. Figure 2 illustrates part of this page.

Figure 2. The HitEx web page

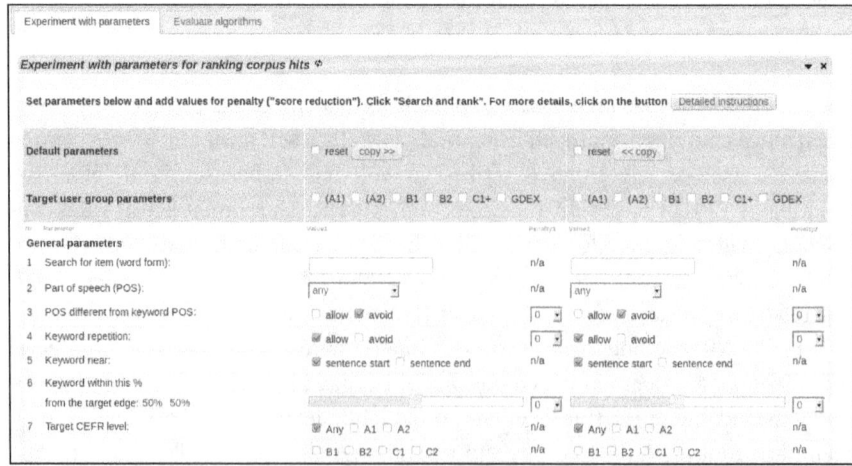

On the left hand side 26 selection criteria, or *parameters*, are listed (only part of these are visible in Figure 2), grouped in three categories: general, structural and lexical. General parameters include basic information about the sentences to select, namely the word to search for (*keyword*), its POS, the corpora from where to choose the examples, etc. Through structural parameters morphosyntactic preferences can be defined. These consist of parameters such as average sentence and word length, percentage of relative pronouns as well as the optional avoidance of participles and modal verbs.

Finally, lexical parameters contain the avoidance of proper names, the allowed percentage of words above the selected CEFR level, etc. Each parameter value can be associated with a *penalty score*, determining the final *ranking* of the sentences based on how well they satisfy the search criteria. A predefined setting is currently available for levels B1, B2, C1+, together with a setting for lexicographers (GDEX). As the presence of the two columns for the parameter values indicates in Figure 2, it is also possible to experiment with two different settings simultaneously.

Instead of using only parameters, the ML component, which we called LäSAS (Lätt/Läs Svenska som Andra Språk [Easy / Read Swedish as a Second Language]), can be selected to be used in combination with some of the parameters. LäSAS classifies sentences based on a large number of linguistic features such as the average number of senses per word, the frequency and CEFR level of words and aspects of syntactic complexity. Such features are based on Swedish L1 readability studies (Heimann Mühlenbock, 2013; Sjöholm, 2012), L2 readability research for other languages (François & Fairon, 2012; Vajjala & Meurers, 2012) and CEFR based course book syllabuses (Levy Scherrer & Lindemalm, 2009). Currently, LäSAS can determine with 70% accuracy whether a sentence is understandable at B1 level or not.

Figure 3 below presents the structure of the readability module and the process of sentence selection. Once users provide their preferences through the dedicated web page in Lärka, the corpus tool, Korp, searches for sentences containing the keyword in Swedish L1 texts. In the next step, sentences undergo a selection with the method previously chosen by the user, which is either purely based on parameters or is a combination of parameters and ML classification with LäSAS. Finally, the resulting filtered set of sentences is displayed on the web page where they can be edited and downloaded to a file. The sentence selection methods are also available as a web service, thus they can be easily integrated in other applications.

Figure 3. The structure of the HitEx readability module

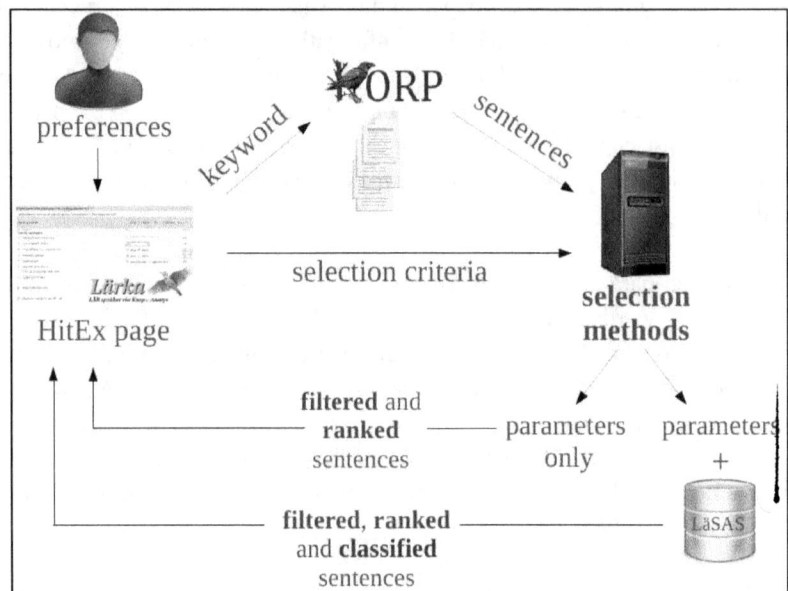

## 4. Evaluation

To verify whether the sentences selected by our systems are suitable for L2 learning purposes, we carried out an evaluation with altogether 34 participants, including L2 Swedish teachers, students and linguists (including one lexicographer). The respondents had to evaluate a list of 196 sentences chosen with our two selection approaches. Students were required to tell us whether they understood the sentences, whilst teachers and linguists needed to decide whether, according to their judgements, B1 learners would comprehend the sentences. Altogether 73% of the presented items were considered understandable. There was, however, a significant difference among the percentages of understandable examples according to the subgroup of respondents. Figure 4 below shows this discrepancy.

Teachers were considerably stricter than linguists when judging understandability, regarding 17% fewer sentences acceptable. The first subgroup of learners (adults with university-level education) understood 10% more sentences than students above 16 years with mixed educational background (*Students2*) and 34% more than 15-year-old high-school students (*Students3*). Learners understood overall 69% of the examples, 4% more than teachers predicted.

Besides the aspect of understandability, teachers and linguists were also asked to decide whether the sentences would be suitable as exercise items or as examples for vocabulary illustration. About six out of ten sentences corresponded to these criteria. For all three aspects investigated, the purely rule-based approach was slightly preferred (by 3%) to the combined method.

Figure 4. Percentage of understandable sentences per respondent subgroup

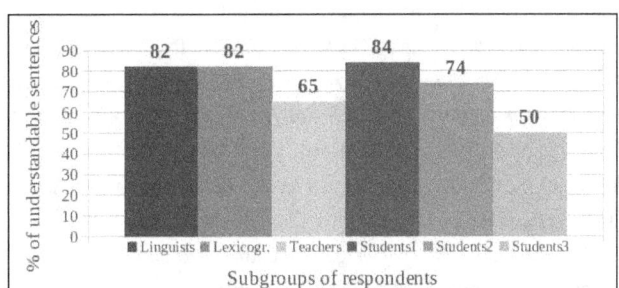

During the evaluation, qualitative data has also been collected, which consisted of respondents' comments about difficult or undesirable elements in the sentences. These included, for example, atypical word order, subordinates and the presence of infrequent idioms. Moreover, the lack of sufficient amount of context, informal spelling and a preference for illustrating the most frequent usage of a word have also been mentioned.

## 5. Conclusions

We proposed two methods for the selection of sentences from native language corpora which are suitable for L2 learning purposes. According to the results of an empirical evaluation, the approach based only on parameters was somewhat more successful than the one combining rules and ML techniques. The results are encouraging, about 70% of the sentences proved to be of an appropriate level of difficulty. About 10% less were suitable as exercise items and example sentences for vocabulary item illustration. The selection methods found their practical application in an ICALL platform in exercise generation and they are also available as a web service. In the future, we intend to extend the selection to all CEFR levels and we also plan to refine the methods further in attempt to improve the suitability of the sentences chosen.

**Acknowledgements.** We would like to thank all the linguists, teachers and students who completed our evaluation. We also wish to express our appreciation to the publishing house *Liber* for making available materials in electronic format for our study.

## References

Borin, L., Forsberg, M., & Roxendal, J. (2012). Korp – the corpus infrastructure of Språkbanken. In *Proceedings of LREC 2012. Istanbul: ELRA* (pp. 474-478). Retrieved from http://www.lrec-conf.org/proceedings/lrec2012/pdf/248_Paper.pdf

François, T., & Fairon, C. (2012). An AI readability formula for French as a foreign language. In *Proceedings of the 2012 Joint Conference on Empirical Methods in Natural Language Processing and Computational Natural Language Learning* (pp. 466-477). Retrieved from http://aclweb.org/anthology//D/D12/D12-1043.pdf

Heimann Mühlenbock, K. (2013). *I see what you mean – Assessing readability for specific target groups*. PhD Thesis. Data linguistica. University of Gothenburg.

Husák, M. (2008). *Automatic retrieval of good dictionary examples*. Bachelor Thesis. Brno. Retrieved from http://is.muni.cz/th/172590/fi_b/bachelor_thesis.pdf

Kilgarriff, A., Husák, M., McAdam, K., Rundell, M., & Rychlý, P. (2008). GDEX: Automatically finding good dictionary examples in a corpus. In *Proc. Euralex*.

Levy Scherrer, P., & Lindemalm, K. (2009). *Rivstart B1+B2 Textbok*. Stockholm: Natur & Kultur.

Segler, T. M. (2007). *Investigating the selection of example sentences for unknown target words in ICALL reading texts for L2 German*. Doctoral Thesis. University of Edinburgh: Scotland. Retrieved from https://www.era.lib.ed.ac.uk/handle/1842/1750

Sjöholm, J. (2012). *Probability as readability: a new machine learning approach to readability assessment for written Swedish*. Doctoral dissertation. Linköping University, Sweden. Retrieved from http://www.ida.liu.se/projects/webblattlast/Rapporter/lasbarhet.pdf

Vajjala, S., & Meurers, D. (2012). On improving the accuracy of readability classification using insights from second language acquisition. In *Proceedings of the 7th Workshop on Innovative Use of NLP for Building Educational Applications (BEA7)* (pp. 163-173). Retrieved from http://www.sfs.uni-tuebingen.de/~dm/papers/vajjala-meurers-12.pdf

Volodina, E., Borin, L., Loftsson, H., Arnbjörnsdóttir, B., & Leifsson, G. Ö. (2012). Waste not, want not: towards a system architecture for ICALL based on NLP component re-use. In *Proceedings of the SLTC 2012 workshop on NLP for CALL* (pp. 47-58). Retrieved from http://www.ep.liu.se/ecp/080/006/ecp12080006.pdf

Volodina, E., & Johansson Kokkinakis, S. (2012). Introducing Swedish Kelly-list, a new lexical e-resource for Swedish. In *LREC 2012, Turkey* (pp. 1040-1046). Retrieved from http://www.lrec-conf.org/proceedings/lrec2012/pdf/264_Paper.pdf

Volodina, E., Johansson, R., & Johansson Kokkinakis, S. (2012). Semi-automatic selection of best corpus examples for Swedish: initial algorithm evaluation. In *Proceedings of the SLTC 2012 workshop on NLP for CALL*, Lund. Linköping Electronic Conference Proceedings. Retrieved from http://www.ep.liu.se/ecp/080/007/ecp12080007.pdf

Volodina, E., Pijetlovic, D., Pilán, I., & Johansson Kokkinakis, S. (2013). Towards a gold standard for Swedish CEFR-based ICALL. In *Proceedings of the Second Workshop on NLP for Computer-Assisted Language Learning*. Oslo, Norway. Retrieved from http://www.ep.liu.se/ecp/086/005/ecp13086005.pdf

# Further Investigation Into the Reuse of OERs for Language Teaching

## Hélène Pulker[1]

**Abstract**. The use of Open Educational Resources (OERs) to support language teaching and learning in higher education has become standard practice in recent years. While OER initiatives have given considerable attention to teacher's engagement as well as the sharing of culture and the creation and uploading of OERs, there is little evidence about specific reuse by teachers in the classroom. This paper builds on a previous study conducted in December 2012 and presents further reflection on the reuse of OERs for teaching French beginners online. The initial enquiry was a case study based on interviews with four teachers of an online beginners' French course at a distance education institution, the Open University, UK. The results of the initial study show that even when resources meet all the criteria teachers are looking for, material adaptation is still occurring. Teachers adapt the resources to fit their own teaching styles and gain ownership of the materials, but above all, materials are adapted according to teachers' own beliefs about online teaching. This paper revisits the types of changes made to original resources and provides further observation about the changes, suggesting that whatever the modification made to the original resource is, the pedagogical intent will always be changed. This paper is of relevance to language teaching practitioners as well as course developers who are interested in reuse of language teaching materials for online language teaching.

**Keywords**: OER, reuse, re-appropriation, material adaptation, online synchronous language teaching.

---

1. The Open University, Department of Languages, Walton Hall, Milton Keynes, UK; helene.pulker@open.ac.uk

**How to cite this article**: Pulker, H. (2013). Further Investigation Into the Reuse of OERs for Language Teaching. In L. Bradley & S. Thouësny (Eds.), *20 Years of EUROCALL: Learning from the Past, Looking to the Future. Proceedings of the 2013 EUROCALL Conference, Évora, Portugal* (pp. 226-230). Dublin/Voillans: © Research-publishing.net.

## 1. Introduction

Teachers play a crucial role in computing-assisted language learning, making decisions that can have significant impact on students' learning experience. In the context of synchronous online language teaching, those decisions include creating materials from scratch, selecting ready-made OERs available through repositories for example, or adapting them to fit specific teaching objectives or specific contexts. Several OER projects such as MERLOT, JORUM, the LORO project at the Open University, the Humbox, the Community Café and the FAVOR projects at the University of Southampton suggest that using online content and resources is becoming increasingly normalised in language teaching. Research and scholarship initiatives related to these OER projects for language teaching (Comas-Quinn, Beaven, Pleines, Pulker, & de los Arcos, 2011; Comas-Quinn, Wild, & Carter, 2013) have given considerable attention to factors contributing to the use of OERs and teachers' engagement with Open Educational Resources and Open Educational Practices. Research reports and findings suggest that there is little need to convince academics of the value of reuse. However, there has been little focus on how the resources are specifically used or repurposed in the virtual classroom.

The report of the initial small-scale study (Pulker & Calvi, 2013), on which this paper is based, was an attempt to provide evidence of teachers' reuse and adaptation of online resources. The resources under investigation were designed broadly in line with communicative and task-based pedagogies, including stimuli for class use and methodological resources, and were also broadly based on the affordances of an online resource described by McGreal (2004). They are:

- accessible from the institutional repository LORO;

- written to be adapted and re-used in any context;

- based on specific objectives of a French beginners course (A1-A2 CEFR);

- free of copyright.

The investigation into the types of changes was based on theories on materials adaptation. Madsen and Bowen (1978, cited in Tomlinson, 2012) point out that good teachers always adapt the materials they are using in order to achieve the optimal congruence between materials, methodology, learners, objectives, the target language, and the teacher's personality and teaching style. Tomlinson (2011) argues that while evaluating and adapting materials, teachers are consciously or unconsciously guided by a set of criteria based on their own beliefs about teaching and learning. McGrath (2002) specifically studied adaptation and suggests that there are two different forms of it:

- **addition**. Teachers will add to the content of a resource; they will provide additional examples, explanations, exercises to do more of the same or to further exploit the materials;

- **change**. Teachers will modify the resource; they will replace some of its content or reuse the resource in a different way.

The initial study's aim was to identify the most common types of adaptation made to resources. This paper focuses more closely on adaptation as change, when the changes made to a resource impact on its original pedagogical intent.

## 2. Method

The initial survey was conducted with four teachers who volunteered to take part in semi-structured interviews online. During the interviews, participants were asked to explain the reasons for choosing a particular resource and to outline their approach to teaching online at beginners' level. In the second part of the interview, participants provided and commented upon a few examples of resources that they had used and adapted. The semi-structured interviews revealed the complexities of explaining a teaching approach and allowed the researchers to clarify what teachers understood by the term 'communicative approach'.

## 3. Discussion

During the interviews, the four teachers said that they seek to adopt a communicative approach in their interactive online tutorials, although one explained that she devotes more tutorial time to grammar and to what she calls the 'theoretical aspects of the language' than to communicative activities. Generally, the examples provided by the teachers confirmed this. The cases of adaptations provided by each teacher demonstrate that their beliefs about teaching French beginners online are reflected in the changes they make when they re-appropriate the original resources. Although the four teachers were all in agreement that the resources created by course developers suited their teaching approach and they indicated that the objective, methods and content of activities proposed were suitable, the examples of adaptation they provided in the interviews demonstrate that all teachers changed the pedagogical intent of the original resource. For instance, Teacher 1 preferred to extend the activities suggested to cover controlled and freer practice with the same resource rather than using the sequence of resources available to progress from controlled to freer practice. Teacher 2 also preferred to modify the OERs used. He was keen to give additional prompts to students to allow for more student autonomy and more oral exchanges proposing to do more practice with a same resource rather than using the full sequence. Here again, the change is not to the resource itself but what he did with it. Teacher 3 tended to use the original resource content but adapted the activities to do more grammar and to develop language acquisition further. As for Teacher 4, she wanted to encourage 'genuine' communicative tasks so sometimes designed her own screens to elicit vocabulary or structures learned previously, rather than giving the prompts to students automatically.

The initial study provided evidence of repurposing OERs for language teaching. However, the examples demonstrate that the change occurs mostly in the learning design and not so much in the content of the resources. The four teachers interviewed were extremely clear and conscious about their teaching approach but their beliefs and understanding of communicative language teaching varied considerably as shown by the examples and the reasons evoked for the changes made. It therefore seems that adaptation does not only occur to suit teaching styles and methods but to suit those strong beliefs. This paper shows that material appropriation and adaptation vary quite considerably according to how teachers interpret communicative approach for online teaching. It also shows that, no matter what the teachers adapt in the resources, they will always change their pedagogical approach. This further reflection on the types of changes also indicates that the term 'reuse' can have different meanings.

## 4. Conclusions

The initial study presented similar findings to the research currently done in the field of use and reuse of OERs in language teaching (Beaven, 2013; Borthwick & Dickens, 2012) which is that teachers modify the resources to suit their teaching style and what is considered as a change is not universally clear. Sometimes changing the colour of a resource, or adding a small prompt is not seen as a major change, when in fact, it is. This paper adds a dimension to findings as it seeks to demonstrate that re-appropriation of materials does not only occur to suit teaching styles but has deeper roots as it seeks to suit strong beliefs and perceptions that teachers have of what constitutes a 'good' online session, and this is demonstrated by the fact that the pedagogical approach for activities based on the resource will always be changed. Most teachers want to adapt teaching materials to their styles and beliefs as to what is effective and OERs by definition allow repurposing and adaptation in a way that many other 'ready-made' materials do not. Further research into the frequent types of changes that are made to OERs for language teaching is needed to study the relationship between teachers' beliefs and their use and reuse of OERs more closely and the impact this may have on language learning.

## References

Beaven, T. (2013). Use and reuse of OER: Professional conversations with language teachers. *Journal of e-Learning and Knowledge Society (JeLKS)*, 9(1), 59-71. Retrieved from http://www.je-lks.org/ojs/index.php/Je-LKS_EN/article/view/802/792

Borthwick, K., & Dickens, A. (2012). One size doesn't fit all: Contrasting approaches to building communities of OER users amongst the language teaching community. In L. Bradley & S. Thouësny (Eds.), *CALL: Using, Learning, Knowing, EUROCALL Conference, Gothenburg, Sweden, 22-25 August 2012, Proceedings* (pp. 26-31). Dublin: Research-publishing.net. Retrieved from http://research-publishing.net/publications/2012-eurocall-proceedings/

Comas-Quinn, A., Beaven, T., Pleines, C., Pulker, H., & de los Arcos, B. (2011). Languages Open Resources Online (LORO): Fostering a culture of collaboration and sharing. *The EuroCALL Review, 18*(March). Retrieved from http://www.eurocall-languages.org/review/18/#loro

Comas-Quinn, A., Wild, J., & Carter, J. (2013). Leveraging passion for open practice. In *OER13, Creating a Virtuous Circle, 26-27 March 2013, Nottingham, UK*. Retrieved from http://oro.open.ac.uk/37551/2/432978F3.pdf

Madsen, H. S., & Bowen, J. D. (1978). *Adaptation in Language Teaching*. Rowley, MA: Newbury House.

McGrath, I. (2002). *Materials Evaluation and Design for Language Teaching*. Edinburgh: Edinburgh University Press.

McGreal, R. (Ed.). (2004). *Online education using learning objects (Open and Flexible Learning Series)*. London: RoutledgeFalmer.

Pulker, H., & Calvi, A. (2013). The evaluation and re-use of Open Educational Resources in language teaching – a case study. In *OER13, Creating a Virtuous Circle, 26-27 March 2013, Nottingham, UK*. Retrieved from http://oro.open.ac.uk/38056/2/9FAE2C09.pdf

Tomlinson, B. (2011). *Developing materials for language teaching*. London: Continuum.

Tomlinson, B. (2012). Materials development for language learning and teaching. *Language Teaching, 45*(2), 143-179. doi: 10.1017/S0261444811000528

# Categorization of Digital Games in English Language Learning Studies: Introducing the SSI Model

## Pia Sundqvist[1]

**Abstract.** The main aim of the present paper is to introduce a model for digital game categorization suitable for use in English language learning studies: the Scale of Social Interaction (SSI) Model (original idea published as Sundqvist, 2013). The SSI Model proposes a classification of commercial off-the-shelf (COTS) digital games into three categories: singleplayer (the smallest scale), multiplayer, and massively multiplayer online games (MMOs, the largest scale). The potential for naturalistic learning (Benson, 2011) of English is hypothesized to be greater the larger the scale of in-game social interaction. A secondary aim is to present preliminary findings regarding the validation of the SSI Model based on data collected from Swedish learners (9th grade) in an ongoing 3-year study about the relation between out-of-school digital gameplay and vocabulary acquisition. The results reveal, for example, that it is more common that learners who play games frequently play multiplayer games and/or MMOs than singleplayer games. Moreover, the results provide partial evidence of the validity of the SSI Model in that the learners who are categorized as playing multiplayer games and MMOs score higher on two vocabulary tests than the learners categorized as playing singleplayer games.

**Keywords**: CALL, computer games, digital games, COTS, MMO, vocabulary acquisition, naturalistic learning, ESL, EFL, social interaction, self-assessment.

## 1. Introduction

Over the years, a number of ways of categorizing digital games have been suggested. Game categorization is necessary for researchers who are interested

---

1. Karlstad University, Faculty of Arts and Social Sciences, Karlstad, Sweden; pia.sundqvist@kau.se

**How to cite this article**: Sundqvist, P. (2013). Categorization of Digital Games in English Language Learning Studies: Introducing the SSI Model. In L. Bradley & S. Thouësny (Eds.), *20 Years of EUROCALL: Learning from the Past, Looking to the Future. Proceedings of the 2013 EUROCALL Conference, Évora, Portugal* (pp. 231-237). Dublin/Voillans: © Research-publishing.net.

in exploring the relations between digital gameplay and language learning. However, within the gaming industry, there is little consensus about how to classify games (Apperley, 2006; Dickey, 2006; Harteveld & Bekebrede, 2011).

Likewise, I have found it difficult to find an approach for categorization within the broad field of second language acquisition, even though some models have been proposed (e.g. deHaan, 2005; Greenberg, Sherry, Lachlan, Lucas, & Holmstrom, 2010; Kinzie & Joseph, 2008). Kinzie and Joseph (2008), for instance, bring forward six activity modes (active, explorative, problem-solving, strategic, social, and creative) to describe digital gameplay. In all these, a game such as *World of Warcraft* ends up being classified into several modes/genres. This makes analytical procedures complex, especially if a quantitative method is adopted.

In the SSI Model, a game taxonomy that springs from one single mode/axis is used, namely the scale of the social interaction in the game, which is directly linked to the number of players simultaneously involved in playing the game (for a detailed description, see Sundqvist, 2013). The present paper aims to introduce the SSI Model to CALL researchers and to present some preliminary findings regarding its validation.

## 2. Method

### 2.1. Participants and materials

This article is based on data collected during the first year of an ongoing 3-year study (2011–2014) about the relation between extramural English (Sundqvist, 2009, 2011) and vocabulary acquisition among Swedish 15- and 16-year-olds ($N = 280$). More specifically, the focus is on one extramural/out-of-school activity: digital gameplay.

Several sets of data are collected each school year, including a questionnaire, two vocabulary tests (shortened versions of the Productive Levels Test and the Vocabulary Levels Test, Laufer & Nation, 1999; Nation, 2001), and the school leaving certificate. The questionnaire provides information about the participants' first language, computer habits in English (e.g. digital gameplay activity: time played and types of games played), speaking anxiety, beliefs about language learning, and self-assessed English ability. The Productive Levels Test (PLT) is taken in the fall semester and the Vocabulary Levels Test (VLT) in the spring. For the present paper, questionnaire data about digital gaming habits are used along with data from the vocabulary tests.

## 2.2. Design

The sample was divided into five groups depending on their responses to a questionnaire item that asked about how frequently the learners played digital games and also about example(s) of game title(s). Brief group descriptions are provided in Table 1. In Table 2, the distribution of learners in groups 2–5 are cross-tabulated with the frequency of gameplay ($\chi^2$ = 344.538, $df$ = 12, $p$ = .000, $\varphi_c$ = .650; see Analytic procedure). For validation of the SSI Model, the non-gamers in group 1 are irrelevant and, therefore, excluded.

Table 1. Five groups based on frequency of gameplay and provision of game title(s)

| Group | N | % |
|---|---|---|
| 1. Non-gamers | 108 | 38.6 |
| 2. Gamers who do not provide any game title(s) | 22 | 7.9 |
| 3. Gamers who provide only singleplayer game title(s) | 31 | 11.1 |
| 4. Gamers who provide multiplayer game title(s) and possibly also singleplayer game title(s), but no massively multiplayer game title(s) | 82 | 29.3 |
| 5. Gamers who provide massively multiplayer game title(s) and possibly also singleplayer and multiplayer game title(s) | 29 | 10.4 |
| Missing | 8 | 2.9 |
| **Total** | **280** | **100** |

Table 2. Distribution of learners across groups 1–5 compared with frequency of gameplay (hours per week)*

| Frequency of digital gameplay | Group 1 "Non-gamers" | Group 2 "No title given" | Group 3 "Singleplayer" | Group 4 "Multiplayer" | Group 5 "Massively multiplayer" | Total |
|---|---|---|---|---|---|---|
| 0 hrs/w | 108 | 1 | 0 | 1 | 0 | 110 |
| < 3 hrs/w | 0 | 10 | 19 | 14 | 3 | 46 |
| 3–9 hrs/w | 0 | 10 | 11 | 23 | 8 | 52 |
| > 9 hrs/w | 0 | 1 | 1 | 44 | 18 | 64 |
| Total | 108 | 22 | 31 | 82 | 29 | 272 |

*Three cells (15.0%) have expected count less than 5.

## 2.3. Analytic procedure

To compute significance and effect sizes for tests with numeric variables, one-way analysis of variance (ANOVA) together with classical eta squared ($\eta^2$) was used. In line with Cohen's (1988) convention for $r^2$, $\eta^2$ = .01 is a small effect size, $\eta^2$ = .06 is medium, and $\eta^2$ = .14 is large (Dörnyei, 2007). Gabriel's post-hoc test was used to examine which groups differed from which within the general between-groups differences. Due to the uneven distribution of learners across the groups, Gabriel's test was preferred over, for example, S-N-K. To compute significance and effect sizes for tests with nominal variables, Pearson's chi-squared ($\chi^2$) and Cramér's (1946) V ($\varphi_c$) were used. In line with Cohen's (1988) convention for $d$ which is also often used for Cramér's V, $\varphi_c = .2$ is a small effect size, $\varphi_c = .5$ is medium, and $\varphi_c = .8$ is large (Aron, Aron, & Coups, 2005).

## 3. Results

Internal consistency measures showed that the PLT and VLT were reliable ($r = .778$, $p = .000$; Cronbach's $\alpha = .777$). Results for both tests are shown in Table 3. Group 4 scored the highest on the PLT, followed by Group 5, 3, and 1. Analysis of variance indicated that there was no significant difference of mean scores among the groups ($F(3, 155) = 1.59$, $p = .193$). For the VLT, again Group 4 scored the highest, and the other groups followed as for the PLT. ANOVA indicated that there was a significant difference of mean scores among the four groups for the VLT ($F(3, 147) = 3.61$, $p = .015$). Gabriel's post-hoc test showed that the score for Group 2 was different from Group 4 ($p = .005$), but that the remaining group comparisons were indistinguishable from one another. Finally, effect sizes were small for the PLT, a test of productive vocabulary size ($\eta^2 = .030$), and medium for the VLT, a test of receptive vocabulary size ($\eta^2 = .069$).

Although the scores for the non-gamers (Group 1) are irrelevant for the validation of the SSI Model, they are relevant from the perspective of the relation between digital gameplay and vocabulary acquisition and, therefore, provided in Table 4.

Table 3. PLT and VLT scores for groups 2–5

|  |  | Group 2 "No title given" | Group 3 "Singleplayer" | Group 4 "Multiplayer" | Group 5 "Massively multiplayer" | Significance Effect size |
|---|---|---|---|---|---|---|
| PLT (max: 45) | | | | | | |
| | mean | 14.90 | 18.65 | 20.19 | 18.79 | |
| | SD | 9.00 | 10.00 | 10.51 | 8.50 | $p = .193$ |
| | n | 21 | 31 | 79 | 28 | $\eta^2 = .030$ |
| VLT (max: 90) | | | | | | |
| | mean | 48.86 | 59.42 | 63.64 | 61.96 | |
| | SD | 18.67 | 18.50 | 18.50 | 19.86 | $p = .015$ |
| | n | 22 | 31 | 75 | 23 | $\eta^2 = .069$ |

Table 4. Scores for Group 1 on the vocabulary tests

|  | PLT (max: 45) | VLT (max: 90) |
|---|---|---|
| mean | 16.26 | 55.99 |
| SD | 9.00 | 17.71 |
| $n$ | 105 | 102 |

## 4. Discussion

Based on sociocultural theory (Vygotsky, 1978), the SSI Model proposes a classification of commercial off-the-shelf digital games into three categories: singleplayer, multiplayer, and massively multiplayer online games. As argued in Sundqvist (2013), the potential for naturalistic learning (Benson, 2011) of English is hypothesized to be greater the larger the scale of the in-game social interaction. In other words, the larger the scale of social interaction offered by particular games, the higher the chances of encountering co-players of different nationalities, making the need for a shared language (i.e. English) for in-game interactions obvious. Subsequently, the more authentic English interactions there are, the higher the chances for naturalistic language learning to occur. The scale of social interaction is viewed as a continuum, from small scale (singleplayer games) to large scale (MMOs). From the perspective of language learning, the SSI Model suggests that MMOs are more beneficial than multiplayer games which, in turn, are more beneficial than singleplayer games.

The results reveal that it is more common that learners who play games frequently play multiplayer games and/or MMOs. Further, the results provide partial evidence of the validity of the SSI Model in that the learners categorized into Groups 4 and 5 score higher than Groups 3 and 2.

## 5. Concluding remarks

This study provides evidence for partial validation of the SSI Model. It was not possible to verify that learners categorized as playing MMOs (Group 5) score significantly higher than learners categorized as playing multiplayer games (Group 4) but, on the other hand, as hypothesized, learners categorized as playing singleplayer games (Group 3) nevertheless scored lower than both Groups 4 and 5, and the lowest scores were found among learners who failed to provide any game titles (Group 2). Upon completion of the 3-year study, which should include a sample of around 1,000 learners, final validation of the SSI Model can be made.

**Acknowledgements.** An early version of the SSI Model has been published as Sundqvist (2013). I would like to thank the Center for Language and Literature in Education, Karlstad University, for funding the last two years of the project.

# References

Apperley, T. H. (2006). Genre and game studies: Toward a critical approach to video game genres. *Simulation & Gaming, 37*(1), 6-23. doi:10.1177/1046878105282278

Aron, A., Aron, E. N., & Coups, E. J. (2005). *Statistics for the behavioral and social sciences: A brief course* (3rd ed.). London: Prentice Hall International.

Benson, P. (2011). *Teaching and researching autonomy* (2nd ed.). Harlow: Pearson Education.

Cohen, J. (1988). *Statistical power analysis for the behavioral sciences* (2nd ed.). New Jersey: Lawrence Erlbaum.

Cramér, H. (1946). *Mathematical methods of statistics*. Princeton: Princeton University Press.

deHaan, J. (2005). Learning language through video games: A theoretical framework, an evaluation of game genres and questions for future research. In S. P. Schaffer & M. L. Price (Eds.), *Interactive convergence: critical issues in multimedia* (pp. 229-239). Oxford: Interdisciplinary Press.

Dickey, M. D. (2006). Game design narrative for learning: Appropriating adventure game design narrative devices and techniques for the design of interactive learning environments. *Educational Technology Research & Development, 54*(3), 245-263. doi: 10.1007/s11423-006-8806-y

Dörnyei, Z. (2007). *Research methods in applied linguistics*. Oxford: Oxford University Press.

Greenberg, B. S., Sherry, J., Lachlan, K., Lucas, K., & Holmstrom, A. (2010). Orientations to video games among gender and age groups. *Simulation & Gaming, 41*(2), 238-259. doi: 10.1177/1046878108319930

Harteveld, C., & Bekebrede, G. (2011). Learning in single- versus multiplayer games: The more the merrier? *Simulation & Gaming, 42*(1), 43-63. doi: 10.1177/1046878110378706

Kinzie, M. B., & Joseph, D. R. D. (2008). Gender differences in game activity preferences of middle school children: implications for educational game design. *Educational Technology Research and Development, 56*(5/6), 643-663. doi: 10.1007/s11423-007-9076-z

Laufer, B., & Nation, P. (1999). A vocabulary-size test of controlled productive ability. *Language Testing, 16*(1), 33-51. doi: 10.1177/026553229901600103

Nation, P. (2001). *Learning vocabulary in another language*. Cambridge: Cambridge University Press.

Sundqvist, P. (2009). *Extramural English matters: Out-of-school English and its impact on Swedish ninth graders' oral proficiency and vocabulary*. PhD, Karlstad University, Karlstad.

Sundqvist, P. (2011). A possible path to progress: Out-of-school English language learners in Sweden. In P. Benson & H. Reinders (Eds.), *Beyond the language classroom* (pp. 106-118). Basingstoke: Palgrave Macmillan.

Sundqvist, P. (2013). The SSI Model: Categorization of digital games in EFL studies. *European Journal of Applied Linguistics and TEFL, 1*(3), **89-104**.

Vygotsky, L. S. (1978). *Mind in society: The development of higher psychological processes.* Cole, M., John-Steiner, V., Scribner, S., & Souberman, E. (Eds.). Cambridge, MA: Harvard University Press.

# Use of Discussion Board and PaperShow in Translation Class

## Mika Takewa[1]

**Abstract**. This report presents how the learning technologies Discussion Board and PaperShow are incorporated into postgraduate translation modules by means of observing their impact on students' learning. Initially and mainly for administrative reasons as well as being encouraged to make use of the university's virtual learning environment (VLE), I set up discussion forums to collect students' translation work. It soon became clear that the forums had the potential to facilitate student-centred learning and increase students' responsibility toward learning. In this paper, the use of Discussion Board on the VLE, which forms the foundation of in-class discussion and student participation, is described. Then, students' learning is evaluated from an 'active learning' aspect. It can be said that Discussion Board enhances students' active learning and promotes quality learning experiences for them. PaperShow, which is used in class to support a student who has a hearing disability, is also discussed. PaperShow is useful for all who wish to revise important points raised in class, which are saved and included in the presentations made available online. Both Discussion Board and PaperShow proved to be more pedagogically useful than initially anticipated. The paper concludes with suggestions for possible areas of language learning in which these pieces of technology could be applicable.

**Keywords**: translation, active learning, student-centred learning, Discussion Board, PaperShow.

## 1. Introduction

This paper discusses students' 'active learning' in the two technologies Discussion Board and PaperShow. The background to this study is the notion that the number of students affects the tutor as to how they prepare for a class. When I started teaching

---

1. University of Leeds, United Kingdom; M.Takewa@leeds.ac.uk

**How to cite this article**: Takewa, M. (2013). Use of Discussion Board and PaperShow in Translation Class. In L. Bradley & S. Thouësny (Eds.), *20 Years of EUROCALL: Learning from the Past, Looking to the Future*. Proceedings of the 2013 EUROCALL Conference, Évora, Portugal (pp. 238-243). Dublin/Voillans: © Research-publishing.net.

specialised English-Japanese (E-J) translation, groups were small and collecting students' work was easy. Since then, the class became larger and Discussion Board on the VLE has been used to collect students' work. The initial motivations were mainly administrative reasons. However, the potential it had to ensure student-centred learning and increase students' responsibility for learning soon became clear.

This paper first describes the use of Discussion Board on the VLE which forms the foundation of in-class discussion and student participation in it. Then, students' learning is evaluated from the point of 'active learning' suggested by Fink (2003). Discussion Board can be said to enhance students' active learning and promote quality learning experiences for them. A shorter description of PaperShow, another technology used in class to support a student who has a hearing disability follows. PaperShow is useful to clarify the important points in class, which are then saved and uploaded online for students to go back and recall discussions.

The paper concludes with suggesting other possible areas of language learning where these pieces of technology could be applicable.

## 2. Class structure of specialised translation modules

Specialised translation modules are offered as part of taught postgraduate programmes at the Centre for Translation Studies at the University of Leeds. These modules are for students to apply the theories and methods they learnt in other modules. One of the learning outcomes of specialised English-Japanese (E-J) translation is for the students to become able to translate texts of a variety of fields written in English into Japanese confidently, which is a subject-specific outcome and closely related to the students' future career.

There is one specialised E-J translation in semester one and another in semester two. They deal with different genres and most students take both. These modules are strongly vocational, and therefore, they are experiential. Students are expected to produce a translation every week. The cycle of one session starts with the students receiving a source text (ST) a week before its translations are discussed in class. Students translate it and post their work on Discussion Board. They then read the translations produced by classmates and leave comments.

The class is for two hours and it begins with a short presentation about the ST of the week by a student in semester one and about a particular issue in translation by the tutor in semester two, and then a discussion follows. Students are encouraged to take part in the discussion; bringing in the comments they received online, questions that remain unsolved, etc. Following the discussion in each session, students are encouraged to edit their translations to their satisfaction in their own time.

## 3. Discussion Board in specialised English-Japanese translation modules

### 3.1. Introducing Discussion Board into the modules

Technology has changed several aspects of the translation process such as communication with clients and colleagues, the speed and amount of information that can be retrieved, and the way texts are created and handled (Gil & Pym, 2006). Translators are expected to be capable of using technology, especially profession-specific Information Technology (IT) tools such as translation memory tools. However, trainees have different levels of experience with computer applications (Knops, 2008). Recently, VLE has been establishing itself as an indispensable learning environment. Although initial motivations to incorporate Discussion Board to the specialised E-J translation modules were administrative reasons, extending the use of the VLE and familiarising students to useful functions available on it were also considered. It is suggested that adding discussion forums does not require a change in the curriculum or focus of the class (Guzdial & Turns, 2000) and they are easy to integrate in existing learning circumstances.

Burston (2006) states that careful examination is needed before incorporating IT into a course because of how it contributes to the realisation of pedagogical aims as well as to how it fits into the academic environment. JISC InfoNet (2006) lists some of the advantages and disadvantages of computer-mediated conferencing, which is similar to Discussion Board.

**Advantages**

- Time and place independence.
- Time lapse between messages allows for reflection.
- Questions can be asked without waiting for a turn.
- Many-to-many interaction may enhance peer learning.

**Disadvantages**

- Paralinguistic cues where speakers' intentions are not available.

- The normal repair strategies of face-to-face communication are not available and misunderstandings may be harder to overcome.

As well as being aware of the disadvantages listed above, "recognis[ing] differences in learning styles among students and facilitat[ing] learning across various learning styles" is important (Levy, 2006, p. 22). Students of specialised E-J translation are dominantly Japanese but not exclusively. Students' first language, background, experience in general and translation vary. Japanese students tend to be quiet and passive in class. Discussion Board is expected to facilitate different types of students with their active and autonomous learning.

### 3.2. Observation of student participation and learning

Specialised translation modules are experiential. Source texts as primary resources are provided by the tutor but it is the students who assemble and provide their own learning materials to be used in class. Without the students' contribution at this stage, classroom discussion will not function. This makes the modules highly student-centred. Students are responsible for their own learning as well as their classmates'.

Students are expected to read all the translations posted online and are encouraged to leave comments on at least one translation before class. It is useful for them to give and receive feedback to/from peers. Their feedback is appropriate in general. They do not hold lengthy discussions online and their comments include suggestions to raise something as an issue or ask questions on a specific subject in class. They create a link between preparation and in-class discussion. Sometimes there are fewer comments than in the other weeks. It could be lack of time, being afraid to appear criticising, or not used to this type of learning. Over time, however, they realise that receiving comments on their own work has positive effects on them and commenting on others' is the same. They feel less threatened to voice their opinions and a positive group dynamic starts to establish.

Discussion Board facilitates students' active learning, which Fink (2003) explains consists of four types of learning. The four aspects, as illustrated in Figure 1, exist in the learning process of specialised translation. Students translate a text (doing), read classmates' translations (observing), reflect their own translation after reading others' (dialogue with self), and take part in discussion in class (dialogue with others). Amongst these, Discussion Board more strongly promoted 'observing' and 'dialogue with self' than before it was introduced. Fry, Ketteridge, and Marshall (2003) confirm that "deliberate and conscious reflections are a requirement for effective experiential learning to take place" (p. 136). Based on these two aspects mentioned above, which are 'observing' and 'dialogue with self', 'dialogue with others' takes place, reinforcing the reflections.

Figure 1. Aspects of active learning (adapted from Fink, 2003)

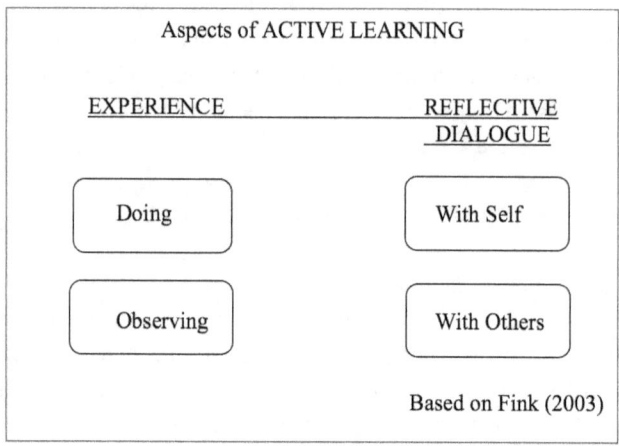

Dengler (2008) claims that citing comments students have made online allows the instructor to increase the voice of the quieter individuals, which leads them to feel confident in contributing in classes. This happens in specialised translation class. It can be said that the use of Discussion Board facilitates classroom learning by reinforcing students' independent study.

Students' feedback indicates the majority of them express gratitude with their learning experiences, both in and outside class.

## 4. PaperShow

PaperShow is similar to overhead projectors but connected to the computer. Slides from PowerPoint Presentations (PPP) that are printed on the PaperShow printing paper are linked to the projected screen and the comments written on the PaperShow printing paper using the PaperShow pen appear on the screen as they are written. This is useful to make sure that a student with a hearing difficulty keeps up with the class alongside the help of a note-taker in class. PaperShow has a function to save PPPs with the added comments included. Thus, important points of discussion that appeared in class can be recorded and made available on the VLE. PaperShow was originally meant for the student with a hearing impairment. However, it proved to be useful for others as well. Writing while talking reduces speed but ensures that everyone can reflect on what is important.

## 5. Conclusions

Discussion Board proved to be more useful pedagogically than initially anticipated. It may be useful for language learning such as reading or grammar exercises. PaperShow also has potential to be valuable but the balance must be measured between the time spent on writing and the importance of the information being written. PaperShow may be suitable for lower level composition as well as grammar exercises.

**Acknowledgements.** I would like to thank Dragos Ciobanu, Caroline Rose, Serge Sharoff and Martin Thomas for their continuous support.

## References

Burston, J. (2006). Working towards effective assessment of CALL. In R. P. Donaldson & M. A. Haggstrom (Eds.), *Changing Language Education through CALL* (pp. 249-270). Oxon: Routledge.

Dengler, M. (2008). Classroom active learning complemented by an online discussion forum to teach sustainability. *Journal of Geography in Higher Education, 32*(3), 481-494. doi: 10.1080/03098260701514108

Fink, L. D. (2003). *A self-directed guide to designing courses for significant learning.* Retrieved from http://trc.virginia.edu/Workshops/2004/Fink_Designing_Courses_2004.pdf

Fry, H., Ketteridge, S., & Marshall, S. (2003). *A handbook for teaching & learning in higher education, enhancing academic practice.* London and New York: Routledge.

Gil, J. R. B., & Pym, A. (2006). Technology and translation (a pedagogical overview). In A. Pym, A. Perekrestenko, & B. Starink (Eds.), *Translation Technology and its Teaching (with much mention of localization).* Retrieved from isg.urv.es/library/papers/isgbook.pdf

Guzdial, M., & Turns, J. (2000). Effective discussion through a computer-mediated anchored forum. *Journal of the Learning Sciences, 9*(4), 437-469. doi: 10.1207/S15327809JLS0904_3

JISC InfoNet. (2006). *Effective use of VLEs: Computer-mediated conferencing (applied infokit).* Retrieved from http://www.jiscinfonet.ac.uk

Knops, U. (2008). Resource management for future translators and translation project management. In R. Dimitriu & K-H. Freigang (Eds.), *Translation Technology in Translation Classes* (pp. 184-192). Romania: Institutul European.

Levy, M. (2006). Effective use of CALL technologies: Finding the right balance. In R. P. Donaldson & M. A. Haggstrom (Eds.), *Changing Language Education through CALL* (pp. 1-18). Oxon: Routledge.

# Designing Pro-telecollaboration Teacher Training: Some Insights Based on the OCEAN Personality Measures

## Anna Turula[1]

**Abstract.** With telecollaboration gaining in popularity, we obtain more insight into how representatives of different cultures interact and co-work online. We learn that while some exchanges may be smooth, others give raise to problems that need some remedial measures. In my paper, I argue that alongside implicit pedagogy, such measures may take on the form of explicit, focused instruction, involving various forms of raising awareness. Departing from this, I present the results of action research into such a pro-telecollaboration course taught online to 11 novice teachers/teacher trainees in the years 2012-2013. I specifically analyse the participants' attitudes to collaboration as well as their affiliation levels, both in relation to personality measures of the course participants obtained by means of Costa and McCrae's (1992) NEO Five-Factor Inventory (NEO-FFI).

Keywords: telecollaboration, personality, attitudes, teamwork, affiliation.

## 1. Introduction

Potential advantages of telecollaboration can be traced in its very definition. Such intercultural exchanges involve "the application of online communication tools to bring together classes of language learners in geographically distant locations to develop their foreign language skills and intercultural competence through collaborative tasks and project work" during which students are "challenged to reflect on their own culture or their stereotypical views of the target culture" (O'Dowd, 2011, pp. 342-344). Consequently, telecollaboration results in: (i)

---

1. University of Social Sciences, Warsaw, Poland; anna.turula@gmail.com

**How to cite this article**: Turula, A. (2013). Designing Pro-telecollaboration Teacher Training: Some Insights Based on the OCEAN Personality Measures. In L. Bradley & S. Thouësny (Eds.), *20 Years of EUROCALL: Learning from the Past, Looking to the Future. Proceedings of the 2013 EUROCALL Conference, Évora, Portugal* (pp. 244-249). Dublin/Voillans: © Research-publishing.net.

experiential learning of target language and culture; (ii) different aspects of computer literacy based on the knowledge of a wide variety of CMC tools; and (iii) challenging students to step out of the comfort zones of their long-held beliefs in regard to their own and others' cultures.

However, especially in the face of cultural differences between partnering groups, pedagogical mediation is indispensable to actually bring out the advantages of telecollaboration. It most popularly takes the form of in-class meetings in which students reflect on their experience and problems are dealt with as they appear in the course of the exchange. The legitimacy of such a pedagogical approach is unquestionable: experiential – or inductive – education is a classic learning mode of proven effectiveness. However, sometimes prevention may be better than medication; some individual differences require a more traditional, teacher-fronted type of instruction. This is why, on occasion, *a posteriori* pedagogy may need to give way to its deductive *a priori* counterpart.

## 2. Method

### 2.1. Collaboractive Online – introduction to action research

In order to verify the idea of a deductive, pro-telecollaboration training, a course including this type of instruction was designed and implemented online (November 2012 – April 2013). Called *Collaboractive* or *Language as a Social Semiotic* (henceforth *Collaboractive Online*), the course consisted of a series of activities in which: (i) language and culture awareness were raised and (ii) the dialogic nature of collaboration was emphasised, with special regard to labour division, modes of cooperation and the language of feedback. Task-based and experiential, the course included three online lectures in which problems pertaining to areas (i) and (ii) above were explicitly addressed.

During the course a number of aspects of collaboration were investigated in the action-research mode. In this article I focus on attitudes to teamwork and affiliation. Both will be analysed in relation to the course participants' personality profiles.

*2.1.1. Research sample*

The research sample consisted of the 11 participants of *Collaboractive Online*: graduates (7) or ongoing students (4) of the English Studies programmes at various universities at home (Poland; 9) and abroad (UK; 1 - Luxembourg; 1). The group included 8 women and 3 men, average age was 26.5 ($SD = 2.94$).

*2.1.2. Research tools and procedures*

In the case of the attitudes study[2], the tool was a self-reflection diary. In the course of data elaboration, the contents of each participant's diary were subject to quantitative discourse analysis as regards utterances indicative of deference (group reference and focus) and demeanor (self-reference and focus). The percentage rates of both types of utterances were calculated for each participant.

When it comes to the affiliation study, the main tool was a 0-3 affiliation scale[3] applied three times: at the beginning, after a month, and at the end of the course. Before the analysis, the numerical results of each testee were translated into stens (standardised testing out of ten) and divided into two categories; *how-I-see-others* and *how-others-see-me*.

The tool used in both of the studies was a 60-item NEO FFI personality inventory (Costa & McCrae, 1992). The results of both studies were correlated with the participants' sten scores on this inventory.

*2.1.3. Research data*

When it comes to the results of the attitudes study, they show a fairly noteworthy correlation in the following areas: deference and extravertism ($p = 0.43$), deference and conscientiousness ($p = 0.42$), demeanor and neuroticism ($p = 0.46$), as well as demeanor and openness ($p = 0.47$).

In the affiliation study, in turn, the correlation differs based on the time of measurement and category. The strongest positive correlation between personality traits and *how-I-see-others* can be noted at the beginning for openness ($p = 0.47$); a tendency that seems to reverse later in the course. There are also positive but weaker course-onset correlations of the self-perceived affiliation with extravertism and conscientiousness ($p$'s bordering on 0.33 and 0.34, respectively). When it comes to *how-others-see-me*, it is strongly related to the individual's conscientiousness ($p = 0.7$), and negatively to neuroticism

---

2. For a detailed report of this study, see Turula (2013); available at http://www.tewtjournal.org/VOL%2013/ISSUE%202/ARTICLE1.pdf

3. The scale corresponds to Brown's (2001) affiliation levels of acquaintance-membership-camaraderie.

($p = -0.34$). Later in the course, *others* affiliate with extraverts ($p = 0.55$) and avoid those characterised by openness ($p = -0.38$).

## 3. Discussion

The data serve as basis to a number of observations regarding the relationship between personality types and the two important aspects of collaboration examined here: attitudes to teamwork and levels of affiliation.

As regards the attitudes:

- the high correlation between deference and extravertism as well as neuroticism and demeanor seems rather uncontroversial;

- the correlation between openness and demeanor as well as deference and consciousness appears to be group specific: in these participants, courage is combined with independence, and the conscientious students are probably the most eager to satisfy their tutor's wish for collaboration-as-dialogue expressed explicitly in the three lectures;

- finally, agreeableness and deference correlate quite weakly. Apparently, in this particular group there is an attitude which can be summarised by one diary quote: "*I am quite open to dialogue, even if I don't agree with my interlocutors and stick to my guns*".

In turn, the correlation between NEO FFI scores and affiliation levels leads to the following observations:

- those open to new experiences are more likely to achieve higher affiliation levels faster. This refers to *how-I-see-others* and course onset only: most probably *others* see open people as slightly intimidating on first encounters, and slightly offensive when those more adventurous become bored with the rest;

- neuroticism correlates negatively with levels of affiliation at the beginning of the course, both self-perceived and others-perceived. Simultaneously, there is a growing attachment to extraverts (a moderate positive correlation noted later in the course). While people-orientation prevails as the course continues, the participants seem to become less sensitive to egocentric behaviours or such behaviours become less frequent as the sense of belonging grows;

- the prevailing others-orientation with a simultaneous decrease in task focus is also confirmed by the fact that conscientious people are perceived by others as more closely affiliated with them at the beginning of the course only;

- agreeableness – similarly to the attitudes study, and potentially for the same reason – seems unrelated to affiliation.

## 4. Conclusions

Considering the small size of the sample ($N = 11$), the conclusions can only be interim and are in demand of further research[4]. However, at this point there already emerge several important points to be taken into account.

When it comes to the quality of collaboration, we definitely need a balance between other-orientation and self-orientation, even though collaboration per se seems more in demand of the former attitude. In a course like *Collaboractive Online* such a balance will mean training for deference combined with acknowledging individual, personality-related needs for being recognised.

As regards levels of affiliation, there appears to be a need for continued people focus as the course develops. Responding to such needs may require more than the initial warm-up activity; it may amount to interspersing telecollaborative content tasks with affiliation-oriented information exchanges continuing throughout the whole course.

**Acknowledgements**. I would like to thank the participants of *Collaboractive Online* – for voluntarily devoting six months of their life to my course, and agreeing to let me use the data as research material.

## References

Brown, R. E. (2001). The process of community building in distance learning classes. *Journal of Asynchronous Learning Networks, 5*(2), 18-35. Retrieved from http://sloanconsortium.org/sites/default/files/v5n2_brown_1.pdf

Costa, P. T., Jr., & McCrae, R. R. (1992). *Revised NEO Personality Inventory (NEO-PI-R) and NEO Five-Factor Inventory (NEO-FFI) manual*. Odessa, FL: Psychological Assessment Resources.

---

4. To be carried out soon, as the second edition of *Collaboractive Online* is going to start in November 2013.

O'Dowd, R. (2011). Intercultural communicative competence through telecollaboration. In J. Jackson (Ed.), *The Routledge Handbook of Language and Intercultural Communication* (pp. 342-258). London: Routledge.

Turula, A. (2013). Between deference and demeanor: the outstanding mind in online collaboration contexts. Some insights based on the five-factor model of personality traits. *Teaching English with Technology, 13*(2), 3-22. Retrieved from http://www.tewtjournal.org/VOL%2013/ISSUE%202/ARTICLE1.pdf

# Do Students Share the Same Experience in an Online Language Exchange Programme? – The Chinese-French eTandem Case

### Jue Wang Szilas[1], Ling Zhang[2], and Claudia Berger[3]

**Abstract.** This article presents the findings of an eTandem Chinese-French exchange course during two academic years, the year 2010-2011 when the course was not credited, and the year 2011-2012 when the course was credited in one university but not in the other. It focuses on the students' perspective about the language exchange experience. The participants are second year language students from both universities – Level B1-B2 according to the Common European Framework of Reference for Languages (CEFR, 2001). The course includes theme-based asynchronous learning activities in the Learning Management System (LMS) Moodle of theme-based exercises, and writing a forum post in their mother tongue for language partners, as well as task-based synchronous oral communication via Skype. A course evaluation was done after each academic year and the data were collected. The findings showed that the fact that the course was credited really affected the students' appreciation of the exchange experience, even though it was only credited in one side.

**Keywords**: telecollaboration, online language exchange, eTandem, Chinese as a foreign language, French as a foreign language.

## 1. Introduction

eTandem language learning, as one of the main telecollaboration forms (O'Rourke, 2007), has been practised by many language teachers and researchers around the

---

1. The University of Geneva, Geneva, Switzerland; INALCO, Paris, France; jue.wangszilas@unige.ch
2. Hubei University, Wuhan, China
3. The University of Geneva, Geneva, Switzerland

**How to cite this article**: Wang Szilas, J., Zhang, L., & Berger, C. (2013). Do Students Share the Same Experience in an Online Language Exchange Programme? – The Chinese-French eTandem Case. In L. Bradley & S. Thouësny (Eds.), *20 Years of EUROCALL: Learning from the Past, Looking to the Future. Proceedings of the 2013 EUROCALL Conference, Évora, Portugal* (pp. 250-257). Dublin/Voillans: © Research-publishing.net.

world (Brammerts,1996; Chung, Graves, Wesche, & Barfurth, 2005; Cziko, 2004; Kabata & Edasawa, 2011; Kötter, 2003; Little & Ushioda, 1998; Mullen, Appel, & Shanklin, 2009; Stickler & Lewis, 2008; Telles & Vassallo, 2006; Tian & Wang, 2010).

However, most language projects were conducted among European languages, experiments involving non-European languages (Asian, Semitic languages, etc.) are not common (Belz, 2003). The eTandem Chinese-French course discussed in this article was initiated in 2009 by the Unit of Chinese Studies of the University of Geneva as an important part of the Chinese blended-learning programme called ChineWeb (initiated in 2006), collaborating with the French Department of Hubei University in China.

The participants were the second year language students from both sides (Level B1-B2). The course includes theme-based asynchronous learning activities in Moodle as well as task-based synchronous oral communication via Skype. The course aimed mainly to develop the students' linguistic competence through communication with native speakers and to help them to better know and understand each other's culture.

Based on the pilot research result (Wang, Berger, & Szilas, 2012), the course was re-designed and was expanded in the academic year 2010-2011 as supplementary learning activities for students from both universities. In the academic year 2011-2012, the course was credited in the University of Geneva, but not in the Hubei University for administrative reasons.

The participants of the eTandem Chinese-French course are from two distant languages and cultures. What is more, the pedagogical focuses of the two universities are different, as one strengthens the development of students' Chinese history and literature knowledge, while the other pays more attention on fostering students' linguistic skills. However, the pre-course survey result showed that students from both sides shared the expectations of "improving oral communication skills, establishing a good friendship or a stable collaborative relationship with their language partners, exchanging cultural knowledge, and improving oral comprehension" (Wang Szilas, Berger, & Zhang, 2013).

In this study, our research interest will be focused on the students' post-course feedback. The research questions are as follows:

- Did the students from both universities share the same learning experience?

- Did the students have different opinions toward the language exchange course?

- Did the integration of the eTandem course in the curriculum influence the students' course participation?

## 2. Method

### 2.1. Data collection

The data mainly came from the annual course evaluation questionnaire administrated by the University of Geneva. It consisted of twelve 5-scale questions about the course content and its organisation, teaching evaluation, as well as global appreciation, and four specific questions on the eTandem exchange, together with three open-ended questions about the comments or suggestions on the exchange. The questionnaire was translated into Chinese and was sent to Hubei University, where the data were then processed separately.

The online self-evaluation questionnaires of each exchange session served as complementary data. It contained questions concerning problems encountered during the exchange, the course preparation, the course completion as well as the tutoring. The questionnaire also served as proof of course presence and all students were required to finish it immediately after the exchange.

The face-to-face interviews organised at the end of each semester by both universities contributed to the data too. Open questions were asked about students' opinion toward their partners and how they communicate with each other, especially when they were allowed to set the exchange time themselves; whether they respected the reciprocity; how they helped each other during the exchange; and their comments on the course organisation, course content and tutoring.

### 2.2. Subjects

The participants in the academic year 2010-2011 consisted of 49 students; 19 from the University of Geneva (abbreviated as UniGe) and 30 from Hubei University (abbreviated as HubeiU). The participants in the academic year 2011-2012 consisted of 81 students (38 UniGes and 43 HubeiUs), with 7 dropouts at the middle of the course for personal reasons. All the students filled the course evaluation questionnaire. The language partners were formed on a one-to-one or one-to-two basis for unbalanced participant numbers.

## 2.3. Data analysis

We made some interesting comparisons of students' course evaluation with one university as well as between two universities to see how they appreciated the course.

### 2.3.1. Comparison of HubeiU students' course evaluation between 2010-2011 and 2011-2012

Figure 1 showed that the HubeiU students' general satisfaction with the course of 2011-2012 was higher than that of the year 2010-2011, especially concerning the course organisation (with 0.96 over 0.48), knowledge integration in the curriculum (with 0.96 over 0.55) as well as theme complement (with 0.94 over 0.64).

### 2.3.2. Comparison of UniGe students' course evaluation between 2010-2011 and 2011-2012

Figure 2 showed that the UniGe students of year 2010-2011 appreciated the course more than those of year 2011-2012, especially regarding the exchange process (0.88 over 0.53), the course organisation (0.95 over 0.70), and knowledge integration (0.94 over 0.70). The satisfaction with teacher encouragement dropped down a bit however.

### 2.3.3. Comparison of HubeiU and UniGe students' course evaluation for the academic year 2010-2011

Figure 3 showed that the students from Hubei University appreciated more than the UniGe students how the course was organised and the way their learning materials were integrated in the course, with 0.95 and 0.94 from the HubeiU students over 0.48 and 0.55 from the UniGe students respectively. However, the UniGe students showed greater satisfaction with the theme complement (1.0) than the HubeiU students (0.64). Both expressed successful attainment of learning objectives. Technology was considered a big obstacle for the exchange by both sides. The exchange process was satisfying for both sides.

### 2.3.4. Comparison of HubeiU and UniGe students' course evaluation for the academic year 2011-2012

Figure 4 revealed that in general the UniGe students appreciated the course less than the HubeiU students. The UniGe students' evaluation of the preparation and the exchange process was much lower than their counterpart, with 0.42 and 0.53

from the UniGe students and 0.79 and 0.91 from the HubeiU students. The same difference could be found regarding how the course was organised (0.70 from the UniGe and 0.96 from the HubeiU). However, the HubeiU students showed lower satisfaction on the knowledge integration (0.70, while 0.96 from the UniGe).

Figure 1. HubeiU students' course evaluation, year 2010-2011 and 2011-2012

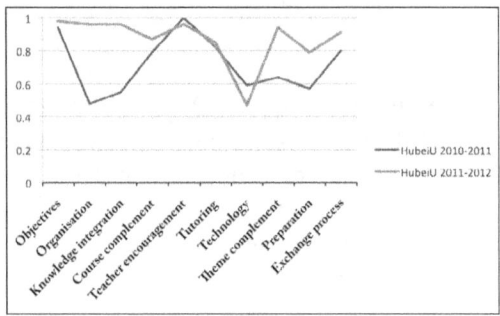

Figure 2. UniGe students' course evaluation, year 2010-2011 and 2011-2012

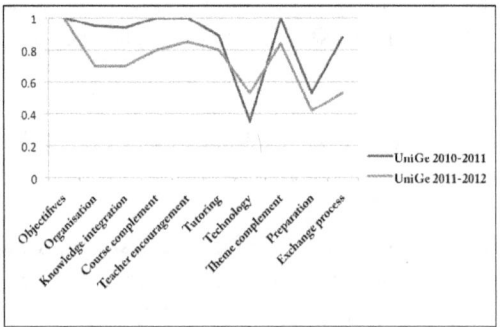

Figure 3. HubeiU and UniGe students' course evaluation, 2010-2011

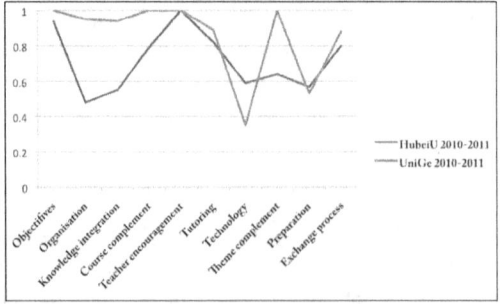

Figure 4. HubeiU and UniGe students' course evaluation, 2011-2012

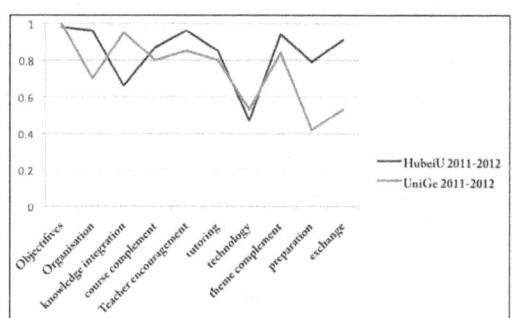

## 3. Discussion

To answer the research questions, the students participating in the eTandem course shared some positive learning experiences regarding the attainment of their learning objectives, teacher encouragement, tutoring and theme complement, which was confirmed by the face-to-face interviews. As for the negative part of the course, both agreed that technological problems remained big obstacles for a smooth exchange.

The fact that the course was integrated in the curriculum of the University of Geneva had an impact on students' participation. The students from the University of Geneva evaluated the course much lower than when it was not credited, while the students from Hubei University appreciated the course more than when it was not credited. The HubeiU students' high satisfaction was mainly due to the course organisation, teacher encouragement, theme complement and exchange process, while the UniGe students' low satisfaction was due to the exchange process and course preparation. More information from the online self-evaluation questionnaire and the face-to-face interviews helped us to have better explanations.

The lack of respect of the reciprocity principle (Little & Brammerts, 1996) as well as the failed communication between language partners mainly explained the UniGe students' unsatisfaction with the exchange process. The UniGe students complained that the HubeiU students did not respect the time allocation for each language (30 minutes in Chinese, 30 minutes in French) during the online exchange session. They were also annoyed by the fact that the HubeiU students corrected their mistakes only when they "forced" them to do so. During the second semester, the students were requested to set online exchange times with their partners. The

UniGe students preferred using emails to communicate with their tandems, while HubeiU students preferred leaving messages on Skype or QQ (an instant messaging software in China), which brought a lot of communication problems.

After the course was credited in the year 2011-2012, the UniGe students found that they were obliged to better prepare the course before each exchange. The online self-evaluation questionnaire showed that most of them spent around 2 hours to prepare the exchange, which was regarded as a big workload for them.

The UniGes felt a bit restricted by the course organisation and they asked for a looser structure, while their partners thought that the course structure should be tightened.

## 4. Conclusions

The above case study revealed that the students of both universities shared the same learning experience in that the course helped them to communicate with "true" native speakers of their own age and to make friends with them. The integration of the course in the curriculum in one university had an impact on their learning experience, both positive and negative. These results, if confirmed by further studies, may have implications on the future pedagogical design for eTandem courses and can be served as guidance for future tutoring. In addition, it would be interesting to make a study on the perspectives of the teachers and the tutors involved in the project to study their perception.

**Acknowledgements**. We would like to thank La Commission Informatique (COINF) and La Formation Continue (Lifelong Education Service) of the University of Geneva for their financial support of the project.

## References

Belz, J. A. (2003). From the special issue editor. *Language learning & technology, 7*(2), 2-5. Retrieved from http://llt.msu.edu/vol7num2/pdf/speced.pdf

Brammerts, H. (1996). Language learning in tandem using the Internet. In M. Warschauer (Ed.), *Telecollaboration in foreign language learning* (pp. 121–130). Honolulu: University of Hawaii Press.

Chung, Y.-G., Graves, B., Wesche, M., & Barfurth, M. (2005). Computer-Mediated Communication in Korean-English Chat Rooms: Tandem Learning in an International Languages Program. *The Canadian Modern Language Review / La revue canadienne des langues vivantes, 62*(1), 49-86. doi: 10.1353/cml.2005.0040

CEFR. (2001). The Common European Framework of Reference for Languages: Learning, Teaching, Assessment. Council of Europe. 2001. Cambridge: Cambridge University Press. Retrieved from http://www.coe.int/t/dg4/linguistic/Source/Framework_en.pdf

Cziko, G. A. (2004). Electronic Tandem Language Learning (eTandem): A Third Approach to Second Language Learning for the 21st Century. *Calico Journal, 22*(1), 25-40. Retrieved from https://calico.org/html/article_172.pdf

Kabata, K., & Edasawa, Y. (2011). Tandem language learning through a cross-cultural keypal project. *Language Learning & Technology, 15*(1), 104-121. Retrieved from http://llt.msu.edu/issues/february2011/kabataedasawa.pdf

Kötter, M. (2003). Negotiation of meaning and codeswitching in online tandems. *Language Learning & Technology, 7*(2), 145-172. Retrieved from http://www.llt.msu.edu/vol7num2/pdf/kotter.pdf

Little, D., & Brammerts, H. (1996). *A Guide to Language Learning in Tandem via the Internet.* Dublin: CLCS Occasional Paper No. 46.

Little, D., & Ushioda, E. (1998). Designing, implementing and evaluating a project in tandem language learning via e-mail. *RECALL, 10*(1), 95-101. doi: 10.1017/S0958344000004304

Mullen, T., Appel, C., & Shanklin, T. (2009). Skypebased tandem language learning and web 2.0. In M. Thomas (Ed.), *Handbook of research on Web 2.0 and second language learning.* Information Science Reference.

O'Rourke, B. (2007). Models of telecollaboration (1): eTandem. In R. O'Dowd (Ed.), *Online Intercultural Exchange: An Introduction for Foreign Language Teachers* (pp. 41-61). Multilingual Matters.

Stickler, U., & Lewis, T. (2008). Collaborative language learning strategies in an email tandem exchange. In S. Hurd & T. Lewis (Eds), *Language Learning Strategies in Independent Settings* (pp. 237-261). Bristol, UK: Multilingual Matters.

Telles, J. A., & Vassallo, M. L. (2006). Foreign language learning in tandem: Teletandem as an alternative proposal in CALLT. *The ESPecialist, 27*(2), 189-212. Retrieved from http://revistas.pucsp.br/index.php/esp/article/view/1629/1048

Tian, J., & Wang, Y. (2010). Taking language learning outside the classroom: learners' perspectives of eTandem learning via Skype. *Innovation in Language Learning and Teaching, 4*(3), 181-197. doi: 10.1080/17501229.2010.513443

Wang J., Berger C., & Szilas, N. (2012). Pedagogical Design of an eTandem Chinese-French Writing Course. *Journal of Universal Computer Science, 18*(3), 393-409. doi: 10.3217/jucs-018-03-0393

Wang Szilas J., Berger C., & Zhang F. (2013). eTandem Language Learning Integrated in the Curriculum: Reflection from Students' Perspectives. *Proceedings of the European Distance and E-Learning Network 2013 Annual Conference* (pp. 93-102). Oslo: The Joy of Learning. Retrieved from http://www.unige.ch/formcont/ressources/publications/e-Tandem.pdf

# C⁴ (C quad): Development of the Application for Language Learning Based on Social and Cognitive Presences

### Masanori Yamada[1], Yoshiko Goda[2], Hideya Matsukawa[3], Kojiro Hata[4], and Seisuke Yasunami[5]

**Abstract**. This research aims to develop collaborative language learning systems based on social and cognitive presence for learning settings out of class, and evaluate their effects on learning attitude and performance. The main purpose of this system is focusing on the building of a learning community, therefore the Community of Inquiry (CoI) framework suggested by Garrison, Anderson, and Archer (2000) was considered to design this system. This system "C⁴" (spelled out as C quad) consists of three functions: chatbot, constitutive chat, and contribution visualization for the enhancement of social and cognitive presence. In this paper, we explain system design and architecture, and discuss future work.

**Keywords**: computer-supported collaborative language learning, social presence, cognitive presence, learning community.

## 1. Introduction

Recent language learning tends to be communicative language learning using Computer-Mediated Communication (CMC) in a context of learner-centered learning in order to foster practical communication proficiency (e.g. Lee, 2002).

---

1. Kyushu University, Fukuoka, Japan; mark@mark-lab.net
2. Kumamoto University, Kumamoto, Japan
3. Osaka University, Osaka, Japan
4. Otemae University, Hyogo, Japan
5. Kumamoto University, Kumamoto, Japan

How to cite this article: Yamada, M., Goda, Y., Matsukawa, H., Hata, K., & Yasunami, S. (2013). C4 (C quad): Development of the Application for Language Learning Based on Social and Cognitive Presences. In L. Bradley & S. Thouësny (Eds.), *20 Years of EUROCALL: Learning from the Past, Looking to the Future*. Proceedings of the 2013 EUROCALL Conference, Évora, Portugal (pp. 258-264). Dublin/Voillans: © Research-publishing.net.

Previous research indicates positive effects of CMC on language learning, such as promotion of negotiation of meaning (e.g. Morris, 2005). It is suggested that CMC is effective on several perspectives of language learning, such as affective and productive performances, but one common issue in CMC-based learning is how to increase opportunities to touch the target language outside class, as well as active interaction between learners. In order to promote active interaction in CMC, building a learning community is one of the essential points for continuing online language learning. This study aims to design and develop a language learning support system "$C^4$ (Constitutive, Cognitive, Collaborative Chat)" with reference to "Community of Inquiry", in particular, social and cognitive presences.

The CoI framework consists of three elements: social presence, cognitive presence, and teaching presence. CoI, "composed of instructors and learners as the key participants in the educational process" (Rourke, Anderson, Garrison, & Archer, 1999, p. 52), provides "the environment in which students can take responsibility and control of their learning through negotiating meaning, diagnosing misconceptions, and challenging accepted beliefs—essential ingredients for deep and meaningful learning outcomes" (Garrison, 2011, p. 22). Social presence is defined as "the ability of participants to identify with the group, communicate purposefully in a trusting environment, and develop personal and affective relationships by way of projecting their individual personalities" (Garrison, 2011, p. 23). Cognitive presence is enhanced by integrating ideas, exploration for relevant information, and so on (Garrison et al., 2000). Social presence is an important factor for promoting learning in distance learning (McIsaac & Gunawardena, 1996). It is said to be effective emotionally. Additionally, social presence seems to increase the learners' satisfaction with learning (Gunawardena & Zittle, 1997). Yamada and Akahori (2008) indicated that social presence in the use of synchronous CMC encouraged active interaction between learners using the target language, promoting the use of social cues. Several studies have revealed the effects of a learning support system based on social presence (e.g. Yamada, 2010; Yamada, Nishiyama, & Goda, 2012). Moreover, Yamada and Kitamura (2011) indicated that social presence has two aspects: perceived and expressive features. These two aspects should be considered for the design of a learning support system for language learning.

Cognitive presence supports critical thinking and learning discourse such as negotiation of meanings, facilitating analysis, and information integration (Garrison, 2011). Cognitive presence consists of four phases: triggering event, exploration, integration, and resolution (Garrison, 2011). In order to create and enhance cognitive presence, integrating shared and private knowledge and thinking through learning discourse should be supported (Garrison, 2011). Finally, teaching presence is defined as "the design, facilitation, and direction of cognitive and social processes for the purpose of realizing personally meaningful and educationally worthwhile learning outcomes" (Anderson, Rourke, Garrison, & Archer, 2001, p. 5). Teaching presence directs learners' awareness to academic purposes of learning activities. Instructors' or teachers' roles and activities in online discussion seem to have influence on the enhancement of teaching presence, unlike social and cognitive presence. This research aims to develop collaborative language learning for the enhancement of social and cognitive presence, and to evaluate its effects on learning. In this paper, we explain the collaborative language learning system that we developed.

## 2. System

Goda and Yamada (2012) suggested the design of a learning community in online discussion using a foreign language, based on three presences: social, cognitive and teaching presences. They suggested three points, viz. (1) students must be supported to enhance social presence; (2) teaching and social presence have effects on the promotion of students' contribution; and (3) teaching and social presence have significant correlation with satisfaction. The system "$C^4$" aims to support the enhancement of learner factors. Therefore, this system focuses on the enhancement of social and cognitive presences. "$C^4$" was developed as a module of the free learning management system (LMS) "Moodle" and it consists of three functions: chatbot, constitutive chat, and contribution visualization. Figure 1, Figure 2, and Figure 3 display the system interfaces.

### 2.1. Chatbot "Mondo"

Chatbot supports learners in constructing their ideas through communication with the chatbot before communication or discussion with other learners in constitutive chat. Chatbot asks questions about the learner's idea or opinion using Socratic questioning. The learner answers the questions. This function is assumed to promote the cognitive process of idea (re) construction. Chatbot seems to be effective in the enhancement of cognitive presence. Communicating with chatbot before discussion may encourage students to organize their ideas in English, and give them opportunities to practice English writing (Jia, 2004). The chatbot "Mondo" was developed based on Eliza (Weizenbaum, 1966), adopting Socratic dialogue methods.

## 2.2. Constitutive chat "CD-Map"

Constitutive chat "CD-Map" is a text-based communication tool with an idea-constitution support function. This function consists of two parts: a communication part in the left pane and idea construction like a mindmap in the right pane. "CD-Map" allows learners to post their ideas and opinions, register postings as "favorite" (similar to the "like" button in Facebook), use emoticons, and make relationships such as cause-and-result between postings. In order to make relationships, learners click and drag a posting object in the left pane to the right pane, and then learners make relationships between postings using arrow lines and the like, as in a mindmap. Learners can share their idea-construction map using their postings. Yamada et al. (2012) suggested that idea construction tools such as mindmaps make learners aware of the learner's contribution, critical thinking, and others' presence. This function is assumed to enhance social and cognitive presence.

## 2.3. Contribution visualization

Contribution visualization is meant to visualize the learner's contribution and log-in frequency, using a facial icon and a background color. If a learner's posting on a chat is registered as a "favorite" or used in idea construction by other learners, the system counts one contribution, and then changes the facial expression to a smile. The background color on the facial icon changes depending on log-in frequency. The change of background color occurs in four patterns: bright blue (log-in), darker blue (from one hour to 23 hours since the last log-in), orange (one day since the last log-in), and gray (over three days since the last log-in). This function supports the enhancement of social presence.

Figure 1. Top page

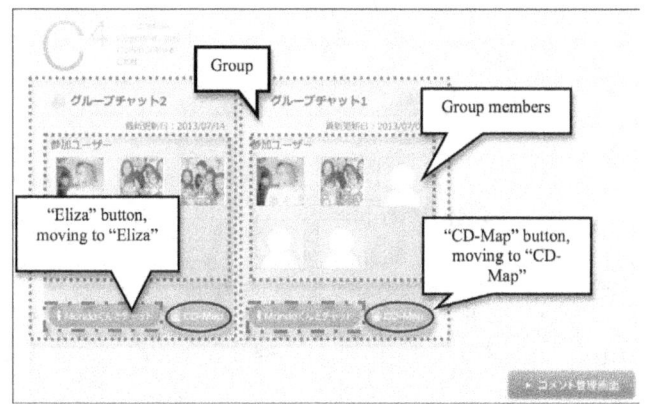

Figure 2. Interface of Chatbot "Mondo"

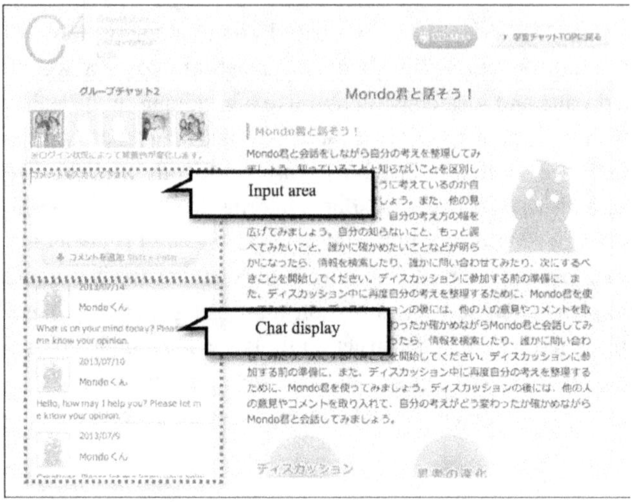

Figure 3. Interface of CD-Map

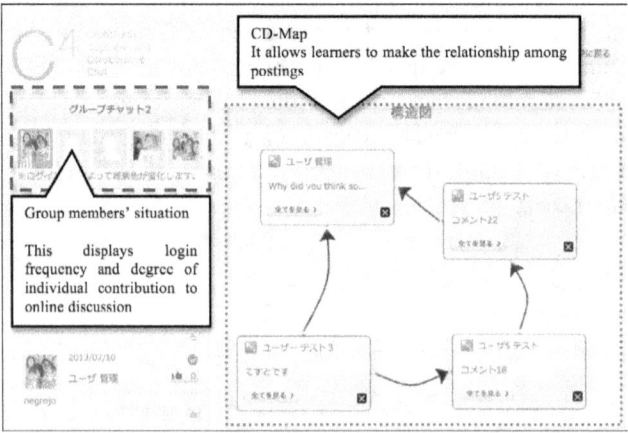

## 3. Conclusion and future works

The purpose of this study was to develop a collaborative language learning system based on social and cognitive presence. It is to be expected that the functions mentioned will be effective for the enhancement of both presence and learning performance. Future avenues of research are recommended as follows:

- Prototype evaluation: formative evaluation should be conducted into whether each function contributes to the promotion of social and cognitive presence.

- System modification: the results of prototype evaluation will suggest several problems with "C⁴". "C⁴" will be modified for a next version based on prototype results.

- Practical evaluation: this research aims to increase the opportunities to use a foreign language out of class. After the modification, effects of "C⁴" will be evaluated in out-of-class learning situations.

**Acknowledgements**. This study has been supported by a Grant-in-Aid for Scientific Research (B) (Grant number 23300304) from the Ministry of Education, Culture, Sports, Science and Technology (MEXT), and the Japan Society for the Promotion of Science (JSPS).

# References

Anderson, T., Rourke, L., Garrison, D. R., & Archer, W. (2001). Assessing teacher presence in a computer conferencing context. *The Journal of Asynchronous Learning Networks (JALN), 5*(2), 1-17. Retrieved from http://sloanconsortium.org/sites/default/files/v5n2_anderson_1.pdf

Garrison, D. R. (2011). *E-learning in the 21st century: a framework for research and practice*. New York, NY: Routledge.

Garrison, D. R., Anderson, T., & Archer, W. (2000). Critical inquiry in a text-based environment: computer conferencing in higher education. *The Internet and Higher Education, 2*(2/3), 87-105. doi: 10.1016/S1096-7516(00)00016-6

Goda, Y., & Yamada, M. (2012). Application of CoI to design CSCL for EFL online asynchronous discussion. In Z. Akyol & D. R. Garrison (Eds), *Educational Community of Inquiry: Theoretical Framework, Research and Practice* (pp. 295-316). Hershey, Pennsylvania, USA: IGI Global.

Gunawardena, C. N., & Zittle, F. J. (1997). Social presence as a predictor of satisfaction within a computer-mediated conferencing environment. *The American Journal of Distance Education, 11*(3), 8-26. doi: 10.1080/08923649709526970

Jia, J. (2004). CSIEC (Computer Simulator in Educational Communication): a virtual context-adaptive chatting partner for foreign language learners. In *Proceedings of the IEEE International Conference on Advanced Learning Technologies (ICALT'04)* (pp. 690-692).

Lee, L. (2002). Synchronous online exchanges: a study of modification devices on non-native discourse. *System, 30*(3), 275-288. doi: 10.1016/S0346-251X(02)00015-5

McIsaac, M. S., & Gunawardena, C. N. (1996). Research in distance education. In D. H. Jonassen (Ed.), *Handbook of research for educational communications and technology* (pp. 403-437). New York, NY: Scholastic Press.

Morris, F. (2005). Child-to-child interaction and corrective feedback in a computer mediated L2 class. *Language Learning & Technology, 9*(1), 29-45. Retrieved from http://llt.msu.edu/vol9num1/pdf/morris.pdf

Rourke, L., Anderson, T., Garrison, D. R., & Archer, W. (1999). Assessing social presence in asynchronous text-based computer conferencing. *Journal of Distance Education, 14*(2), 50-71.

Weizenbaum, J. (1966). ELIZA-A computer program for the study of natural language communication between man and machine. *Communications of the ACM, 9*(1), 36-45.

Yamada, M. (2010). The development and evaluation of CSCL based on social presence. In *Proceedings of World Conference on E-Learning (e-Learn) 2010* (pp. 2304-2309).

Yamada, M., & Akahori, K. (2008). Self awareness and learning performance in videoconferencing with self and partner's image. In *Proceedings of World Conference on Educational Media and Technology (EdMedia) 2008* (pp. 1190-1197).

Yamada, M., & Kitamura, S. (2011). The role of social presence in interactive learning with social software. In B. White, I. King, & P. Tsang (Eds), *Social Media Tools and Platforms in Learning Environments: Present and Future* (pp. 325-335). Heidelberg, Germany: Springer.

Yamada, M., Nishiyama, N., & Goda, Y. (2012). Effects of visualization of social interaction based on social presence theory: formative evaluation of a prototype system. In *Proceedings of International Conference on Education and e-Learning Innovation (ICEELI) 2012* (pp. 86-90). doi: 10.1109/ICEELI.2012.6360624

# Author Index

## A
Aizawa, Kazumi  1
Allen, Christopher  7
Arús-Hita, Jorge  206
Arvanitis, Panagiotis  14
Atkins, Andrew  18

## B
Bárcena, Elena  206
Benini, Silvia  25
Berger, Claudia  250
Bergman, Hilkka  31
Berns, Anke  38
Beuls, Katrien  45
Blin, Françoise  188
Boulton, Alex  51
Brautlacht, Regina  57

## C
Calle-Martínez, Cristina  206
Correia Martins, Maria de Lurdes  64
Cutrim Schmid, Euline  149

## D
Dell'Aria, Carmela  78
De Marco, Anna  71
Ducrocq, Csilla  57

## F
Ferreira, Daniel  86

## G
Gabaudan, Odette  93
Goda, Yoshiko  258

## H
Hamada, Mayumi  98
Hartwell, Laura M.  106

Hata, Kojiro  258

## I
Iino, Atsushi  112
Iloene, George O.  117, 183
Iloene, Modesta I.  117, 183
Incalcaterra McLoughlin, Laura  78
Iso, Tatsuo  1

## J
Jauregi, Kristi  123
Johansson, Richard  218

## K
Kétyi, András  129
Kitao, Kenji  135
Kitao, S. Kathleen  135
Koenraad, Ton  141, 149

## L
Lafond, Celia  158
Leone, Paola  71
Liversidge, Gordon  164
Lopes, António  169

## M
MacKinnon, Teresa  175
Martín-Monje, Elena  206
Matsukawa, Hideya  258
Mbah, Boniface M.  117, 183
Mbah, Evelyn E.  117, 183
Melchor-Couto, Sabela  123
Moreira, António  64
Moreira, Gillian  64
Murray, Liam  25

## N
Nakamura, Yoichi  112

Nocchi, Susanna 188

## O
Obari, Hiroyuki 194

## P
Panagiotidis, Panagiotis 200
Pareja-Lora, Antonio 206
Pijetlovic, Dijana 211
Pilán, Ildikó 218
Pomposo, Lourdes 206
Pulker, Hélène 226

## R
Read, Timothy 206
Rodríguez-Arancón, Pilar 206

## S
Spang Bovey, Nadia 158
Sundqvist, Pia 231

## T
Takewa, Mika 238
Tedremaa-Levorato, Kristiina 31
Turula, Anna 244

## V
Valero-Franco, Concepción 38
Vilar Beltrán, Elina 123
Volodina, Elena 211, 218

## W
Wang Szilas, Jue 250
Whyte, Shona 149

## Y
Yabuta, Yukiko 112
Yamada, Masanori 258
Yasunami, Seisuke 258

## Z
Zhang, Ling 250
Zou, Bin 106

# Name Index

## A

Aceto, Stefania 204
Adeyinka, Adewuyi Ayodele 119, 122
Adika, Lawrence O. 119, 122
Adler, Richard P. 201, 204
Agustiawan, Mohammad Ridwan 202, 205
Ahlers, Robert 39, 44
Aizawa, Kazumi 1, 2, 6
Akahori, K. 259, 264
Allen, Christopher 7
Álvarez, Agustín 85
Amuzie, Grace L. 119, 122
Andersen, Hanne Leth 170, 174
Andersen, Kent vii
Anderson-Hsieh, Janet 82, 84
Anderson, Jonathan 119, 122
Anderson, Lara Lomicka 59, 63
Anderson, Terry 258, 259, 260, 263, 264
Anthony, Laurence 53, 55
Appel, Christine vi, 251, 257
Apperley, Thomas H. 232, 236
Archer, Walter 258, 259, 260, 263, 264
Arnbjörnsdóttir, Birna 219, 224
Aron, Arthur 234, 236
Aron, Elaine N. 234, 236
Arús-Hita, Jorge 206, 208, 210
Arvanitis, Panagiotis 14
Aston, Guy 53
Atkins, Andrew 18, 20, 23

## B

Bainbridge, William Sims 16, 17
Bakhtin, Mikhail M. 188, 190, 193
Bamford, Julian 19, 23
Bañados, Emerita 107, 111
Bárcena, Elena 206, 208, 210
Bardel, Camilla 73, 76

Barfurth, Marion 251, 256
Barker, David 88, 91
Barr, David vi
Bazzanella, Carla 72, 73, 74, 76
Beauchamp, Gary 149, 152, 156, 157
Beaven, Tita 227, 229, 230
Beer, Colin 201, 205
Beglar, David 20, 23
Bekebrede, Geertje 232, 236
Belz, Julie A. 251, 256
Benini, Silvia 25
Bennett, Gena R. 170, 174
Bennett, Sue 26, 30
Benson, Philip 231, 235, 236
Berger, Claudia 250, 251, 257
Bergman, Hilkka 31
Bernal, Jesús 85
Bernhardt, Elizabeth Buchter 19, 21, 22, 23
Berns, Anke 38, 39, 41, 44
Betcher, Chris 166, 168
Beuls, Katrien 45, 48, 49, 50
Blake, Robert J. 62, 63
Blin, Françoise vi, vii, 109, 111, 188, 189, 193
Bobadilla, Jesús 85
Bolinger, Dwight 80, 84
Borin, Lars 211, 212, 213, 217
Borin, Lars 219, 224
Borthwick, Kate 229, 230
Boulton, Alex vi, vii, 51, 55, 170, 174
Bowen, J. Donald 227, 230
Bradin Siskin, Claire vi
Bradley, Linda i, ii
Brammerts, Helmut 251, 255, 256, 257
Brautlacht, Regina 57
Broberg, Megan 182
Broos, Agnetha 26, 30

Name Index

Brown, C. 26, 30
Brown, John Seely 201, 204
Brown, Ruth E. 246, 248
Bruton, Anthony 86, 91
Burston, Jack 240, 243
Byram, Michael 124, 127, 170, 174

C

Calle-Martínez, Cristina 206, 208, 210
Callies, Marcus 170, 174
Calvi, Anna 227, 230
Camacho, David 39, 41, 44
Carmean, Colleen 95, 97
Carter, Jackie 227, 230
Chambers, Angela vi, 53
Chang, Anna C.-S. 19, 23
Charles, Maggie 53, 55
Chatti, Mohamed Amine 202, 205
Chun, Dorothy M. 80, 84
Chung, Yang-Gyun 251, 256
Clancy, Patricia M. 73, 76, 113, 116
Clapham, Caroline 3, 6
Clark, Ken 201, 205
Clark, Vicki L. Plano 27, 30
Clerc, Stéphanie 159, 163
Cloke, Suzanne 107, 111
Cobb, Tom 18, 20, 23, 51, 53, 55
Cohen, Jacob 233, 234, 236
Cole, Simon 20, 23
Colpaert, Jozef vi, 143, 144, 145, 146
Comas-Quinn, Anna 227, 230
Conole, Grainne 8, 13
Corbett, John 170, 174
Correia Martins, Maria de Lurdes 64
Costa, Paul T., Jr 244, 246, 248
Coups, Elliot 234, 236
Cramér, Harald 234, 236
Creswell, John W. 27, 30
Cruttenden, Alan 80, 84
Cunningham, D. Joseph 107, 111
Cutrim Schmid, Euline 149, 152, 156, 157

Czerniewicz, L. 26, 30
Cziko, Gary A. 251, 257

D

Dabbagh, Nada 7, 9, 10, 12, 13
Daisy, Brenda 182
Dalal, Dev K. 95, 97
Dalgarno, Barney 26, 30
Davies, Graham 141, 144, 145, 146, 147
Davies, Mark 170
Day, Richard R. 19, 23
deHaan, Jonathan 232, 236
De Jong, Nivja H. 86, 92
Dell'Aria, Carmela 78, 82, 84
De los Arcos, Bea 227, 230
De Marco, Anna 71, 72, 76, 114, 116
Dengler, Mary 242, 243
Develotte, Christine 110, 111
Devonshire, E. 65, 70
Dickens, Alison 229, 230
Dickerson, Wayne B. 80, 85
Dickey, Michele D. 232, 236
Dodero Beardo, J. 44
Dondi, Claudio 204
Dooly, Melinda 124, 127
Dörnyei, Zoltán 233, 236
Dösinger, Gisela 202, 205
Dowdy, Michael 201, 202, 205
Dragos, Dragos 243
Driskell, James E. 39, 44
Ducate, Lara C. 59, 63
Ducrocq, Csilla 57
Dudeney, Gavin 12, 13

E

Edasawa, Yasuyo 251, 257
Ellis, Rod 9, 13
Elsness, Johan 170, 174

F

Fairon, Cédrick 221, 224

Ferreira, Daniel  86
Ferris, Dana R.  86, 87, 91, 92
Fink, L. Dee  239, 241, 242, 243
Fischer, Kerstin  72, 77
Fletcher, J. D.  80, 85
Forsberg, Markus  212, 213, 217, 219, 224
Foucault, Michel  188, 189, 190, 193
Fowley, Cathy  189, 193
François, Thomas  221, 224
Fratter, Ivana  107, 111
Fry, Heather  241, 243

## G

Gabaudan, Odette  93
Gardner, Robert C.  104, 105
Garrett, Nathan  95, 97
Garrison, D. Randy  258, 259, 260, 263, 264
Garris, Rosemary  39, 44
Gilbert, Judy B.  80, 85
Gil, José Ramón Biau  240, 243
Gillespie, John  vi, vii
Girvan, Carina  189, 193
Goda, Yoshiko  258, 259, 260, 263, 264
Godwin-Jones, Robert  119, 122, 201, 205
Goertler, Senta  119, 122
Gomes, Fernando  vii
Gomez, Pedro  80, 85
Gonzalez-Pardo, Antonio  39, 41, 44
Gorsuch, Greta  19, 23
Graves, Barbara  251, 256
Gray, Kathleen  26, 30
Greenberg, Bradley S.  232, 236
Grgurovic, Maja  182
Grönlund, Åke  129, 134
Grosbois, Muriel  vi
Grundy, Peter  170, 174
Guichon, Nicolas  vi, 143, 145, 146, 147
Gunawardena, Charlotte N.  259, 263, 264
Guth, Sarah  vi, 31, 32, 37, 107, 111
Guzdial, Mark  240, 243

## H

Hachey, Alyse C.  95, 97
Hakel, Milton D.  95, 97
Halliday, M. A. K  15, 17
Hall, Joan Kelly  124, 128
Hamada, Mayumi  98, 99, 105
Hampel, Regine  vi, 113, 116
Harrison, David  122
Harteveld, Casper  232, 236
Hartwell, Laura M.  106
Hasan, Ruqaiya  15, 17
Hata, Kojiro  258
Hattori, Takahiko  19, 23
Hauck, Mirjam  vi, vii
Hegelheimer, Volker  180, 182
Heift, Trude  vi
Heimann Mühlenbock, Katarina  219, 221, 224
Hellermann, John  73, 77
Helm, Francesca  vi, vii, 31, 37, 107, 111
Hennessy, Sara  119, 122
Higgins, Steve  149, 156
Hillier, Emily  152, 156, 157
Hockly, Nicky  12, 13
Holmstrom, Amanda  232, 236
Hsu, Angela Yi-ping  87, 91, 92
Huang, Hsin-chou  137, 140
Hubbard, Phil  vi
Hughes, Joan E.  59, 63
Husák, Miloš  219, 224
Hussey, Jill  94, 97
Hussey, Roger  94, 97
Hymes, Dell H.  15, 17

## I

Iino, Atsushi  112
Iloene, George O.  117, 183
Iloene, Modesta I.  117, 183
Incalcaterra McLoughlin, Laura  78, 84
Ingerman, Bret L.  202, 205
Ip, Albert  65, 70

Name Index

Iso, Tatsuo  1, 2, 6

## J
Jafari, Ali  95, 97
James, Carl  87, 92
Jarke, Matthias  202, 205
Jauregi, Kristi  107, 111, 123
Jia, Jiyou  260, 263
Johansson Kokkinakis, Sofie  213, 217, 219, 224, 225
Johansson, Richard  218, 219, 224
Johns, Tim  51, 52, 53, 54, 55, 56, 136, 140
Jones, Chris  26, 30
Jones, David  201, 205
Jones, Jennifer  16, 17
Joseph, Dolly R. D.  232, 236
Judd, T.  26, 30

## K
Kabata, Kaori  251, 257
Kaptelinin, Victor  189, 193
Kaszubski, Przemysław  53, 56
Kennedy, Gregor  26, 30
Kennewell, Steve  149, 156
Kervin, Lisa  26, 30
Ketteridge, Steve  241, 243
Kétyi, András  129
Kharbach, Mohamed  86, 92
Kilgarriff, Adam  219, 224
Kim, Yu-Jeung  170, 174
King, Philip  51, 56, 136, 140
Kinzie, Mable B.  232, 236
Kirkendall, Sarah R.  95, 97
Kitamura, Satoshi  259, 264
Kitao, Kenji  135, 138, 140
Kitao, S. Kathleen  135, 136, 138, 140
Knight, Rachael-Anne  184, 186
Knops, Uus  240, 243
Koenraad, Ton  141, 149, 154, 156
Koli, Hanne  36, 37
Kötter, Markus  251, 257

Kramsch, Claire  124, 128, 170, 174
Krashen, Stephen D.  87, 92
Krishnan, Reshmy  195, 199
Kuiken, Folkert  86, 92
Kvale, Steinar  175, 178, 182

## L
Lachlan, Kenneth  232, 236
Lafond, Celia  158
Lalande, John F.  87, 92
Lambacher, Stephen  199
Lange, Dale L.  170, 174
Lantolf, James P.  124, 128
Laufer, Batia  232, 236
Lave, Jean  181, 182
Lee, Hukyoung  73, 77
Lee, Icy  86, 92
Lee, Lina  258, 263
Lee, Mal  166, 168
Lee, Mark J. W.  202, 205
Leifsson, Guðmundur Örn  219, 224
Leigh, Elyssebeth  65, 66, 68, 70
Lemke, Jay L.  188, 193
Leone, Paola  71, 72, 76, 114, 116
Leprêtre, Eric  202, 205
Leroy, Sabine  202, 205
Levitan, Steven  138, 140
Levy, Mike  124, 128, 175, 177, 182, 241, 243
Levy Scherrer, Paula  221, 224
Lewis, Tim  251, 257
Lieberman, Philip  80, 85
Ligorio, Maria Beatrice  190, 193
Limentani, Roberto  158, 163
Li, Mimi  62, 63
Lindemalm, Karl  221, 224
Little, David  251, 255, 257
Littlejohn, Allison  26, 30
Liu, Sammi  182
Liversidge, Gordon  164, 165, 167, 168
Livingstone, D. W.  8, 13
Lloyd, Christopher  138, 140

Loftsson, Hrafn 219, 224
Long, Michael H. 87, 92
Lopes, António 169
Lord, Gillian 184, 186
Lowood, Henry 16, 17
Lucas, Kristen 232, 236
Lund, Andreas 143, 144, 145, 146, 147
Lund, Karen 170, 174
Lutters, Wayne 16, 17
Lux, Mathias 202

## M

Madden, Mary 184, 187
Madsen, Harold S. 227, 230
Maes, Pattie 48, 50
Mangenot, François 107, 111
Mantovani, Fabrizia 189, 193
Marçalo, Maria João v, vii
Margaryan, Anoush 26, 30
Marini-Maio, Nicoletta 107, 111
Marshall, Stephanie 241, 243
Marsh, Tim 192, 193
Martindale, Trey 201, 202, 205
Martínez, Rafael 85
Martín-Monje, Elena 206, 208, 210
Marzotto, Paola 204
Maton, Karl 26, 30
Matsukawa, Hideya 258
Mayer, Richard E. 80, 85
Mbah, Boniface M. 117, 183
Mbah, Evelyn E. 117, 183
McAdam, Katy 219, 224
McCrae, Robert R. 244, 246, 248
McGee, Patricia 95, 97
McGrath, Ian 228, 230
McGreal, Rory 227, 230
McIsaac, Marina S. 259, 264
McLester, Susan 16, 17
McLoughlin, Catherine 202, 205
McNerney, Maureen 80, 85
Meara, Paul 2, 6, 19, 20, 23

Melchor-Couto, Sabela 123
Mendelsohn, David 80, 85
Merriam, Sharan B. 94, 97
Meurers, Detmar 221, 224
Miah, Andy 16, 17
Middlebrooks, Katy 182
Miller, Dave 149, 156
Mills, Daniel J. 129, 134
Montredon, Jacques 159, 161, 163
Moon, Jennifer A. 95, 97
Moreira, António 64
Moreira, Gillian 64
Moreno, Nina 59, 63
Morgan, Michael 189, 193
Morris, Frank 259, 264
Moseegaard Hansen, Maj-Britt 72, 77
Mullen, Tony 251, 257
Müller-Hartmann, Andreas 143, 144, 145, 147
Muñoz, Carmen 124, 128
Murray, Liam vi, 25
Myskow, Gordon 19, 23

## N

Nakamura, Yoichi 112
Narayan, Ravi 59, 63
Nardi, Bonnie 189, 193
Nardi, Daniele 48, 50
Nation, Paul 2, 6, 18, 20, 23, 24, 232, 236
Newgarden, Kristi 189, 193
Nieto, Victoria 85
Nigoević, Magdalena 73, 77
Nishiyama, Nobuaki 259, 264
Nocchi, Susanna 188, 189, 193
Norris, John M. 52, 56
Nunan, David 9, 13
Nurmukhamedov, Ulugbek 170, 174

## O

Obari, Hiroyuki 194
Oberhofer, Margret 152, 157

Oblinger, Diana G.  16, 17
Oblinger, James L.  16, 17
O'Dowd, Robert  31, 34, 37, 113, 115, 116, 124, 128, 244, 249
Olinger, Andrea R.  170
Olsson, Leif-Jöran  212, 217
Oluikpe, Benson Omenihu  183, 187
Onguko, Brown  119, 122
Orenha-Ottaiano, Adriane  170, 174
O'Rourke, Breffni  250, 257
Ortega, Lourdes  52, 56
Otto, Sue K.  vi

## P
Paige, R. Michael  170
Palalas, Agnieszka  129, 133
Palomo-Duarte, Manuel  44
Panagiotidis, Panagiotis  200
Pareja-Lora, Antonio  206
Patton, Toni  vii
Paulussen, Hans  vi
Pegrum, Mark  12, 13
Pellet, Stéphanie Hélène  73, 77
Pennington, Martha C.  80, 85
Peters, Martine  180, 182
Peter, Yvan  202, 205
Phil, M.  118, 119, 122
Pijetlovic, Dijana  211, 217, 219, 225
Pilán, Ildikó  213, 217, 218, 219, 225
Plaisir, Jean Y.  95, 97
Pleines, Christine  227, 230
Pomposo, Lourdes  206, 208, 210
Pons Bordería, Salvador  72, 77
Prensky, Marc  16, 17, 25, 26, 29, 30
Pulker, Hélène  226, 227, 230
Pym, Anthony  240, 243

## R
Rainie, Lee  184, 187
Read, Timothy  206
Reid, Joy M.  87, 92
Reo, Rick  7, 9, 10, 12, 13
Reppert, Ketty  182
Rhoten, Diana  16, 17
Richards, Jack C.  80, 85
Risager, Karen  170, 174
Rispail, Marielle  159, 163
Ritella, Giuseppe  190, 193
Riva, Giuseppe  189, 193
Robb, Thomas  87, 91, 92
Roberts, Barrie  87, 91, 92
Rodellar, Víctor  85
Rodríguez-Arancón, Pilar  206, 208, 210
Roe, Keith  26, 30
Rollett, Herwig  202, 205
Rose, Caroline  243
Rose, Kenneth R.  137, 140
Rosser, Elizabeth  65, 66, 70
Ross, Steven  87, 92
Rourke, Liam  259, 260, 263, 264
Roxendal, Johan  212, 217, 219, 224
Rundell, Michael  219, 224
Russel, C.  65, 70
Rychlý, Pavel  219, 224

## S
Samuels, S. Jay  19, 23
Savage, Timothy  189, 193
Savina, Fany  ii
Savina, Raphaël  ii
Schalow, Thomas  104, 105
Schmidt, Johannes  184, 187
Schmidt, Richard  80, 85
Schmitt, Diane  3, 6
Schmitt, Norbert  3, 6
Schulze, Mathias  vi
Schwienhorst, Klaus  39, 44
Sclater, Niall  201, 205
Scott, Mike  52, 54, 56
Searle, John R.  138, 140
Segalowitz, Norman  19, 23
Segler, Thomas M.  219, 224

# Name Index

Semke, Harriet D.  87, 92
Shanklin, Trevor  251, 257
Shao, Binhui  26, 30
Sharoff, Serge  243
Shepherd, J.  65, 70
Sherimon, P. C.  195, 199
Sherry, John  232, 236
Shield, Lesley  vi
Shimizu, M.  164, 168
Shiotsu, Toshihiko  22, 23
Shizuka, Tetsuhito  2, 6
Shortreed, Ian  87, 92
Shyamlee, Solanki D.  118, 119, 122
Siemens, George  203, 205
Silva, Ana Alexandra  v, vii
Sjöholm, Johan  219, 221, 224
Sliter, Michael T.  95, 97
Spang Bovey, Nadia  158
Specht, Marcus  202, 205
Speicher, Oranna  vi, vii
Spindler, Laraine  68, 70
Steel, Caroline  129, 134
Steels, Luc  46, 50
Stickler, Ursula  113, 116, 251, 257
Stockwell, Glenn  vi, 86, 92
Stoerger, Sharon  26, 30
Stotland, Doug  98, 105
Stringer, Ernest T.  64, 67, 70
Strohmaier, Markus  202, 205
Sučić, Patricia  73, 77
Sundqvist, Pia  231, 232, 235, 236, 237
Suzuki, Ryoko  73, 76, 113, 116
Szilas, Nicolas  251, 257

## T

Taalas, Peppi  vi, vii
Taguchi, Etsuo  19, 23
Takewa, Mika  238
Tammelin, Maija  vi
Tanaka, Sachiko  107, 111
Tao, Hongyin  73, 76, 113, 116

Tapscott, Don  184, 187
Tedremaa-Levorato, Kristiina  31
Tella, Adedeji  119, 122
Tella, Adeyinka  119, 122
Telles, João A.  251, 257
Theilheimer, Rachel  95, 97
Thomas, Martin  243
Thomas, Michael  149, 157
Thompson, June  vi
Thompson, Sandra A.  73, 76, 113, 116
Thorne, Steven L.  124
Thouësny, Sylvie  i, ii
Tian, Jianqiu  251, 257
Tian, Shiauping  136, 140
Tobias, Sigmund  80, 85
Tochtermann, Klaus  202, 205
Tognini-Bonelli, Elena  54, 56
Tomlinson, Brian  227, 230
Toyobo, Oluwole Majekodunmi  119, 122
Tribble, Christopher  52, 54, 56
Truscott, John  87, 91, 92
Tschichold, Cornelia  vi
Tumposky, N.  179, 182
Turns, Jennifer  240, 243
Turula, Anna  244, 246, 249

## U

Uchechukwu, Chinedu  119, 122
Underwood, Paul  19, 23
Uppström, Jonatan  212, 217
Ushioda, Ema  251, 257

## V

Vajjala, Sowmya  221, 224
Valero-Franco, Concepción  38, 44
Van Beuningen, Catherine G.  86, 92
Vandergrift, Larry  179, 182
Vanderveken, Daniel  138, 140
Van Harmelen, M.  204, 205
Van Hazebrouck Thompson, Sanderin  152, 157

# Name Index

Van Lier, Leo 9, 13
Van Maanen, John 94, 97
Van Trijp, Remi 48, 50
Vassalo, Maria Luisa 251, 257
Vergun, Andrea 73, 77
Viberg, Olga 129, 134
Vigmo, Sylvi vii
Vilar Beltrán, Elina 123
Vinu, P. V. 195, 199
Vojt, Gabrielle 26, 30
Volodina, Elena 211, 212, 213, 217, 218, 219, 224, 225
Vyatkina, Nina 86, 87, 91, 92, 107, 111
Vygotsky, Lev Semenovich 8, 13, 62, 63, 235, 237

## W

Wamakote, Leonard 122
Wang Szilas, Jue 250, 251, 257
Wang, Yuping 251, 257
Waring, Rob 19, 24
Waterworth, Eva L. 189, 193
Waterworth, John A. 189, 193
Waycott, J. 30
Waycott, Jenny 26, 30
Webb, Stuart 20, 24
Weizenbaum, Joseph 260, 264
Wellens, Peter 48, 50
Weller, Martin 8, 13
Wenger, Etienne 177, 181, 182
Wesche, Mari 251, 256
White, Jeremy 129, 134
Whyte, Shona 149, 152, 155, 156, 157
Wild, Joanna 227, 230
Willis, Jane 9, 13
Wills, Sandra 65, 66, 70
Winke, Paula 119, 122

## X

Xing, Xiong 119, 122

## Y

Yabuta, Yukiko 112
Yamada, Masanori 258, 259, 260, 261, 263, 264
Yang, Catherine 202, 205
Yasunami, Seisuke 258
Yngve, Victor H. 73, 77

## Z

Zarate, Geneviève 159, 163
Zhang, Ling 250, 251, 257
Zhao, Yong 119, 122
Zheng, Dongping 189, 193
Zittle, Frank J. 259, 263
Zou, Bin 106
Zur, A. 26, 30
Zur, Ofer 26, 30

www.ingramcontent.com/pod-product-compliance
Lightning Source LLC
Chambersburg PA
CBHW050841230426
43667CB00012B/2100